Getting Started with Citrix XenApp 6

Design and implement Citrix farms based on XenApp 6

Guillermo Musumeci

BIRMINGHAM - MUMBAI

Getting Started with Citrix XenApp 6

Copyright © 2011 Packt Publishing

All rights reserved. No part of this book may be reproduced, stored in a retrieval system, or transmitted in any form or by any means, without the prior written permission of the publisher, except in the case of brief quotations embedded in critical articles or reviews.

Every effort has been made in the preparation of this book to ensure the accuracy of the information presented. However, the information contained in this book is sold without warranty, either express or implied. Neither the author nor Packt Publishing, and its dealers and distributors will be held liable for any damages caused or alleged to be caused directly or indirectly by this book.

Packt Publishing has endeavored to provide trademark information about all of the companies and products mentioned in this book by the appropriate use of capitals. However, Packt Publishing cannot guarantee the accuracy of this information.

First published: June 2011

Production Reference: 1090611

Published by Packt Publishing Ltd.
32 Lincoln Road
Olton
Birmingham, B27 6PA, UK.

ISBN 978-1-849681-28-5

www.packtpub.com

Cover Image by David Guettirrez (bilbaorocker@yahoo.co.uk)

Credits

Author
Guillermo Musumeci

Reviewers
Christopher Buford
Bart Jacobs
Shankha Mukherjee

Acquisition Editor
Amey Kanse

Development Editor
Alina Lewis

Technical Editor
Manasi Poonthottam

Copy Editor
Leonard D'Silva

Project Coordinator
Vishal Bodwani

Proofreader
Linda Morris

Indexer
Rekha Nair
Monica Ajmera Mehta

Graphics
Geetanjali Sawant

Production Coordinator
Shantanu Zagade

Cover Work
Shantanu Zagade

About the Author

Guillermo Musumeci is a Windows Infrastructure Architect specialized in Citrix and virtualization with 16 years of experience. He has a passion for designing, building, deploying, and supporting enterprise architectures using Citrix, Microsoft, and VMware products.

He worked as Project Manager and Senior Consultant in medium to large Citrix and virtualization projects in America, Europe, and recently he relocated to Asia, where he lives with his wife and two children.

Guillermo is also the founder and developer of the popular site CtxAdmTools, which provides free tools to manage Citrix environments, Active Directory, and more.

He holds more than 25 Citrix, Microsoft, and VMware certifications.

> This book is dedicated to my beautiful and adorable wife, Paola and to my amazing kids: my little girl, Ornella and my incredible son, Stefano. I love you all!
>
> I would also like to thank my family and friends for their support.
>
> And finally, I would not have written this book without the terrific support of my project coordinator Vishal Bodwani, my Acquisition Editor Amey Kanse, my development editor Alina Lewis, and all technical reviewers and editors at Packt Publishing. Thank you!

About the Reviewers

Christopher Buford, a cloud computing/hosting and virtualization evangelist, is also the President and co-owner of SMB Technology Solutions, LLC, an Atlanta Ga. based technology company which specializes in cloud computing and virtualization for small-midsized businesses, as well as offering virtualization sub-contracting services to larger virtualization partners

Christopher has been working in the Citrix industry for over 12 years. He has served at several fortune 500 companies as well as midsized businesses.

Christopher has recently developed the Citrix Professional toolbar, which is a web-based toolbar specifically for those in the Citrix virtualization industry. Christopher is also working on a short e-book which is based on implementing a Citrix XenApp solution on VMware vSphere.

Christopher states he has a dream to use cloud computing and virtualization to help close the technology gap with people in under-served communities. Someday, he would like to operate a non-profit organization which not only teaches technology but also offers IT certification training along with job-placement services.

When asked who he admires in the IT industry. Christopher stated "*I really admire the people who do so much for the industry and their communities without a lot of fanfare. If I could accomplish 1/1000th of what Mr. David Steward of World Wide Technology in St. Louis has for the technology industry and more importantly, the lives of people, I would definitely consider myself a very successful man*".

> I would like to thank my Lord, Jesus Christ as well as my family for supporting me as I attempt to leave the world a better place.

Bart Jacobs is a Senior System Engineer/Consultant based in Belgium. He started his career back in 1998. One of the first projects he worked on in those days was Citrix Metaframe 1.8 on Microsoft Windows NT 4 Terminal Server "Hydra". Over the years, Citrix technology has always been a major theme in his professional career, resulting in becoming a true technical expert in the matter. In the last few years, he has also become an expert in virtualization technology, with a special interest in a real challenger in this business: Citrix XenServer.

From 1998 to 2010, he has worked in three Belgian IT companies, working for customer projects all over the Benelux. In 2007, he founded his own company BJ IT, alongside a job as Senior System Engineer. In late 2010, BJ IT evolved into a full-time job and Bart Jacobs is now the CEO/Owner.

> I would also like to thank all of my customers and former colleagues, to give me the possibility to take my experience to the next level. And last, but not least, my wife Sandra and the children in our family Elle, Joshua, and Joke for their patience for all those late nights.

Shankha Mukherjee has four years of experience in Citrix XenApp (the new name for Presentation Server). He has worked on almost all the versions of Citrix XenApp starting from Metaframe XP. He is currently working as a Level 2 administrator for WINTEL (Windows Intel / Citrix XenApp / VMware), giving support to client infrastructure remotely.

Shankha Mukherjee is a B-Tech Engineer in Information Technology.

> I am thankful to Maitreya Bhakal and Vishal Bodwani, the Development Editor and Project Coordinator at Packt, for giving me this opportunity.

www.PacktPub.com

Support files, eBooks, discount offers, and more

You might want to visit www.PacktPub.com for support files and downloads related to your book.

Did you know that Packt offers eBook versions of every book published, with PDF and ePub files available? You can upgrade to the eBook version at www.PacktPub.com and, as a print book customer, you are entitled to a discount on the eBook copy. Get in touch with us at service@packtpub.com for more details.

At www.PacktPub.com, you can also read a collection of free technical articles, sign up for a range of free newsletters, and receive exclusive discounts and offers on Packt books and eBooks.

http://PacktLib.PacktPub.com

Do you need instant solutions to your IT questions? PacktLib is Packt's online digital book library. Here, you can access, read, and search across Packt's entire library of books.

Why subscribe?

- Fully searchable across every book published by Packt
- Copy and paste, print, and bookmark content
- On demand and accessible via web browser

Free access for Packt account holders

If you have an account with Packt at www.PacktPub.com, you can use this to access PacktLib today and view nine entirely free books. Simply use your login credentials for immediate access.

Instant updates on new Packt books

Get notified! Find out when new books are published by following @PacktEnterprise on Twitter, or the *Packt Enterprise* Facebook page.

Table of Contents

Preface	**1**
Chapter 1: Getting Started with XenApp 6	**7**
Introducing XenApp 6	**8**
XenApp feature overview	**11**
System requirements	**12**
Data store databases	14
Citrix Delivery Services Console	14
License server	15
Clients	15
Summary	**16**
Chapter 2: Designing a XenApp 6 Farm	**17**
Case study: Brick Unit Constructions	**17**
Farm terminology and concepts	**18**
Infrastructure server	20
Virtualization infrastructure	21
Access Infrastructure	22
Designing a basic XenApp architecture	**23**
The pilot plan	**25**
Designing Active Directory integration	26
Building a small test farm	27
Creating a list of applications to publish in our Citrix farm	29
Testing the list of applications	31
Microsoft Office applications	32
Java	33
Summary	**34**

Table of Contents

Chapter 3: Installing XenApp 6 — 35
Installing and Configuring XenApp 6 — 35
Configuring Windows components — 36
   Configuring Windows Firewall — 37
   Configuring IE ESC (Enhanced Security Configuration) — 39
Installing XenApp using the Wizard-based Server Role Manager — 40
Installing License Server and web interface roles in server BRICKXA01 — 43
Configuring Citrix License Server — 44
Installing Citrix Licenses — 46
Installing and configuring XenApp 6 on BRICKXA02 using Wizard-based Server Role Manager (first server of the farm) — 49
Configuring XenApp using the Wizard-based Server Configuration tool — 52
   Configuring the first XenApp server of the farm — 53
   Installing data stores — 54
      Microsoft SQL Server 2008 Express database server — 55
      Microsoft SQL Server 2008 database server — 57
      Oracle database server — 59
Installing and configuring XenApp 6 on BRICKXA03 — 62
Configuring Citrix Web Interface server — 64
   Creating a XenApp website — 64
   Creating a XenApp Services site — 70
Configuring Remote Desktop licensing — 72
   Configuring Remote Desktop licensing mode by using Group Policy — 74
Managing XenApp farms — 75
Summary — 76

Chapter 4: Using Management Tools — 77
Management Consoles — 78
   Citrix Delivery Services Console — 78
   License Administration Console — 80
   Citrix Web Interface Management console — 86
Other administration tools — 93
   Citrix SSL Relay Configuration tool — 93
   Shadow taskbar — 94
   SpeedScreen Latency Reduction Manager — 94
Managing Citrix administrators — 95
   Add a Citrix administrator — 95
   Disable a Citrix administrator — 99
   Modify administrator properties — 100
Summary — **101**

Table of Contents

Chapter 5: Application Publishing — 103
Publishing applications — 103
Choosing the best method to deliver applications — 105
Publishing a hosted application using the Publish Application wizard — 106
Publishing a streaming application using the Publish Application wizard — 118
Publishing content using the Publish Application wizard — 130
Publishing a server desktop using the Publish Application wizard — 138
Configuring content redirection — 148
Enabling content redirection from server to client — 148
Configuring content redirection from client to server — 149
Associating published applications with file types — 150
Updating file type associations — 151
Enabling or Disabling content redirection — 153
Summary — 155

Chapter 6: Application Streaming — 157
Application streaming — 157
System requirements for application streaming — 159
Components for application streaming — 161
Choosing which plugin to use for application streaming — 162
Profiling Microsoft Office 2010 — 163
Installing a profiler workstation — 163
Customizing the Office 2010 installation — 165
    Disabling the Office Welcome Screen — 168
    Disabling some Office popups — 168
    Setting the KMS server name (32-bit target device) — 169
    Setting the KMS server name (64-bit target device) — 170
    Setting the KMS port number (64-bit target device) — 170
    Setting the KMS port number (32-bit target device) — 171
Profiling Microsoft Office 2010 — 173
Publishing Office 2010 on the farm — 183
Specifying trusted servers for streamed services and profiles — 187
Summary — 189

Chapter 7: Managing Policies — 191
Understanding Citrix policies — 191
Working with Citrix policies — 192
Best practices for creating Citrix policies — 193
Guidelines for working with policies — 193
Working with management consoles — 194
Using the Group Policy Management Console — 194
Using the Delivery Services Console — 195

[iii]

Using the Local Group Policy Editor	196
Creating Citrix policies	**198**
Creating a policy using consoles	198
Applying policies to sessions	**202**
Unfiltered policies	203
Using multiple policies	205
Troubleshooting policies	**206**
Using the Citrix Policy Modeling Wizard	207
Simulate connection scenarios with Citrix policies	207
Citrix settings precedence over Windows settings	211
Searching policies and settings	211
Importing and migrating existing policies	213
Summary	**213**
Chapter 8: Printing in XenApp Environments	**215**
Windows printing concepts	**215**
Print job spooling	216
Printing on Citrix XenApp	**217**
Printing pathway	218
Client local printing	219
Client network printing	220
Server network printing	220
Assigning network printers to users	221
Adding session printers settings to a Citrix policy	221
Setting a default printer for a session	222
Modifying settings of session printers	223
Server local printers	224
Configuring server local printers	225
Managing printer drivers	**225**
Controlling printer driver automatic installation	226
Modifying the printer driver compatibility list	227
Replicating print drivers in XenApp	229
Using the Citrix Universal Printer	**230**
Setting up an auto-create generic universal printer	232
Setting up universal driver priority	233
Configuring the Universal Printer Driver on sessions	235
Setting up universal printing preview preference	236
Change the default settings on the Universal Printer	236
Implementing Printers	**236**
Auto-creation	237
Auto-creating client machine printers	237
Auto-creating network printers	238
Configuring printer auto-creation settings	238

Configuring legacy client printer support	239
User provisioning	240
Publishing the Windows Add Printer wizard	240
Publishing the ICA Client Printer Configuration tool	241
Storing users' printer properties	241
General locations of printing preferences	244
Printing for mobile users	**244**
SmoothRoaming	245
Proximity printing	245
Configuring printers for mobile users	245
Improving printing performance	246
Limit printing bandwidth	247
Third-party printing solutions	**247**
XenApp Printing Optimization Pack	**247**
Universal printing EMF processing mode	248
Universal printing image compression limit	249
Universal printing optimization defaults	250
Universal printing print quality limit	251
Summary	**251**
Chapter 9: Multimedia Content on XenApp	**253**
Description of Citrix HDX technologies	**253**
Using HDX 3D technologies to improve image display	**254**
Using HDX 3D Image Acceleration to reduce bandwidth	255
Using HDX 3D Progressive Display to improve the display of images	256
Reduce CPU use by moving processing to GPU	258
Using HDX Broadcast Display settings	**259**
Using HDX MediaStream Multimedia Acceleration	**262**
Using Citrix policies to configure HDX MediaStream	264
Configuring echo cancellation	267
Using HDX MediaStream for Flash to optimize Flash content	**267**
Enabling HDX MediaStream at server side	268
System requirements for HDX MediaStream for Flash	269
Install/uninstall HDX MediaStream for Flash	269
Configuring HDX MediaStream for Flash settings	270
Setting up Flash Acceleration	270
Enable server-side event logging	271
Configuring HDX MediaStream for Flash on the client machine	274
Configuring audio using policies	**276**
Audio policy settings	276
Bandwidth policy settings	279
Configuring audio for user sessions	**280**

Table of Contents

HDX Experience Monitor for XenApp	**281**
Summary	**287**
Chapter 10: Managing Sessions	**289**
Understanding sessions	**289**
Monitoring XenApp sessions	**291**
Managing XenApp sessions	**293**
Disconnecting, resetting, and logging off sessions	293
Terminating processes in a user session	294
Sending messages to users	295
Viewing XenApp sessions	**296**
Viewing sessions using the Shadow Taskbar	297
Starting the Shadow Taskbar	298
Initiating shadowing	298
Ending a shadowing session	299
Enabling logging for shadowing	299
Enabling user-to-user shadowing	300
Creating a shadowing policy	301
Maintaining session activity	**304**
Configuring Session Reliability	304
Configuring automatic client reconnection	305
Configuring ICA keep-alive	307
Customizing user environments in XenApp	**308**
Controlling the appearance of user logons	309
Controlling access to devices and ports	309
Mapping drives	310
Redirecting COM ports and audio	310
Limiting concurrent connections	**311**
Limit the number of sessions per server	311
Limiting application instances	312
Logging connection denial events	313
Sharing sessions and connections	314
Preventing user connections during farm maintenance	315
Optimizing user sessions for XenApp	**316**
Mouse click feedback	316
Local text echo	317
Configuring SpeedScreen Latency Reduction	318
Redirection of Local Special Folders in sessions	**319**
Enable Special Folder Redirection in the web interface	320
Enable Special Folder Redirection for the Citrix Online Plug-in	321
Using Group Policy to redirect Special Folders	322
Summary	**324**

Chapter 11: Receiver and Plugins Management — 325
Introduction to Citrix Receiver — 325
  Citrix Receiver features — 326
  Citrix Receiver plugin compatibility — 326
  Citrix Receiver system requirements and compatibility — 327
    Citrix Receiver for Windows — 327
    Citrix Receiver for Macintosh — 328
Installing Citrix Receiver — 328
  Deploying Citrix Receiver for internal users with administrative rights — 328
  Installing Citrix Receiver for Windows — 329
  Installing Citrix Receiver on XenApp servers — 330
  Installing Citrix Receiver for Macintosh — 331
  Deploying Citrix Receiver for internal Windows users without administrative rights — 331
  Deploying Citrix Receiver for remote users — 332
  Instructions to edit the sample download page — 334
Setting up Citrix Merchandising Server 2.1 — 334
  Installing Merchandising Server software — 335
  Merchandising Server System requirements — 335
  Importing the virtual appliance into VMware vSphere 4.1 — 336
  Importing the virtual appliance into Citrix XenServer 5.6 — 338
  Setup Merchandising Server — 340
  Configuring administrator users — 341
  Installing plugins — 343
  Create recipient rules — 344
  Creating deliveries — 346
  Configure SSL certificates — 348
  Creating a self-signed SSL certificate — 349
  Creating a Certificate Signing Request — 350
  Importing SSL certificates — 351
  Creating a signing request for Microsoft certificate services — 352
  Installing SSL certificates on client machines — 353
Summary — 353
Chapter 12: Scripting Programming — 355
MFCOM and PowerShell — 355
Installing XenApp Commands on XenApp Servers — 356
  Installing Citrix XenApp 6 PowerShell SDK — 357
  Installing PowerShell XenApp Commands — 357
Using PowerShell for basic administrative tasks — 358
  Installing Citrix XenApp Commands snap-in — 358
  Using PowerShell for farm management — 360

Using PowerShell Commands from .NET applications — 366
Creating a sample VB.NET application — 366
Adding references — 366
Creating and opening a runspace — 367
Running a cmdlet — 368
Display results — 369
Passing parameters to cmdlets — 371
Creating a sample C#.NET application — 371
Adding references — 371
Creating and opening a runspace — 372
Running a cmdlet — 373
Display results — 373
Passing parameters to cmdlets — 376
Using MFCOM on XenApp — 376
Convert MFCOM scripts to PowerShell — 376
Summary — 377

Chapter 13: Virtualizing XenApp Farms — 379
Deploying XenApp 6 in a virtualized environment — 379
Virtual machine performance and host scalability — 381
Choosing the right virtualization platform — 382
Deploying XenApp6 on Citrix XenServer — 383
Install XenApp Evaluation Virtual Appliance on XenServer — 384
Creating a new XenApp 6 VM in XenServer — 385
Deploying XenApp6 on Microsoft Hyper-V — 389
Installing XenApp Evaluation Virtual Appliance on Hyper-V — 390
Creating a new XenApp 6 VM in Hyper-V — 392
Deploying XenApp 6 on VMware vSphere — 395
Create a new XenApp 6 VM in VMware vSphere — 396
Cloning XenApp 6 virtual machines — 403
Unattended Install of XenApp 6 — 406
Unattended Install of XenApp Components — 406
Summary — 411

Index — 413

Preface

XenApp 6 is the leader in application hosting and virtualization delivery, allowing users from different platforms such as Windows, Mac, Linux, and mobile devices to connect to their business applications. It reduces resources and costs for application distribution and management. Using Citrix XenApp 6, you can deploy secure applications quickly to thousands of users.

Getting Started with Citrix XenApp 6 provides comprehensive details on how to design, implement, and maintain Citrix farms based on XenApp 6. Additionally, you will learn how to use management tools and scripts for daily tasks such as managing servers, published resources, printers, and connections.

Getting Started with Citrix XenApp 6 starts by introducing the basics of XenApp such as installing servers and configuring components, and it then teaches you how to publish applications and resources on the client device before moving on to configuring content redirection. Author Guillermo Musumeci includes a use case throughout the book to explain advanced topics like creating management scripts and deploying and optimizing XenApp for Citrix XenServer, VMware ESX, and Microsoft Hyper-V virtual machines. It will guide you through an unattended installation of XenApp and components on physical servers. By the end of this book, you will have enough knowledge to successfully design and manage your own XenApp 6 Farms.

What this book covers

Chapter 1, *Getting Started with XenApp 6*, provides an introduction to XenApp 6 and discusses the new features in the product. This chapter also covers the requirements to deploy XenApp 6.

Chapter 2, *Designing a XenApp 6 Farm*, explains Citrix farm terminologies and concepts, and how to design a basic XenApp architecture and a basic pilot plan to deploy XenApp. Also, how to choose applications and implement them on XenApp is discussed with the help of a case study.

Preface

Chapter 3, Installing XenApp 6, describes how to install and configure XenApp 6, including XenApp, Licensing Service, and Web Interface roles using the new XenApp Server Role Manager. Configuring Remote Desktop Services and installing the new Citrix Delivery Services management console are also discussed in this chapter.

Chapter 4, Using Management Tools, presents the Citrix Delivery Services Console, License Administration, and Citrix Web Interface Management Consoles. It shows other tools like Citrix SSL Relay Configuration tool, Shadow taskbar, and SpeedScreen Latency Reduction Manager. Finally, it shows how to create and manage Citrix administrator's accounts.

Chapter 5, Application Publishing, discusses how to publish different types of resources in XenApp: hosted and streamed applications, content and server desktops. Also, it discovers content redirection, from server to client and client to server, and explains how to set up and update file type associations.

Chapter 6, Application Streaming, explains the installation, configuration, and delivery of streaming applications. It describes system requirements and components for application streaming. It chooses plugins for application streaming and describes how to profile and publish Microsoft Office 2010 on a XenApp farm.

Chapter 7, Managing Policies, describes Citrix policies and how to create, manage, and apply Citrix policies. It explains the use of the Group Policy Management Console, Citrix Delivery Services Console, and Local Group Policy Editor to manage Citrix Policies. Also, troubleshooting Citrix Policies is discussed in this chapter.

Chapter 8, Printing in XenApp Environments, describes Windows and Citrix XenApp printing concepts. It explains how to assign network printers to users using Citrix policies. It presents the new XenApp Printing Optimization Pack. It shows how to manage printer drivers, use the Citrix universal printer, and implement printers. It also explains printing for mobile users.

Chapter 9, Multimedia Content on XenApp 6, explains how to optimize user sessions for XenApp using different Citrix HDX features like HDX MediaStream Multimedia Acceleration, HDX 3D Image Acceleration, HDX 3D Progressive Display, HDX MediaStream for Flash, and more. It describes how to configure HDX MediaStream for Flash on the Server and different multimedia, audio, and video settings using Citrix policies.

Chapter 10, Managing Sessions, describes sessions and explains how to manage and monitor sessions using Citrix Delivery Services Console, including viewing and shadowing of sessions. It discusses how to customize user environments in XenApp and limit concurrent connections. It also shows how to optimize user sessions, redirect local Special folders in sessions, and maintain session Activity using Session Reliability, Auto Client Reconnect, and ICA keep-alive.

Chapter 11, Receiver and Plugins Management, presents Citrix Receiver, including features and compatibility and explains how to install Citrix Receiver for Windows and Macintosh. It describes how to deploy a Citrix Merchandising Server on VMware, XenServer Virtual Machines, and configure Merchandising Server and Receiver Plugins.

Chapter 12, Scripting Programming, shows how to install and configure PowerShell to manage XenApp farms and how to use cmdlets to manage XenApp servers. It explains how to use PowerShell commands from inside VB.NET and C#.NET code. It discusses how to convert MFCOM scripts to PowerShell and access MFCOM objects and manage previous versions of XenApp from PowerShell.

Chapter 13, Virtualizing XenApp Farms, explains how to deploy XenApp 6 in a virtualized environment, including advantages and disadvantages of virtualization, virtual machine performance, host scalability, and more. It describes how to deploy XenApp6 on Citrix XenServer, Microsoft Hyper-V, and VMware vSphere virtual machines, and how to clone XenApp6 virtual machines. It also shows how to use an unattended installation of XenApp 6.

What you need for this book

The following are the software requirements for this book:

- Microsoft Windows Server 2008 R2 and Citrix XenApp 6 are required to install and configure XenApp 6 servers
- Optional: dedicated database server running Microsoft SQL Server 2005 or later or Oracle 11g R2 is required in *Chapter 3, Installing XenApp 6*
- Microsoft Office 2010 is required to setup Application Streaming for *Chapter 6, Application Streaming*
- Microsoft Visual Basic.NET or Microsoft C#.NET to create applications in *Chapter 12, Scripting Programming*
- One hypervisor like Citrix XenServer, Microsoft Hyper-V, and VMware vSphere to create virtual machines discussed in *Chapter 13, Virtualizing XenApp Farms*

Who this book is for

If you are a system administrator or consultant who wants to implement and administer Citrix XenApp 6 farms, then this book is for you. This book will help both new and experienced XenApp professionals to deliver virtualized applications.

Conventions

In this book, you will find a number of styles of text that distinguish between different kinds of information. Here are some examples of these styles, and an explanation of their meaning.

Code words in text are shown as follows: "To use the cmdlets included with XenApp Commands, we must call it using an instance of the RunspaceConfiguration class".

A block of code is set as follows:

```
Imports System.Collections.Generic
Imports System.Collections.ObjectModel
PublicClass Form1
   Sub ShowXAServers()
Dim rsConfig As RunspaceConfiguration
   rsConfig = RunspaceConfiguration.Create()
Dim info As PSSnapInInfo
Dim snapInException AsNew PSSnapInException
```

When we wish to draw your attention to a particular part of a code block, the relevant lines or items are set in bold:

```
Command myCommand = newCommand("Get-XAServer")
myCommand.Parameters.Add("ZoneName", "US-ZONE")
pipeLine.Commands.Add(myCommand)
```

Any command-line input or output is written as follows:

C:\>RUNAS /user:brickunit\wempire CMD

New terms and **important words** are shown in bold. Words that you see on the screen, in menus or dialog boxes for example, appear in the text like this: "The **Server Farms** option on the **Edit Settings** pane helps us to set up XML Broker(s) and Citrix farm(s) accessible to the web interface".

> Warnings or important notes appear in a box like this.

> Tips and tricks appear like this.

Reader feedback

Feedback from our readers is always welcome. Let us know what you think about this book—what you liked or may have disliked. Reader feedback is important for us to develop titles that you really get the most out of.

To send us general feedback, simply send an e-mail to feedback@packtpub.com, and mention the book title via the subject of your message.

If there is a book that you need and would like to see us publish, please send us a note in the **SUGGEST A TITLE** form on www.packtpub.com or e-mail suggest@packtpub.com. If there is a topic that you have expertise in and you are interested in either writing or contributing to a book, see our author guide on www.packtpub.com/authors.

Customer support

Now that you are the proud owner of a Packt book, we have a number of things to help you to get the most from your purchase.

Downloading the example code

You can download the example code files for all Packt books you have purchased from your account at http://www.PacktPub.com. If you purchased this book elsewhere, you can visit http://www.PacktPub.com/support and register to have the files e-mailed directly to you.

Errata

Although we have taken every care to ensure the accuracy of our content, mistakes do happen. If you find a mistake in one of our books—maybe a mistake in the text or the code—we would be grateful if you would report this to us. By doing so, you can save other readers from frustration and help us improve subsequent versions of this book. If you find any errata, please report them by visiting http://www.packtpub.com/support, selecting your book, clicking on the **errata submission form** link, and entering the details of your errata. Once your errata are verified, your submission will be accepted and the errata will be uploaded on our website, or added to any list of existing errata, under the Errata section of that title. Any existing errata can be viewed by selecting your title from http://www.packtpub.com/support.

Piracy

Piracy of copyright material on the Internet is an ongoing problem across all media. At Packt, we take the protection of our copyright and licenses very seriously. If you come across any illegal copies of our works, in any form, on the Internet, please provide us with the location address or website name immediately so that we can pursue a remedy.

Please contact us at `copyright@packtpub.com` with a link to the suspected pirated material.

We appreciate your help in protecting our authors, and our ability to bring you valuable content.

Questions

You can contact us at `questions@packtpub.com` if you are having a problem with any aspect of the book, and we will do our best to address it.

1
Getting Started with XenApp 6

Citrix XenApp is now the leader of application virtualization or application delivery. Several years ago, back when the word Virtualization didn't exist, people used to talk about application hosting. Citrix was founded in 1989 and they developed the first successful product in 1993 called WinView. It provided remote access to DOS and Windows 3.1 applications on a multiuser platform. Citrix licensed Microsoft's Windows NT 3.51 source code from Microsoft; and in 1995, they shipped a multiuser version of Windows NT based on MultiWin engine, known as WinFrame. This allowed multiple users to logon and execute applications on a WinFrame server. Citrix in 1996 licensed the MultiWin technology to Microsoft, establishing the foundation of Microsoft's Terminal Services.

I remember the first time I was in touch with application hosting. It was in 1997 and I was working at Microsoft in Argentina as a Technical Support Engineer. I was invited for MCSE certification training on a Saturday morning. We had been building a lab with several machines, when I saw several Microsoft Beta CDs on a table.

I took one of them called Hydra and I asked the guy in charge of the training about it. He told me that the CD contained a software to convert a Windows NT 4.0 – a sort of mainframe. I asked him if we could install it on a machine and he told me we did not have enough RAM to install it. I recall walking inside empty offices to open computers and remove the RAM so that we could install Hydra on a computer.

It was a couple of years later, in 1999, when I discovered that Hydra is the Windows 4.0 Terminal Server Edition; I was working with my first Citrix server and that was when I first fell in love with application hosting.

In this chapter, we will learn:

- XenApp 6 and its features
- System requirements for the installation of XenApp 6

Introducing XenApp 6

The new Citrix XenApp 6 runs only on Microsoft Windows Server 2008 R2. Citrix rewrote the code completely for the Windows 64-bit platform. This job provided a great opportunity to optimize the code for performance and scalability (Citrix tested XenApp 6 farms with over 1,000 member servers and 100,000 concurrent sessions) and provided new features.

Here are some of the highlights of the new XenApp 6:

- **Citrix Delivery Services Console** is the new single management console. Only one console is something all users wanted for years. The new management console has been completely redesigned. We still need a separate console to manage web interface servers and licensing. We are going to explore the new **Citrix Delivery Services Console** in *Chapter 4, Using Management Tools*, and *Chapter 5, Application Publishing*.

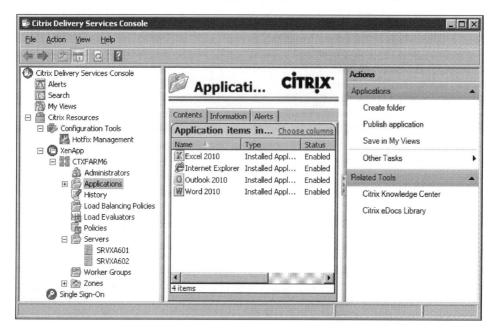

- **Citrix Receiver:** The new Citrix Receiver for Windows supports eight languages and provides support for new plugins including Single sign-On, WAN acceleration, App-V, and more. Also, there is a new receiver for Mac and mobile users. We can use this receiver on iPhone, iPad, Android, or Blackberry to access applications hosted on XenApp 6. We are going to learn about the Citrix Receiver in detail in *Chapter 11, Receiver and Plugins Management*.

- **Citrix Dazzle:** Citrix called Dazzle the first self-service "storefront" for enterprise applications. Dazzle allows corporate employees 24x7 self-service access to the applications they need to work. End users now can subscribe to XenApp applications (including App-V packages) using Dazzle on PC or Mac.

- **Active Directory Group Policy integration**: Now, we can manage XenApp policies and configure XenApp servers and farm settings using Active Directory Group Policies (GPO). *Chapter 7, Managing Policies*, is dedicated to XenApp policies and provides extensive information on how to use the Group Policy Management Console to manage Citrix policies.

- **PowerShell Support:** We can use Microsoft PowerShell to automate common XenApp management tasks. Citrix dropped support for MFCOM (the programming interface for the administration of XenApp servers and farms on previous versions) as the favorite option for developers and added PowerShell 2.0 support. *Chapter 12, Scripting Programming*, is dedicated to scripting programming using PowerShell.

- **Windows service isolation for streamed applications**: This new feature allows applications to install Windows services and they can be profiled and streamed. This new option increases the number of streamed applications supported. Applications like Microsoft Office 2010 or Adobe Creative Suite install a windows service. Now we can profile and stream them, and other applications, using the new service isolation technology. We can learn about Application Streaming in *Chapter 6, Application Streaming*.

- **Citrix HDX technologies:** Provide better multimedia and high-definition experience with support for more USB devices than ever before. Citrix HDX offers great improvements in both audio and video quality. New video conference capabilities and advanced Adobe Flash support are included too. Also, HDX provides multi-monitor support, improving application compatibility when we use multiple monitors. *Chapter 9, Multimedia Content on XenApp 6*, is dedicated to improve the multimedia experience of users using Citrix HDX technologies.

- **Support for Windows portable USB devices:** This feature allows our users to plug in their USB devices like cameras, scanners, and other devices and access them from their published applications on XenApp 6. The **Role-based Setup Wizard** simplifies server deployment and reduces installation time. The new redesigned setup makes installation simple, fast, and intuitive. Now we can install XenApp 6 in a few clicks. Also, by separating the installation from the configuration, we simplified XenApp deployments using Provisioning services or other image management solutions. We use the role-based Setup Wizard in *Chapter 3, Installing XenApp 6*, to install our first XenApp 6 servers.

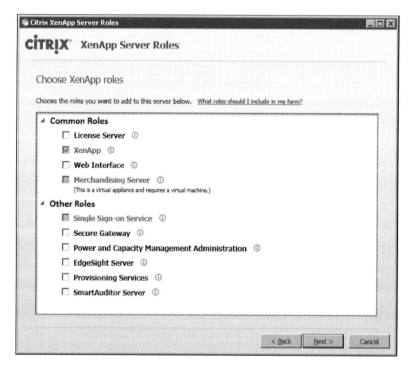

- **Microsoft App-V integration** allows us to manage and deliver both Citrix and Microsoft application delivery from a single point. Also, App-V managed applications can now be delivered via Citrix Dazzle. Administrators can now distribute App-V plugin to end-point devices using Citrix Receiver.
- **Multi-lingual User Interface (MUI):** XenApp now supports MUI. This feature allows multinational companies to deploy one XenApp server to serve users who need access to their applications in their local language.

In addition to these major features and enhancements, XenApp 6 included other features like great **Web Interface**, **Single Sign-on**, and **SmartAuditor** enhancements, new 32-bit color support, Windows 7 smart card support, and so on.

XenApp feature overview

This section provides summary descriptions of some of the most popular XenApp features. This section will help new Citrix customers to understand major features on the last three versions of XenApp (XenApp 4.5, 5.0, 6.0).

- Access applications from any device, anytime, anywhere: We can deliver any published Windows application to an extensive variety of user devices and operating systems, including Windows, Mac, Linux, UNIX, DOS, Java, and mobile devices like iPhone, iPad, Blackberry, and Android devices.
- Active Directory Federation Services support: We can use ADFS to provide business partners access to published applications.
- Application gateway: Citrix provides SSL-proxy, using both hardware (Citrix NetScaler and Citrix Access Gateway) and software (Citrix Secure Gateway) solutions, to allow remote users to access published applications in XenApp, securely.
- CPU utilization management: This feature prevents users and their processes from utilizing the CPU too much and guarantees a consistent performance level for all users on the XenApp server.
- Installation Manager: This feature allows us to remotely install applications to multiple XenApp servers simultaneously.
- Network Management Console Integration: XenApp supports SNMP monitoring and integration with third-party network management tools, including Microsoft System Center Operations Manager (SCOM), Microsoft Operations Manager (MOM), IBM Tivoli, HP OpenView, CAUnicenter.
- Novell eDirectory and NDS Support: XenApp 6 provides support for Novell eDirectory and Domain Services for Windows, allowing XenApp to authenticate Novell users.
- Power and capacity management: We can create system policies to manage server power consumption. This feature can turn on/off XenApp servers. As users log off and idle resources increase, idle servers are shut down. When users arrive in the morning and they log on to the farm, servers are powered up. Also, we can schedule time for powering on and powering off servers.

- Single Sign-On: This feature (formerly known as Password Manager) provides single sign-on access to Windows, web, and terminal emulator applications. The self-service password reset feature included in single sign-on allows users to reset their domain password or unlock their Windows account.
- SmartAuditor: Uses policies to allow us to record the on-screen activity of any user's session, over any type of connection, from any server running XenApp. SmartAuditor records, catalogs, and archives sessions for review.
- Web interface: The web interface allows users access to published applications and content on XenApp through a standard web browser or Citrix Plug-in. Web interface provides built-in support for two-factor, RADIUS, and Smart Card authentication, simple customization through the management console and multilingual support, for the following languages: English, German, Spanish, French, Japanese, Chinese (simplified and traditional), and Korean.

System requirements

The most obvious requirement to install XenApp 6 is the operating system. XenApp6 is only available for Microsoft Windows Server 2008 R2, with two exceptions: Web Server and Core editions. We cannot install XenApp in these two versions.

If we want to deploy XenApp on Microsoft Windows Server 2003 or Microsoft Windows Server 2008 R1 (x86 and x64), we must choose to use XenApp 5. Citrix XenApp 6 does not support mixed farms. Mixed farms are XenApp farms that contain more than one server version.

Until previous versions, Citrix supported XenApp farms that contained different versions of Windows and/or of XenApp. XenApp 6 cannot coexist with any previous versions in the same farm. We can have two separated farms and use web interface to provide users access to both farms using one single interface.

During the wizard-based installation, the XenApp Server Role Manager automatically installs prerequisites for the selected roles. Also, we can choose to install XenApp from command-line installations or using unattended scripts. In that case, we must need to deploy the prerequisites before starting the XenApp role installation. We will talk about unattended install of XenApp 6 in *Chapter 13, Virtualizing XenApp Farms*.

We need to use the `ServerManagerCmd.exe` command or PowerShell to deploy prerequisites like IIS or .NET Framework.

The XenApp Server Role Manager deploys the following software, if it is not already installed:

- .NET Framework 3.5 SP1 (this is a prerequisite for the XenApp Server Role Manager and it is deployed automatically when we choose the XenApp server role)
- Windows Server Remote Desktop Services role (if we do not have this prerequisite installed, the Server Role Manager installs it and enables the RDP client connection option; we will be asked to restart the server and resume the installation when we log in again)
- Windows Application Server role
- Microsoft Visual C++ 2005 SP1 Redistributable (x64)
- Microsoft Visual C++ 2008 SP1 Redistributable (x64)

If the server already has the IIS role services installed, the Citrix XML Service IIS Integration component is selected by default in the wizard-based XenApp installation, and the Citrix XML Service and IIS share a port (the default port is 80).

If the IIS role services are not installed, the Citrix XML Service IIS Integration component is not selected by default in the wizard-based installation. In this case, if we select the checkbox, the Server Role Manager installs the following IIS role services. (If we do not install these services, the Citrix XML Service defaults to standalone mode with its own port settings, which we can configure using the XenApp Server Configuration Tool.)

- **Web Server (IIS) | Common HTTP Features | Default Document**. Selecting this role automatically selects Web Server (IIS), Management Tools, and Management Console (not required for XenApp installation).
- **Web Server (IIS) | Application Development | ASP.NET**. Choosing this role automatically selects **Web Server (IIS) | Application Development | .NET Extensibility**.
- **Web Server (IIS) | Application Development | ISAPI Extensions**.
- **Web Server (IIS) | Application Development | ISAPI Filters**.
- **Web Server (IIS) | Security | Windows Authentication**.
- **Web Server (IIS) | Security | Request Filtering**.
- **Web Server (IIS) | Management Tools | IIS 6 Management Compatibility** (which includes IIS 6 Metabase Compatibility, IIS 6 WMI Compatibility, IIS 6 Scripting Tools, and IIS 6 Management Console).

Data store databases

The following databases are supported for the data store:

- Microsoft SQL Server 2008 Express (the new XenApp Server Configuration Tool can install it when creating a new XenApp farm)
- Microsoft SQL Server 2005
- Microsoft SQL Server 2008 / 2008 R2
- Oracle 11g R2

For more information about supported databases versions, see the Document ID **CTX114501** at http://support.citrix.com/article/CTX114501.

We will use Microsoft SQL Server to configure the Citrix Data store in this book, because this is the most popular option. We will install and configure a SQL Server as a data store database in *Chapter 3, Installing XenApp 6*.

Citrix Delivery Services Console

As we mentioned before, Citrix XenApp 6 includes a new Citrix Delivery Services Console. We can manage our XenApp servers using it. By default, the console is installed on the same XenApp server where we install the XenApp server role; but we can install and run the console on a separate computer.

If we want to administer multiple farms of the different XenApp versions, we need to install multiple versions of management consoles on the same computer.

To install the Citrix Delivery Services Console on a computer, from the XenApp Auto run menu, select **Manually Install Components | Common Components | Management Consoles**. We will install the Citrix Delivery Services Console in *Chapter 3, Installing XenApp 6*.

We can install the Citrix Delivery Services Console in the following operating systems:

- Microsoft Windows XP Professional SP3, 32-bit, and 64-bit editions
- Microsoft Windows Vista SP1(Business, Enterprise, and Ultimate versions), 32-bit and 64-bit editions
- Microsoft Windows 7 (Professional, Enterprise, and Ultimate versions), 32-bit and 64-bit editions
- Microsoft Windows Server 2003 SP2 (Standard, Enterprise, and Datacenter versions), 32-bit and 64-bit editions
- Microsoft Windows Server 2003 R2 (Standard, Enterprise, and Datacenter versions), 32-bit and 64-bit editions

Chapter 1

- Microsoft Windows Server 2008 (Standard, Enterprise, and Datacenter versions), 32-bit and 64-bit editions
- Microsoft Windows Server 2008 R2 (Standard, Enterprise, and Datacenter versions)

Also, the XenApp Server Role Manager deploys the following software, if it is not already installed:

- Microsoft .NET Framework 3.5 SP1
- Microsoft Windows Installer (MSI) 3.0
- Microsoft Windows Group Policy Management Console
- Microsoft Visual C++ 2005 SP1 Redistributable (x64)
- Microsoft Visual C++ 2008 SP1 Redistributable (x64)
- Microsoft Visual C++ 2008 SP1 Redistributable
- Microsoft Visual C++ 2005 SP1 Redistributable
- Microsoft Primary Interoperability Assemblies 2005

> If we install the Delivery Services Console on a computer that previously contained the Microsoft Group Policy Management Console (GPMC) and an earlier version of the Delivery Services Console, we may also need to uninstall and reinstall the Citrix XenApp Group Policy Management Experience (x64) program in order to use the GPMC to configure Citrix policies.

License server

Download and install the latest Citrix License Server or use the version included in the ISO of XenApp 6. License server version recommended is at least 11.6.1 build 10007.

We will install and configure the Citrix License Server in *Chapter 3, Installing XenApp 6*.

Clients

We need to install the most recent version of the Citrix Plug-in (formerly known as ICA Client) to guarantee availability of all features and functionality of XenApp 6 to our users.

To install plugins, connect to www.citrix.com and then go to the **Downloads** option. Choose **Citrix Clients** and then install the **Citrix Online Plug-in** (choose full or web version) and if you're planning to run offline streamed applications, you must install the **Citrix Offline Plug-in** too.

Summary

In this chapter, we learned some new features about XenApp 6. Specifically:

- Enhanced scalability and performance
- Simplified install
- Citrix Receiver and Citrix Dazzle
- Microsoft App-V support
- Windows service isolation for streamed applications
- Multi-lingual User Interface
- Citrix HDX technology
- Single management console
- Active Directory Group Policy integration
- PowerShell SDK

We discussed about these new exciting features, and in particular, the Citrix Delivery Service console, the 64-bit support, the new installation process using role-based setup, Citrix HDX, and more.

In the next chapter, we will discuss how to design a XenApp 6 Farm and how to implement some of these new features.

2
Designing a XenApp 6 Farm

Now that we have learned about the features of XenApp and the new features of XenApp 6, it's now time for us to start the design of our XenApp 6 farm. The most important step before any Citrix deployment is to understand the features of the product and design the architecture before the servers are set up.

In this chapter, we will take a look at the case study that we will use in the book to implement XenApp 6: Brick Unit Constructions.

In this chapter, we will cover the following topics:

- Learning Citrix farm terminology and concepts
- Designing a basic XenApp architecture
- Designing a basic pilot plan
- Creating a list of applications to publish in our Citrix farm
- Reviewing a list of applications and deciding the best method to deliver them

Case study: Brick Unit Constructions

John Charles Empire established a small construction company near Washington DC in 1973. His company started building small homes in the state of Maryland and currently is one of the most important construction companies in the area. In the last 10 years, they increased the revenue, the amount of employees, and construction sites, and now they have several construction sites around the state.

Managing the software installed on computers and other devices in the field is a nightmare for the small IT department of the company and their manager, William Empire, son of John Charles.

When William read about the new XenApp 6, he thought the product could help the company manage the distributed and complex environment of Brick Unit Constructions.

Farm terminology and concepts

Now is the moment to define the terminology we are going to use in this book. If you are new in the Citrix world, please pay attention to this section.

- **Multi-user environment** is when applications are published on servers running remote desktop services and/or XenApp accessed by multiple users simultaneously.

- **XenApp server** is the main software component of the Citrix application delivery infrastructure. The objective of XenApp servers is to deliver applications to user devices.

- **XenApp application servers** are the farm servers that host published applications.

- **XenApp infrastructure servers** are the farm servers that host services such as a license server or web interface. Usually, they do not host published applications.

- **Remote desktop services (RDS)**, formerly known as **Terminal Services**, is one of the components of Microsoft Windows that allows a user to access applications and data on a remote computer over a network. We need to install this component (and appropriate licenses) to setup and run XenApp servers. XenApp extends the functionality of Microsoft Remote Desktop Services, adding flexibility, manageability, security, and performance to RDS.

Applications can be made available by installing in the server or streaming to the client. XenApp 6 supports only Windows 32-bit or Windows 64-bit applications. Running 16-bit applications is NOT supported.

XenApp offers three methods for delivering applications to user devices, servers, and virtual desktops:

- Server-side application virtualization: Applications run on the XenApp servers. XenApp shows the application interface on the user device or client, and transmits user actions from the device, such as keystrokes and mouse actions, back to the application.

- Client-side application virtualization: XenApp streams applications on demand to the user device from the XenApp farm and runs the application on the user device.

- VM hosted application virtualization: Challenging applications or those requiring specific operating systems run inside a desktop on the XenApp server. XenApp shows the application interface on the user device or client, and transmits user actions from the device, such as keystrokes and mouse actions, back to the application.

XenApp server farm is a logical collection or group of XenApp servers that can be managed as a single entity. Usually, Citrix define three types of farms:

- **Design validation farm**: Design validation farm is set up in a laboratory, typically as the design or blueprint for the production farm. Usually, the preferred method to build a design validation farm today is using virtual machines.
- **Pilot farm**: Pilot farm is a preproduction farm used to test a farm design and applications before deploying the farm across the company. The pilot must include users from the entire organization and role. These users should access the farm for their everyday needs.
- **Production farm:** Production farm is in regular use and accessed by all users in the organization.

Farm Architecture defines the plan for the design of the server farm and zones based on current requirements and future expansion plans. Farm architecture requires a strong understanding of the network topology, scalability, failover, and geographic location of the sites and users in the company.

- **Zones**: Zones are used to control the aggregation and replication of data in the farm. A farm should be divided into zones based upon the network topology, where major geographic regions are assigned to separate zones. Each zone elects a data collector, which aggregates dynamic data from the servers in its zone and replicates the data to the data collectors in the other zones.
- **Worker group**: A worker group is a new feature introduced on XenApp 6. It is a collection of XenApp servers in the same farm. Worker groups allow a set of similar servers to be grouped together and managed as one. Worker groups are closely related to the concept of application **silos** (silos usually are servers dedicated to run critical or resource-intensive applications). All servers in the worker group share the same list of published applications and identical XenApp server settings.
- **Data collector**: A collector stores information about servers and published applications inside a group and acts as a gateway between data collectors in other groups. In large XenApp server farm environments, it is a good idea to have a dedicated server and restrict it from delivering applications. A dedicated data collector improves load balancing decisions and reduces session logon time.

User device is where the client software is installed to access data anywhere:

- **Citrix Receiver:** Citrix Receiver is the first universal client for IT service delivery. Users can use any device—it runs on smartphones, laptops, desktops, and netbooks (PC or Mac). With Citrix Receiver installed on a device, IT can deliver applications and desktops as an on-demand service with no need to manage, own, or care about the physical device or its location. Citrix Receiver is a lightweight software client with an extensible browser-like "plugin" architecture that communicates with head-end infrastructure in the Citrix Delivery Center product family including XenApp and XenDesktop. Citrix Receiver was formerly known as Citrix ICA Client.

- **Citrix Dazzle** and the self-service storefront: Citrix Dazzle, the self-service enterprise application storefront, offers a personal and easy-to-use interface for subscribing to applications. Administrators can distribute the Dazzle plug-in using Citrix Receiver, and users can choose their published application subscriptions. Dazzle also downloads and pre-caches streamed applications. The self-service storefront is available for both Windows and Mac users.

- **Merchandising Server** provides easy management, setup, and distribution of Citrix Receiver and related plugins and updates. Users simply point any browser to the setup site included with Merchandising Server, and within two clicks, the setup process starts. Merchandising Server software is delivered as a virtual appliance for Citrix XenServer or VMware.

Infrastructure server

Infrastructure servers are farm servers that host services such as license server or web interface. Usually, they do not host published applications.

XenApp farms have two types of infrastructure servers:

- **Virtualization infrastructure** consists of the XenApp servers that deliver virtualized applications and VM hosted applications and roles that support sessions and administration, such as the data store, data collector, Citrix XML broker, Citrix License Server, configuration logging database (optional), load testing services database (optional), service monitoring agents, and so on.

- **Access Infrastructure** consists of roles such as the web interface, secure gateway (optional), and access gateway (optional) that provide access to users.

In small deployments, we can group one or more roles together. In large deployments, we provide services on one or multiple dedicated servers.

Virtualization infrastructure

Virtualization infrastructure represents a series of servers that control and monitor application environments.

Now, we will see different types of infrastructure servers:

- Citrix licensing: A Citrix License Server is required for all XenApp deployments. Install the license server on either a shared or standalone server, depending on your farm's size. After we install the license server, we need to download the appropriate license files from the `MyCitrix.com` website and install them in the license server. We can share a license server with multiple Citrix products. We are going to install and configure a license server in the next chapter.

- Data store database: Data store database is a repository of persistent farm information, including server's information, published applications, administrators, printers, and so on. We can host the data store database on a SQL Server Express database running on one of our XenApp servers in a small farm, use a dedicated SQL Server, or an Oracle database server in medium to large farms. We are going to install and configure a data store in the next chapter.

- Citrix XML Broker acts as an intermediary between the web interface and other servers in the farm. When a user logs in to the web interface, the XML Broker receives the user's credentials from the web interface and queries the server farm for a list of published applications that the user has permission to access. The XML Broker obtains this application set from the IMA (Independent Management Architecture) system and returns it to the web interface.

- Citrix XML Service: The XML Broker is a component of the Citrix XML Service. By default, the XML Service is installed on every server during XenApp setup. However, only the XML Service on the server specified in the web interface acts as the broker. In a small farm, the XML Broker runs on a server with multiple infrastructure functions. In a large farm, the XML Broker might be configured on one or more dedicated servers. Configuring a dedicated XML server is a simple task, we need to set up a dedicated XenApp server without any published applications.

- Single sign-on (optional): Single sign-on provides password management for published applications. Single sign-on can use Active Directory or a NTFS share to store password information. Single sign-on was formerly known as password manager and requires a Platinum license. Installation and configuration of single sign-on is out the scope of this book.

- Service monitoring (optional) is based on CitrixEdgesight and enables the administrator to collect, monitor, and report server resource metrics to estimate servers required to deploy a XenApp farm or to analyze the load of production servers. This feature requires a Platinum license. Installation and configuration of Edgesight is out the scope of this book.

- Provisioning Services (optional) assist administrators to manage the entire XenApp farm of application hosting servers, both physical and virtual, using one or multiple standardized server image. PVS can rollback to a previous working image in the time it takes to reboot. This feature requires a Platinum license. Installation and configuration of Provisioning Services is out the scope of this book.

- SmartAuditor (optional) allows an administrator to record the onscreen activity of any user's session, over any type of connection, from any server running XenApp. SmartAuditor uses policies to record, catalog, and archive sessions for retrieval and playback. This feature requires a Platinum license. Installation and configuration of SmartAuditor is out the scope of this book.

- Power and Capacity Management (optional) enables administrators to reduce power consumption and manage server capacity by dynamically scaling the number of online servers or powering on/off servers based on specific times. This feature requires a Platinum license. Installation and configuration of Power and Capacity Management is out the scope of this book.

Access Infrastructure

Access Infrastructure represents a series of servers deployed within the local network or the DMZ to provide access to different types of users (local or remote) to resources published on XenApp servers.

XenApp farms have three types of access infrastructure servers:

- Web interface provides users with access to resources published on one or multiple XenApp farms through a standard web browser or through the Citrix Online Plug-in.

- Access Gateway (optional) is a universal SSL VPN appliance that can be used to secure client connections to XenApp farms and provide secure access to other internal network resources. XenApp Platinum Edition licenses include a universal Access Gateway license, which can be used with any Access Gateway edition. The Access Gateway appliance, also known as **Netscaler**, must be purchased separately.

- Secure Gateway (optional) assists administrators to secure access to enterprise network computers running XenApp and provides a secure Internet gateway between XenApp farms and client devices. The Secure Gateway transparently encrypts and authenticates all user connections to help protect against data tampering and theft. All data traversing the Internet between a remote workstation and the Secure Gateway is encrypted using the Secure Sockets Layer (SSL) or Transport Layer Security (TLS) protocol. The Secure Gateway is an application that runs as a service on a server that is deployed in the demilitarized zone (DMZ).

Designing a basic XenApp architecture

Let's learn more about Brick Unit Constructions. The HQ of the company is located near Frederick in Maryland. The company had around 120 users working there. Currently, they have 17 sites under construction around the state located in a 150 miles radius from HQ. Each of these sites has 10 to 25 computers, accessing applications installed on the site server or in each user computer. So we have around 400 users between HQ and construction sites. Almost 20 percent of all these users utilize laptops, work on a few projects at the same time, and travel between sites. All these sites are connected in a MPLS network between HQ and sites using T1 links.

Usually, these projects are short-term, between 6 months to 2 years. When the project is completed, IT needs to take a full backup of every machine and the server and reassign them to a new project. None of these sites has its own IT personnel, so the management of these servers and computers (backups, installing new applications, printers, and so on) is centralized from HQ, making the administration very complicated.

Users with laptops are having issues with printers and access to files located on different servers. William wants to resolve this issue by moving all data in remote file servers to a centralized file server on a NAS (Network Attached Storage) device, and migrate all printer queues located on remote sites to a new printer server on HQ. The migration of printers will help him to clean up print server drivers and check the compatibility of the current printers with Citrix.

The other issue these users are having is related to an in-house developed financial application installed on construction sites servers. Users must have these applications installed multiple times (one per site).

The following diagram is the Brick Unit Construction's current infrastructure:

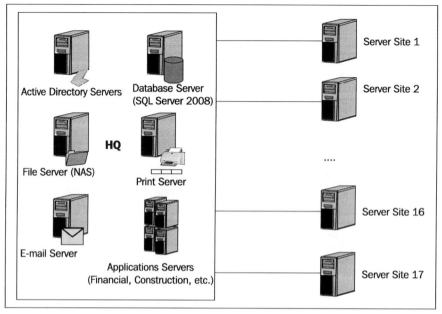

William is concerned about the following:

- Deciding whether he would want to run XenApp on virtual machines or physical servers
- Budget: The cost of all Terminal Server and Citrix licenses will require a large expenditure
- Virtual machines will provide a lot of benefits, but will require a large investment in a SAN (Storage Area Network), the increase of memory RAM of existing servers, and the cost of the virtualization server software

William's idea is to move all applications installed on a client's machine or servers in remote sites to a XenApp farm, migrate all data in these sites to the HQ file, print servers, remove servers from field, and reuse them (these servers are pretty new) to build more XenApp servers or virtualization hosts to run XenApp on virtual machines.

Moving all applications to XenApp will help IT to reduce the license cost of applications and simplify the deployment of new versions.

Centralizing all data in a NAS file server will help to reduce backup costs (hardware and software) and simplify administration. Also, it will reduce the time to restore information.

Currently, the most popular option to implement XenApp 6 is using virtual machines and William decided to use it for the deployment of Brick Unit's farm. We are going to learn how to implement XenApp on virtualized environments in *Chapter 13*, *Virtualizing XenApp Farms*.

The pilot plan

William wants to build a very simple infrastructure to test the product with some users and later add more features (and servers) to the deployment.

He, hence, creates a basic task list to deploy the XenAppDesign Validation Farm:

1. Design Active Directory integration.
2. Build a small test farm in the lab with three servers to test XenApp and applications and get some experience with the product.
3. Create a list of applications to publish in the Citrix farm.
4. Test the list of applications and decide the best method to deliver them.

If we are satisfied with the results, the next step will be to create a XenApp pilot farm or extend our XenApp Design Validation Farm and provide some users access to the farm. This will be discussed in more detail in the next chapter. However, a few tasks are described as follows:

- Estimate the amount of XenApp application servers: In this step, we need to calculate the number of XenApp application servers required. We can obtain an estimate based on the amount of memory and CPU required per user when they are executing the applications. Then, we can add extra servers based on how critical these applications are and the future growth of the company. The pilot phase will confirm if these estimations are realistic or not.

- Determine the number of XenApp infrastructure servers we need for our farm: Based on the size of the farm (and our budget), we need to estimate how many Citrix Infrastructure Servers we need. Is one web interface server enough or do we need at least two? Are we going to use one (or more) dedicated data collectors?

- Define the installation processes: In this step, we need to decide the method to build the XenApp servers. Are we going to use Microsoft WDS (Windows Deployment Services), unattended scripts, or a manual process to install the operating system in physical servers? Or are we going to use virtual machines and just clone the template?

- Build and test XenApp application servers: In this step, we are going to choose how we are going to build the application servers. Are we going to use virtual machines and deploy a template with all applications? Clone and deploy images to physical servers with all applications installed? Use Active Directory GPOs or script to install applications?

- Design, build, and test XenApp infrastructure servers: Here, we need to decide the appropriate way to build infrastructure servers. Are we going to build these servers as virtual machines or use physical servers? Can some infrastructure servers run on small or old servers? Can we re-use any existing servers?

- Create and test a preproduction pilot farm based on our farm design: In this phase, after we have our servers ready, a small amount of users, usually from the IT department, test applications on XenApp servers.

- Select and make a list of pilot users from different business groups: In this step, managers from every area of the company will select a few users from each department to test the farm and applications.

- Provide access to pilot users to the pilot farm: In this phase, we need to create Active Directory groups and assign the pilot users selected in the previous phase to these groups. After that, we will assign these groups to published applications and users can start the pilot phase.

- Release the server to production: In this final phase, after we successfully test the farm for several weeks or months, and all errors and issues are resolved, we can provide access to all users in the organization to the new farm.

Designing Active Directory integration

The Active Directory design is very important for a successful Citrix implementation and now in XenApp 6 more than ever because XenApp policies and farm and server settings have been added to Active Directory group policies.

Following is a check list of the basic recommendations:

- Put all XenApp servers in their own AD OUs (Organizational Units), this will help us easily manage servers using Worker Groups.
- If we use dedicated servers for some applications (silos) create an OU for each of them and keep servers organized in their own OUs.
- All XenApp servers must reside in the same domain.
- The server farm needs to be in a single Active Directory forest. If our farm has servers in more than one forest, users cannot log on using UPNs (User Principal Names). UPN logons use the format *username@UPN*.

XenApp supports Active Directory Federated Services (ADFS) when used with the Citrix web interface. If we provide access to published applications to a business partner, ADFS will provide a great alternative than creating multiple new user accounts on our AD domain.

Building a small test farm

Installing a small test farm is the first step to gain some experience with the product.

We have two options:

- Build a single server test farm: If we want to learn about XenApp 6 or deploying a very small internal farm for a few users, we can install all these components in a single server. The following is a list of steps required to build a single-server small test farm:
    - Install Windows Server 2008 R2 on the server. Requirements are in *Chapter 1, Getting Started with XenApp 6*.
    - Join the server to the Active Directory domain. Although we can run XenApp on a workgroup, I don't recommend it.
    - Follow the instructions in *Chapter 3, Installing XenApp 6*, to configure Windows components such as Windows Firewall and IE ESC (Enhanced Security Configuration).
    - Using instructions in *Chapter 3, Installing XenApp 6*, to install and configure these components on the server: Web Interface, License Server, and XenApp.
    - When XenApp setup asks about the database, we need to choose **New Database**. This option will install SQL Server 2008 Express Edition on the same server.
    - After the setup is completed and the server is rebooted, we need to download and install a XenApp Evaluation license from www.citrix.com. Instructions are located in *Chapter 3, Installing XenApp 6*.
    - Optionally, we can setup Remote Desktop licenses. This step is not required if we are going to use this test environment for less than 120 days.
- Build a multiple-server test farm: If we are planning a pilot farm for a medium or large company, we would probably want to build a few XenApp servers, usually a separate web interface server (or two if we want some redundancy), and install the License server on one of the web interface servers. Also, we probably want to use a separate SQL Server. This scenario is covered in detail in *Chapter 3, Installing XenApp 6*.

Designing a XenApp 6 Farm

William wants to test basic features of XenApp 6. Later, he can add more infrastructure servers for other roles or increase redundancy.

The following diagram shows a graphic of the components of a small Citrix farm:

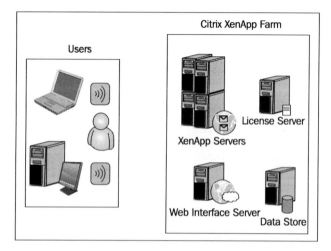

There are three roles he will use in the test farm: Citrix XenApp, Citrix Web Interface, and Citrix License Server.

William will use two servers with two CPUs (Quad Core) with 8 GB RAM and at least two hard drives with RAID 1 (more about disk configuration is discussed in the next chapter) for XenApp testing servers.

Both Citrix License Service and Citrix Web Interface Server are not intensive services so he decides to put both together in the same server. He will use a single processor server with 2 GB of RAM.

Because Brick Unit Construction had one existing SQL Server 2008 dedicated server, William will create the Citrix data store on it.

This is the new proposed architecture of infrastructure servers at Brick Unit Construction:

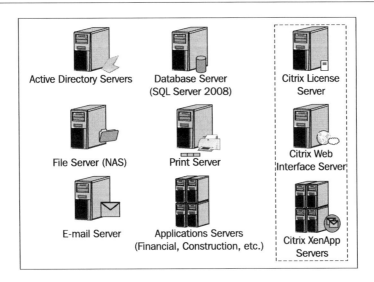

Creating a list of applications to publish in our Citrix farm

The first step to deploy applications on a multi-user environment is to decide which applications we want to run on Citrix.

Citrix is especially useful when we have applications that are old and infrequently used, difficult to manage, or frequently updated.

Following are some parameters we can use to select applications we want to move to our XenApp 6 farm:

- Citrix XenApp lets us to efficiently deploy and maintain software in an enterprise environment. You can easily deploy applications from a central location (our datacenter). Because you install the programs on the XenApp 6 server and not on the client machine, applications are easier to upgrade and to maintain.
- Testing new versions of a new application is easy and we can run multiple versions of the same application at the same time, using multiple servers or streaming the application to the client. For example, we can run Office 2007 and Office 2010 or both 32-bit and 64-bit versions of Microsoft Office 2010 at the same time.

- Are we going to provide remote access to applications published on Citrix in the near future? Remote users can access programs that are running on XenApp farm from devices such as home computers, kiosks, mobile devices, and operating systems other than Windows, like MAC and Linux.
- Applications accessing remote databases or data stores can improve its performance and reduce network utilization by moving the application from branch offices or remote sites to our datacenter.
- Reduce license expenses is the other advantage when we move applications to a XenApp farm. We can limit the amount of sessions of a specific application.

William decided to move all Microsoft Office suite applications in use in the company (Microsoft Word, Microsoft Excel, Microsoft Outlook, Microsoft PowerPoint, Microsoft Project, and Microsoft Visio) to the Citrix farm. This decision will reduce the time the IT department spends updating Office in remote machines and simplify the license management of Microsoft Project and Microsoft Visio.

Brick Unit Constructions don't have enough licenses of Microsoft Project and Microsoft Visio for all employees, and usually the change of roles of several users make license management complicated and deployment of these applications slow. The creation of the AD group for all project managers will simplify the Microsoft Project and Microsoft Visio management and provide instant access for users of these applications.

Moving the Microsoft Office suite to Citrix will simplify printing and file storage and management too.

The next application William picks to move to XenApp is the financial application used in each construction site. This is an in-house application known internally as BrickFin. This application is very difficult to deploy because it requires us to install a client in every computer and then setup manually multiple connections to access all financial information for the site.

Brick Unit Constructions use another in-house application for architects and engineers. This is an offline application used in the construction site in laptops, to take notes and photos and document the project. This application is called **BrickDocProject**.

Finally, the company has two more applications, one for time tracking called **BrickTime** and another used for expenses tracking called **BrickExpenses** used for all users. These applications are web applications, so publishing them in the farm is pretty easy.

Testing the list of applications

The next step is to test the list of applications and decide the best method to deliver them.

Most Windows 32-bit programs will work on the 64-bit version of Windows like Windows Server 2008 R2. One of the exceptions is antivirus programs. They use 32-bit kernel-mode device drivers and 32-bit drivers don't run on 64-bit operating systems.

The same applies to any device driver. Printers will require 64-bit print drivers. We will talk later about printing on a XenApp 6 environment in *Chapter 8, Printing in XenApp Environments*.

The WOW64 (known as Windows 32-bit on Windows 64-bit) subsystem allows 32-bit Windows-based applications to run flawlessly on 64-bit Windows operating systems.

Some 32-bit programs may run slower on Windows Server 2008 R2 than they would on 32-bit versions of Windows Server 2003/2008.

The WOW64 subsystem isolates 32-bit binaries from 64-bit binaries by redirecting registry and file system calls. The WOW64 subsystem isolates the binaries to prevent a 32-bit binary from accidentally accessing data from a 64-bit binary. For example, a 32-bit binary that runs a .DLL file from the %systemroot%\System32 folder might accidentally try to access a 64-bit .DLL file that is not compatible with the 32-bit binary. To prevent this, the WOW64 subsystem redirects the access from the %systemroot%\System32 folder to the %systemroot%\SysWOW64 folder. This redirection prevents compatibility errors because it requires the .DLL file to be specifically designed to work with 32-bit programs.

Running 32-bit applications on a 64-bit operating system can cause overload because WOW64 creates a 32-bit environment for any application to load 32-bit DLLs and isolate it from 64-bit applications.

> For more information about this topic, see the *Running 32-bit Applications* in the 64-Bit Windows section of the Microsoft Platform SDK documentation.
> http://msdn2.microsoft.com/en-us/library/aa384249.aspx

One of the best practices for installing applications is to install related applications or applications that have dependencies on other local applications on the same Citrix servers.

If the application has compatibility issues or excessive use of resources that might affect other programs on the same server, deploy it on silo servers using Worker Groups.

Before installing any application on Remote Desktop (formerly known as Terminal Server) or XenApp server, it is a good idea to check the vendor website to ensure the application can run on multi-user environment. If the application has issues, usually vendors provide compatibility scripts or fixes. If the application is not supported on multi-user environment, we must try to stream the application to the client machine.

Websites that use old ActiveX controls in Microsoft Internet Explorer must run on the 32-bit version of Microsoft Internet Explorer.

After testing, if any of these solutions do not work, we might need to try finding and fixing the root cause of the issue.

To identify root application issues, consider using tools such as the Microsoft Application Compatibility Toolkit (ACT) or Microsoft Sysinternals tools like Process Monitor.

Sysinternals tools are available at `http://technet.microsoft.com/sysinternals`.

Examples of common issues include the following:

- Custom or in-house applications developed with hardcoded paths in the registry
- Applications that use the computer name or the IP address as credential or for identification purposes
- `.INI` files that contain hardcoded file path names, database connection settings, and read/write file.

Microsoft Office applications

The Microsoft Office suite is one of the most popular products delivered in Citrix environments. Here we have some advice to deliver them successfully:

- If we have an application that requires Microsoft Excel to export results, install them on the same server.
- Install all Microsoft Office applications (Microsoft Office, Microsoft Project, Microsoft Visio, and so on) on the same server. Microsoft Office shares a lot of components between different products.
- Avoid mixing different versions of Microsoft Office products on the same server (for example, Office 2003 and Visio 2007 on the same server).
- If we need to deliver multiple versions of Office products (Office 2003, Office 2007, and Office 2010) at the same time and we can't use a dedicated server for each one, we need to use application stream.

- Office 2010 is the first edition of the suite released on both native 32-bit and 64-bit versions. Curiously, Microsoft recommends installing the 32-bit version instead of the 64-bit version. Installing 32-bit Office 2010 applications that run on 64-bit operating systems allow for better compatibility with ActiveX controls, COM add-ins, and VBA code.
- Some Microsoft Office 2010 compatibility issues on the native 64-bit version are as follows:
    - **Microsoft Access MDE/ADE/ACCDE** files created on the 32-bit version cannot run on 64-bit editions of Office 2010 and vice versa.
    - **ActiveX controls and COM DLLs add-ins** that were written for 32-bit Office will not work in a 64-bit version. The workaround for resolving this issue is to obtain 64-bit compatible controls and add-ins or to install Office 2010 32-bit (WOW).
    - **Inserting an object** into an Office 2010 application document might fail, if we try to insert a 32-bit object in a 64-bit Office 2010 application document.
    - **Visual Basic for Applications (VBA)** code that uses the `Declare` statement to access the Windows Application Programming Interface (API) or other DLL entry points will see differences between 32-bit and 64-bit versions.

Java

Windows Server 2008 R2 comes with both 32-bit and 64-bit Internet Explorer browsers. 32-bit IE comes as a default. There are different versions of Java software available for download depending on whether you are using 32-bit or 64-bit IE browsers.

If we are using:

- 32-bit Internet Explorer (IE), we need to download and install 32-bit Java
- 64-bit IE, we need to download and install 64-bit Java
- Both 32-bit and 64-bit IE, we need to download and install both 32-bit and 64-bit Java versions

William and his team installed and tested all selected applications and took the following decision to deliver them:

- Microsoft Office suite: They will deploy Office 2010 64-bit: Brick Unit Construction talked with several users and reviewed documents and they found that users don't have any VBA code or 32-bit add-ins and nobody uses Microsoft Access. Using the native 64-bit version will increase the amount of resources used on XenApp servers.
- BrickFin: Installing the application in a XenApp server and creating multiple icons (one for each site) will simplify access to this application. This application requires Excel to export financial results to Excel, so IT will deploy it on the same server as Microsoft Office.
- BrickDocProject: IT decided to stream it to a client computer because it requires offline access.
- Web applications: William and his team tested these two web applications and found one of them, used to manage expenses, uses an old 32-bit ActiveX. So they need to run it on Internet Explorer 32-bit version. This web application used lots of resources on the XenApp server, because users sometimes left it open and updated the time several times a day. That might affect other programs on the same server, so they think they will deploy it on silos servers.

Summary

In this chapter, we learned how to design a Citrix XenApp 6 farm and discovered Brick Unit Construction. Specifically:

- Common farm terminology and concepts used in the Citrix world and some new names used on XenApp 6
- Designing a Basic XenApp Architecture
- Writing a simple pilot plan
- Designing Active Directory integration
- Building a small test farm, used as a design validation farm
- Creating a list of applications to publish on the new farm
- Testing the list of applications and deciding the best method to deliver them

Designing and building a basic XenApp 6 farm is the first step for a successful deployment of the product. Installing and testing applications will help us understand the features of the products and gain experience with it.

In the next chapter, we will leave words aside and we will start building our first XenApp 6 server!

3
Installing XenApp 6

In the last chapter, we learned about common Citrix farm terminology, concepts, and discovered our case study, Brick Unit Construction. We discussed how to design a simple Citrix XenApp 6 farm and wrote a simple pilot plan. Now, we are going to install our first XenApp 6 servers.

Installing and Configuring XenApp 6

Now, let's take a look at the lab created by William to build the pilot farm at Brick Unit Construction, to test XenApp 6. He had two existing servers, an Active Directory domain controller, and a database server running on SQL Server 2008. We will deploy three new XenApp servers.

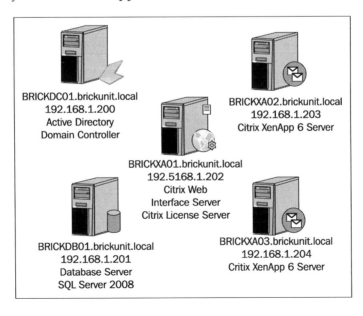

He will deploy Citrix Web Interface and Citrix License Server on one of the servers called BRICKXA01. Later, he will install Citrix XenApp 6 on servers BRICKXA02 and BRICKXA03.

The following is his plan to deploy the pilot farm:

1. Install Windows Server on all servers (Windows Server 2008 R2 is required for all XenApp applications servers, but he can use Windows Server 2008 R1 32-bit or 64-bit for the database server, license server, and Web Interface servers.
2. Join servers to the Active Directory domain.
3. Configure Windows components (Windows Firewall and IE ESC).
    a. Install Citrix Licensing Server and Citrix Web Interface on BRICKXA01.
    b. Configure Citrix Licensing Server.
    c. Install Citrix Licenses.
4. Install and configure XenApp 6 on BRICKXA02 using Wizard-based Server Role Manager (first server of the farm).
5. Install and configure XenApp 6 on BRICKXA03.
6. Configure Citrix Web Interface.
7. Configure Remote Desktop Licensing (formerly known as Terminal Server Licensing).

Configuring Windows components

Before installing XenApp 6, he had two components that depend on his environment that he probably wants to configure:

- Windows Firewall
- IE ESC(Enhanced Security Configuration)

In the previous versions of XenApp, he needed to install Remote Desktop Services (formerly known as Terminal Server) before the XenApp setup. In XenApp 6, the setup process will install Remote Desktop Services automatically.

Configuring Windows Firewall

We have multiple options to configure Windows Firewall:

- Configure Windows Firewall using Active Directory Group Policies (GPO):Open Group Policy Management Editor and expand Computer Configuration/Policies/Administrative templates/Network/Network Connections/Windows Firewall/Domain Profile. Modify appropriate settings.
- **Disable Windows Firewall:** Open command prompt and type the following command:
  `netshadvfirewall set allprofiles state off`
    - Also, we can disable Windows Firewall from the Windows interface. Open **Control Panel** and choose **Windows Firewall**.

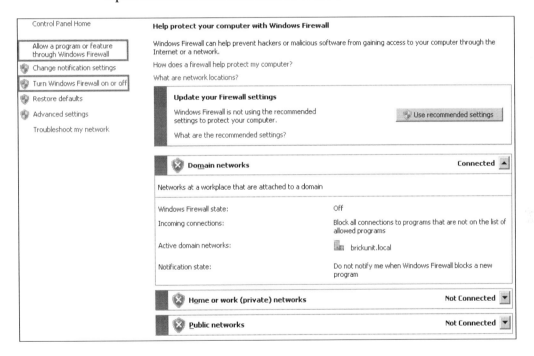

Installing XenApp 6

- ○ Select the **Turn Windows Firewall on or off** option and then select **Turn off Windows Firewall 9 (not recommended)** for all profiles.

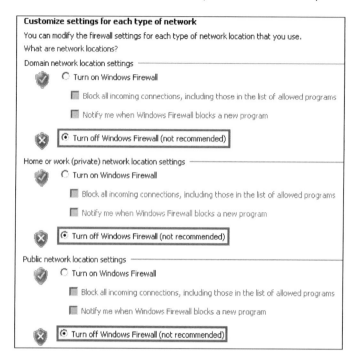

- **Configure Windows Firewall for XenApp:** In order to keep Windows Firewall running after we installed XenApp 6, we need to configure XenApp ports. Open **Control Panel** and select **Windows Firewall**. On the Windows Firewall main page, click on the **Allow a program or feature through Windows Firewall** option and verify that Citrix ports checkboxes for all profiles are enabled.

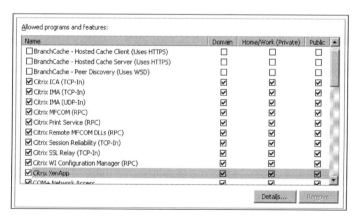

Configuring IE ESC (Enhanced Security Configuration)

Microsoft recommends this best security practice—administrators must have limited access to the Internet to avoid the possibility of an attack on the server by malicious websites. This is a good practice for critical servers like domain controllers or database servers, but impractical for Terminal Servers and XenApp servers.

To disable IE ESC, open **Server Manager (Start | All Programs | Administrative Tools | Server Manager)** and click on **Configure IE ESC**.

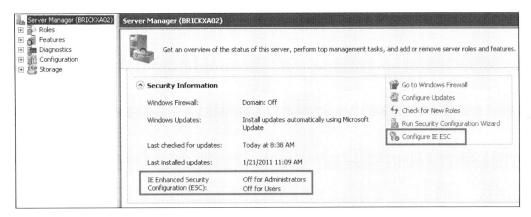

Select **Off** for both **Administrators** and **Users** and click on the **OK** button.

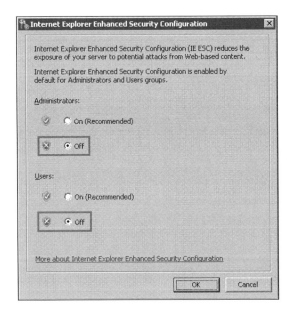

Installing XenApp using the Wizard-based Server Role Manager

There are two different ways to deploy XenApp 6 servers: using the Wizard-based Server Role Manager or using the command line. Usually, the first option is the preferred one when you need to deploy one or two specific roles and the second option is the best when we need to deploy multiple (and identical) servers using scripts. We are going to learn more about deploying an entire server using unattended scripts in the last chapter of this book.

This step is common to all setup processes. To start the setup, we need to open the DVD or mount the .iso file (if we are using a Virtual Machine or a remote console) and run the file autorun.exe in the root of the disk.

1. After autorun.exe has been executed, the Citrix XenApp installation menu is displayed.
2. Select **Install XenApp Server**.

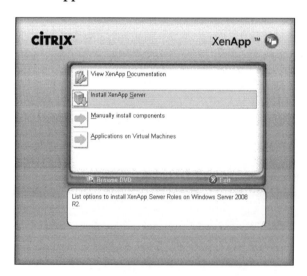

Chapter 3

3. If .NET Framework 3.5 SP1 is not installed on the server, the XenApp wizard will launch the setup of the .NET Framework 3.5. The following pop-up will be displayed:

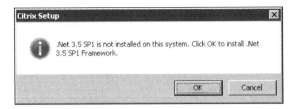

4. Click on the **OK** button to install it.
5. After .NET Framework 3.5 SP1 installation is completed, we need to click again on **Install XenApp**. Then the Citrix XenApp Server Role Manager will be displayed.
6. Click on **Add server roles** to start the setup of the XenApp server.

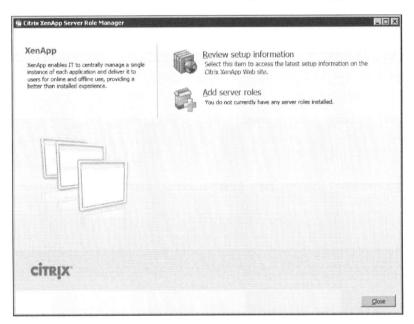

Installing XenApp 6

Choose your XenApp edition. Features available for installation will vary. If you want to test the new XenApp 6 using a 90 day-evaluation license, choose **Platinum Edition**. William is going to use Platinum Edition licenses in this pilot lab, so he can test all features.

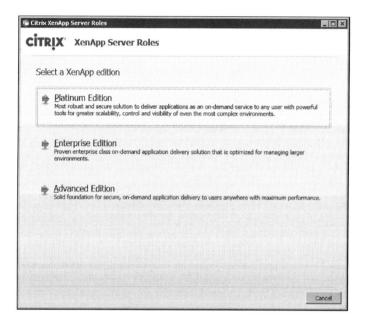

If we have a single server or we just want to test the product, we can install all common roles (License Server, XenApp, and Web Interface) on one server. In his pilot, William is going to going to build multiple XenApp servers, but in *Chapter 2, Designing a XenApp 6 Farm*, there is a list of steps required to build a single server pilot.

After he accepts the Citrix License Agreement, he chooses the roles we want to install on our XenApp server.

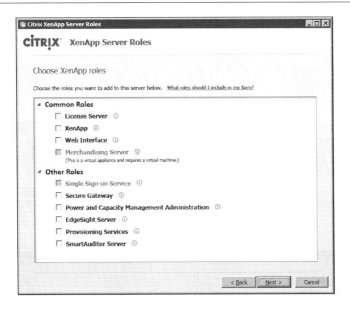

Installing License Server and web interface roles in server BRICKXA01

Now, we will start with our deployment plan, and the first step is to install both the roles on the server BrickXA01. We need to follow the instructions explained in the previous chapter and then choose the **License Server** and **Web Interface** roles and click on the **Next** button to see the role subcomponents:

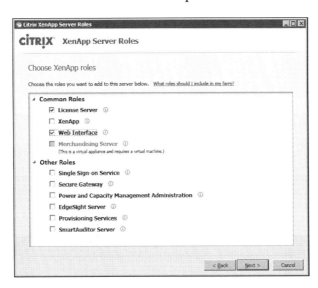

Installing XenApp 6

1. At this moment, XenApp setup will install the missing prerequisites. Click on the **Next** button to continue.
2. Click on the **Install** button to start the setup process.
3. Once the installation is complete. Click on the **Finish** button to close the window.

In this window, the setup process shows both the components installed and the components ready to be configured.

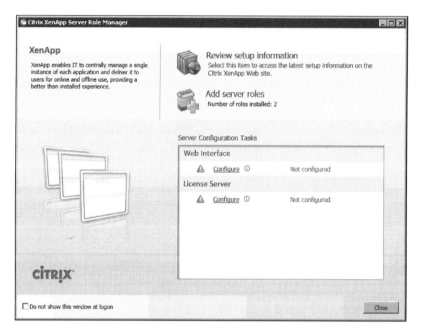

Configuring Citrix License Server

To configure the License Server, click on the **Configure** link. This process will open a window. We need to enter a password and confirm it. We can change ports of services (optional) and click on the **OK** button to apply changes.

The default license server port is **27000** and the **Management Console Web Port** is **8082**. We need to verify whether these ports are open in the firewall. The XenApp setup process will open the required ports on Windows Firewall.

Chapter 3

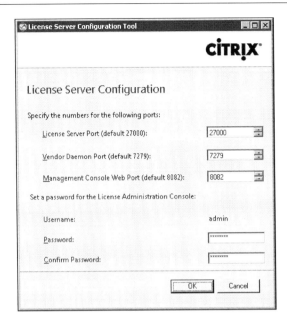

The following screenshot shows that the License Server is configured.

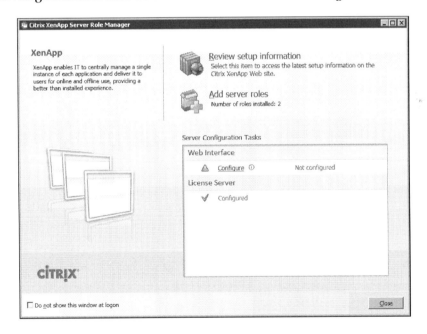

Installing XenApp 6

Installing Citrix Licenses

Now we are going to install Citrix Licenses on our license server. We are also going to install XenApp Evaluation Licenses. These licenses are valid for 90 days and they are perfect to evaluate XenApp.

The first step is to log in to www.citrix.com/mycitrix (this requires a MyCitrix account). In the **Choose a Toolbox** menu, select **Product Previews / Beta Releases – License Retrieval**.

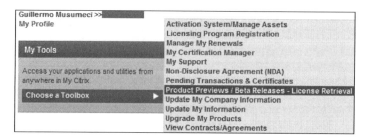

Then select **XenApp Evaluation** from the drop-down menu.

On this page, we need to click on the hyperlink of one of the serial numbers to start the activation process.

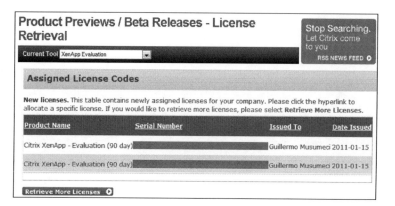

Next, we have the option to choose our **Solution Advisor**.

On this page, we need to select the contact for this license activation.

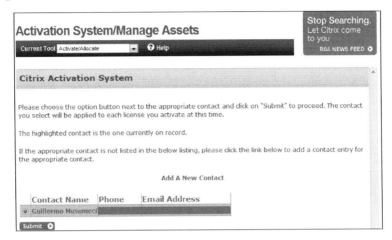

Then we check our information and click on the **Submit** button to continue.

In this step, we need to filter the license and enter the hostname of the Citrix License Server.

The hostname is case sensitive.

To determine the hostname on our license server machine, we need to open a command prompt window and type hostname.

The hostname returned will be in case-sensitive format. Copy this name to the hostname fieldbox in MyCitrix:

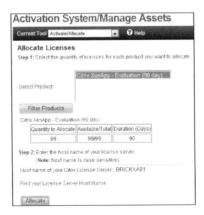

Installing XenApp 6

Then the site asks to confirm or cancel the license allocation. Click **Confirm**.

Finally, we are ready to download the license.

After we download the license and copy it to our license server, we need to install it using the Citrix License Administration Console. We need to click on the **Import License** button located on the **Vendor Daemon Configuration** tab. Detailed information about this procedure is available in the next chapter.

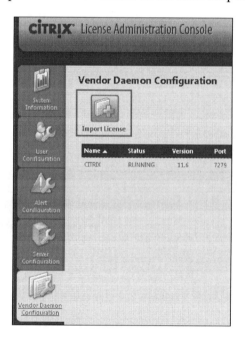

Installing and configuring XenApp 6 on BRICKXA02 using Wizard-based Server Role Manager (first server of the farm)

The next step in the deployment plan is to install the first XenApp server. On the **Choose XenApp Server Roles** page, William needs to select only the **XenApp** role.

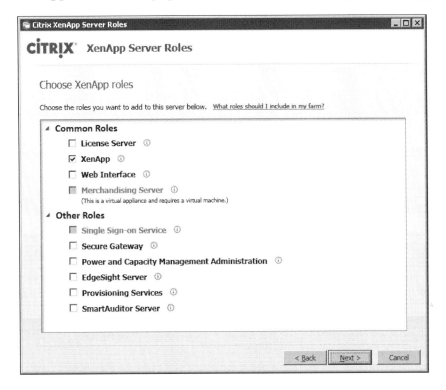

He can choose to install default components or remove XenApp Management.

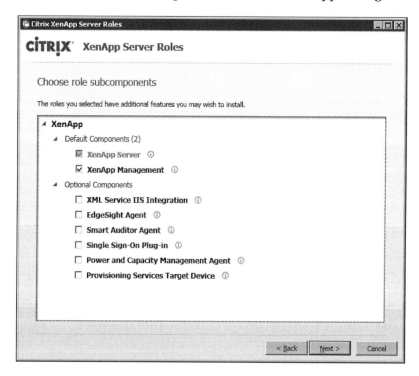

Now, XenApp setup will install the missing prerequisites. William clicks on the **Next** button to continue. One of these prerequisites is Remote Desktop Services (formerly known as Terminal Server); XenApp 6 will install it automatically, if required.

Once he is ready to install all components, he clicks on the **Install** button to continue.

When all components are installed, he needs to restart the server to continue setup and click on the **Finish** button.

He then clicks on the **Reboot** link to restart the server to complete prerequisite installation and configuration.

Chapter 3

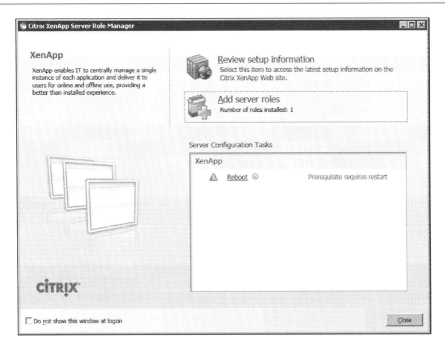

After restarting the BRICK02 server, the **XenApp Server Role Manager** is presented. On **Server Configuration Tasks**, William clicks on the **Resume Install**. Link to continue the XenApp installation.

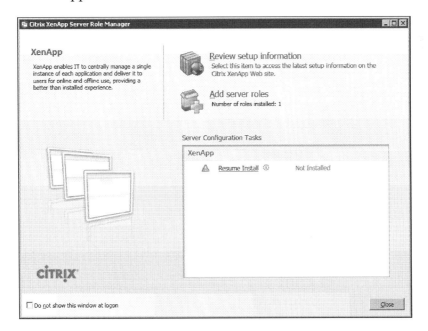

After the list of prerequisites is reviewed, he clicks on the **Install** button to install them.

Once the installation is complete, he clicks on the **Finish** button to continue.

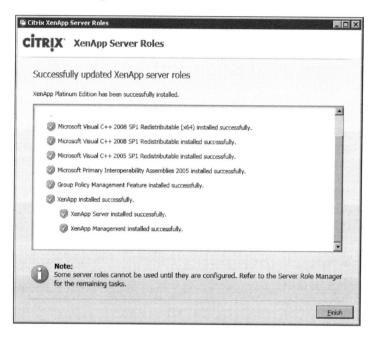

Configuring XenApp using the Wizard-based Server Configuration tool

Once XenApp is set up, it is time to configure the server. We need to click on the **Configure** link to start the configuration process.

During the setup procedure, we can choose to create a new Citrix farm or join our server to an existing Citrix farm and set up the Citrix data store.

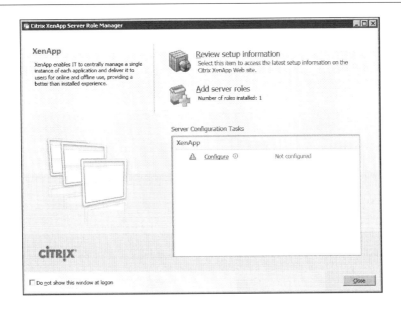

Configuring the first XenApp server of the farm

At this point, we can select if we want to **Create a new server farm** or **Join an existing server farm**. In our case, because this is the first server, we need to choose **Create a new server farm**.

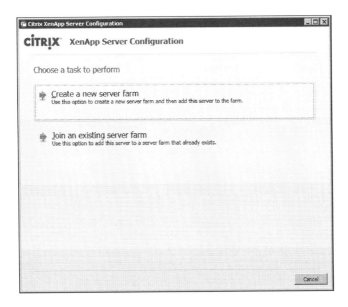

Installing XenApp 6

Here, he needs to enter the name of the new Citrix farm and the first Citrix administrator account. We need to enter a domain account, except when we have a specific reason to use a local account (such as a single test server on a workgroup).

In this step, he can enter the Citrix License Server name, if it is already set up. He changes the port or he can set up the Citrix License Server later using the management console.

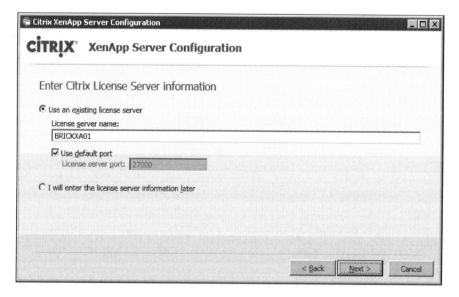

Installing data stores

The next step in the installation process is to choose where we can install our Citrix data store.

We have three options here:

- **New database**: This option will install and set up a Microsoft SQL Server 2008 Express on the current machine. This option is appropriate when you want to build a test or small Citrix Farm, but it is not recommended for medium to large farm or multi-zone farms.
- **Existing Microsoft SQL Server database**: This option will install the data store on an existing SQL server database. You must check with your DBA to create one in advance or check `http://xenapp6.musumeci.com.ar` for detailed instructions to create a new database on a Microsoft SQL Server 2008. For more information on supported databases versions, take a look at the CTX114501 document at `http://support.citrix.com/article/CTX114501`.
- **Existing Oracle database**: This option will install the data store on an existing Oracle database. You must check with your DBA to create one in advance or check `http://xenapp6.musumeci.com.ar` for detailed instructions to create a new database on an Oracle 11g R2 server. For more information about supported database versions, take a look at the CTX114501 document at `http://support.citrix.com/article/CTX114501`.

> The existing Oracle database option is visible only if you previously installed the 32-bit(x86) Oracle client on your XenApp server.

In this lab, William is going to use the SQL Server 2008 standard server, but we are going to see how to install both the versions (Express and Standard).

Microsoft SQL Server 2008 Express database server

This limited version of Microsoft SQL Server 2008 is perfect for testing on small environments because it's free and migration to other versions of Microsoft SQL Server is easy and fast. Express is also recommended for evaluation or PoC (Proof of Concept) implementation because it's easy to set up and doesn't require an extra server.

The configuration process of Microsoft SQL Server Express is pretty simple. Select **New database** and click on the **Next** button and the setup will install SQL server and create a new database for us.

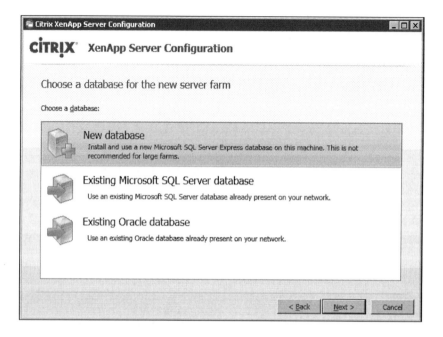

Next, click on the **Enter Credentials** button.

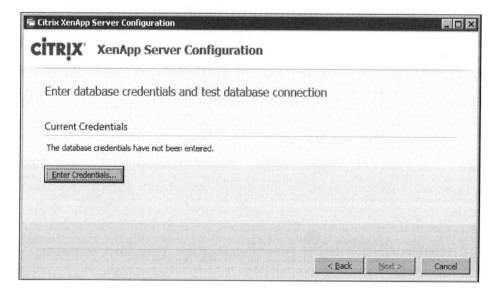

Enter the administrator username and password and click on the **OK** button.

Click on the **Next** button to continue with the installation process.

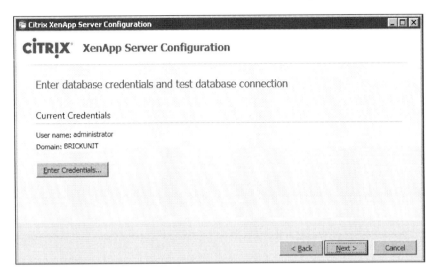

Microsoft SQL Server 2008 database server

Deploying Microsoft SQL Server Standard or Enterprise edition versions is the preferred option for medium to large Citrix implementations.

In this screen, select the **Existing Microsoft SQL Server** database and click on the **Next** button.

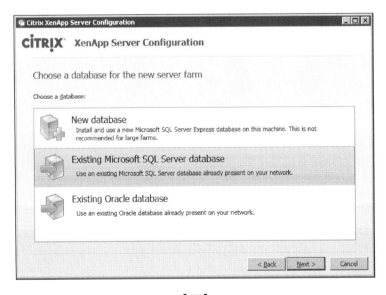

Installing XenApp 6

Here we need to enter the **Database server name** and the name of the database. The database MUST exist before the setup.

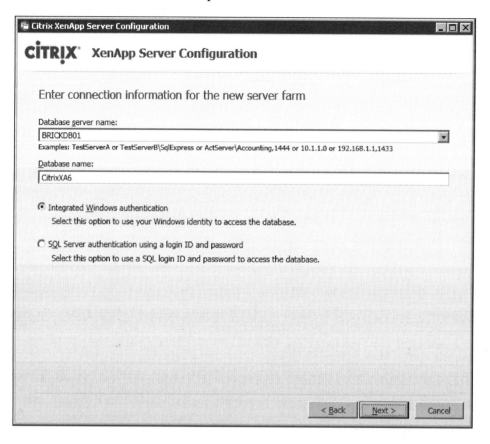

Enter credentials with permissions to access the database specified in the last step and click on the **OK** button.

When the **Test Connection** button returns a **Test Completed Successfully** message, click on the **Next** button to continue with the setup process.

 If you have issues with the **Test Connection** process, try to use the server name followed by 1433, where 1433 is the port of SQL Server. Also, you can try using the IP address of the database server and verify that the firewall on both the machines (SQL server and XenApp server) are not blocking traffic in the SQL port.

Oracle database server

We are going to use Microsoft SQL server to set up the Citrix data store in this book, because it's the most popular method to deploy Citrix data stores.

> Detailed instructions to set up the 32-bit Oracle client and Oracle data stores are available at `http://xenapp6.musumeci.com.ar`.

The data store is ready now and it's time to continue with our configuration process.

Configuring shadowing permits Citrix administrators to take control of users' sessions. On the screen, William enables the **Force a shadow acceptance popup** and **Force logging of all shadow connections** checkboxes. Enabling the first option will not request shadow permissions to users and enabling the second option will log all shadow activities.

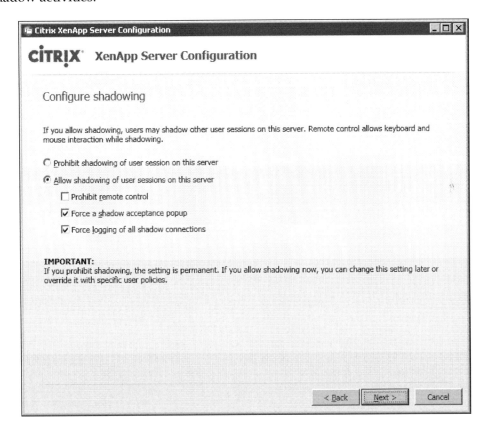

Installing XenApp 6

Here William can enter a custom **Zone name** for the new server. Zones are useful in complex environments where a large number of servers are located in geographically dispersed locations, but multiple zones generate more network traffic. It is not recommended to create multiple zones, if you are installing a test or a small farm.

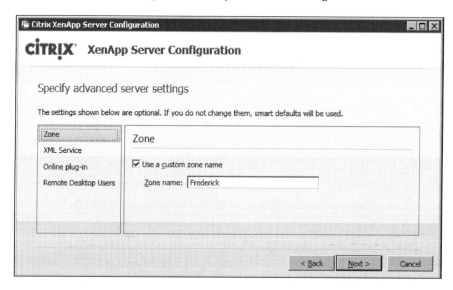

Here he can change the XML port (optional). If we change this port, we need to specify it later when we set up the Web Interface server.

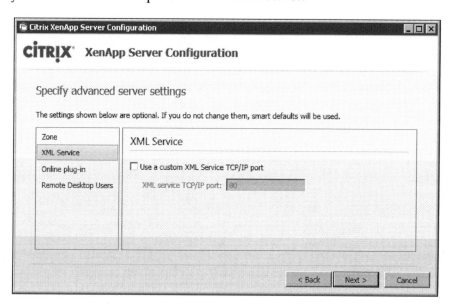

Now, William can enter **Web Interface server name** (optional).

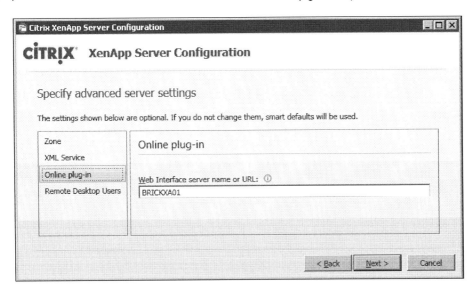

Next, he provides permissions to **Remote Desktop Users** (optional), as shown in the following screenshot. The default settings are listed on the page. Make sure to uncheck the default **Add Anonymous users** checkbox, unless you need it.

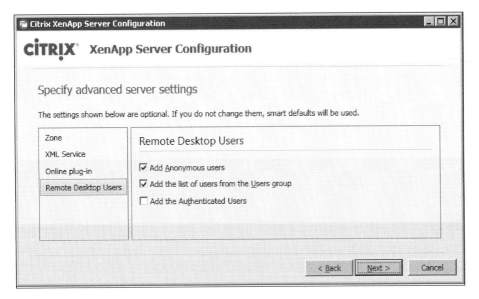

He clicks on the **Apply** button to finish the configuration.

The he clicks on the **Finish** button to close the Setup.

A reboot is required to complete the installation process. Click on the **Reboot** link to restart the server.

Installing and configuring XenApp 6 on BRICKXA03

Now, Continuing with the deployment process, William adds a new XenApp server to the Citrix farm. This process is pretty similar to the installation of the first server of the farm. For this he must:

1. William selects the **Join an existing server farm** option to continue.

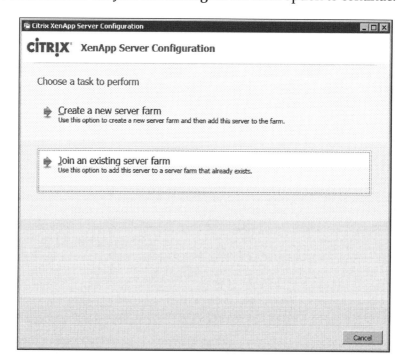

2. He selects the **Existing Microsoft SQL Server** database and clicks on the **Next** button.

Chapter 3

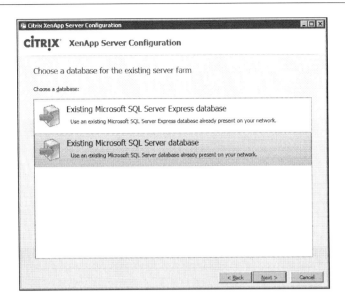

3. He enters the database server name, database name, and credentials and tests the connection.
4. He sets up the Shadowing.
5. Then he chooses **Use the global farm settings for the license server** and clicks on the **Next** button.

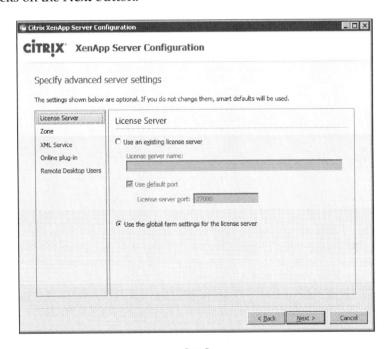

Installing XenApp 6

Now, the configuration process continues in the same way as described in the *Configuring the first XenApp server of the farm* section.

Configuring Citrix Web Interface server

The Web Interface server is the server used by the client to access applications. We can find the following two types of XenApp sites on the Web Interface servers:

- **XenApp Web Sites**: These sites are used when users access applications published on the Citrix farm using a web browser. Once authenticated, users can access online and offline applications using a Citrix client.

- **XenApp Services Sites:** These sites are used to integrate resources with users' desktops. Citrix Online Plug-in provides access to applications, virtual desktops, and online content by clicking icons on the **Start** menu or shortcuts on their desktop. XenApp Services Sites were formerly known as Program Neighborhood Agent.

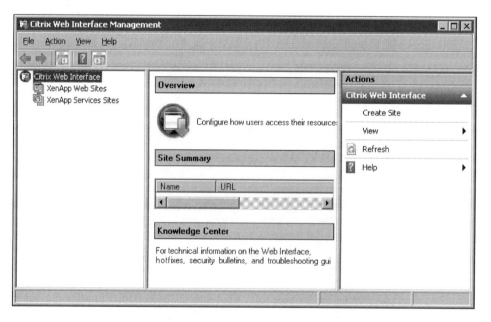

Creating a XenApp website

To create a new site, William needs to open the **Citrix Web Interface Management** console, click on **XenApp Web Site**, and then click on **Create Site** on the right panel. The **Set as the default page for the IIS site** checkbox is used if we have multiple sites.

Chapter 3

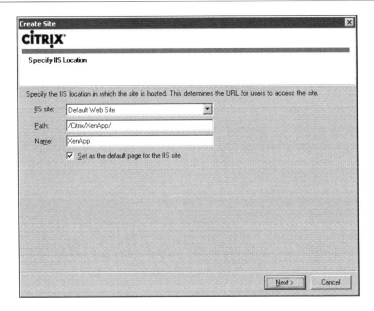

Here he can leave the default authentication (**At Web Interface**) because he is going to access the Web Interface internally only. Then, he clicks on the **Next** button to continue.

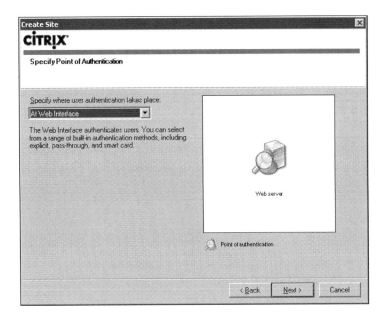

He clicks on the **Next** button until the site is successfully created.

Installing XenApp 6

William needs to enter the **Farm name** and the name of at least one XenApp server running the XML service, as shown in the following screenshot. In small or medium production environments, it is recommended to have two or more XML servers. In large farms, Citrix recommends at least two or more dedicated XML servers. Check if the XML service port is the right one for your environment (usually, the XML port is 80 or 8080).

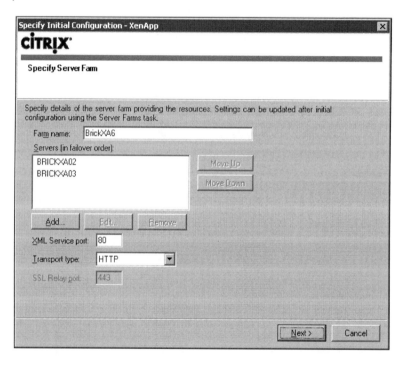

Now he needs to configure authentication methods:

- **Explicit** (XenApp websites) or **Prompt** (XenApp services sites): Users need to log in using a username and a password. Authentication options are User Principal Name (UPN), Microsoft domain-based authentication, and Novell Directory Services (NDS).
- **Pass-through**: Users can authenticate using the credentials they provided when they logged on to their Windows desktop machines. The Citrix client sends their credentials to the Web Interface server and their resource set appears automatically.

- **Pass-through with smart card**: Users are authenticated by inserting a smart card in a smart card reader attached to the user desktop machine or mobile device. If users have installed the Citrix Online Plug-in, they are prompted for their smart card PIN when they log on to the user device. After logging in, users can access their resources without additional logon prompts. Users accessing XenApp websites are not asked for a PIN.
- **Smart card**: Users use a smart card to authenticate. The user is asked for the smart card PIN.
- **Anonymous:** Anonymous users can log on without providing a username and password and access resources published only for anonymous users.

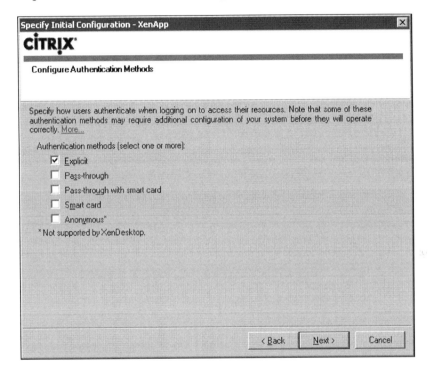

Installing XenApp 6

William can restrict the list of domains with permissions to login into the Citrix Web Interface, as shown in the following screenshot. When we set domain restrictions, the Web Interface will only ask for the username and password. This option is useful to simplify user login.

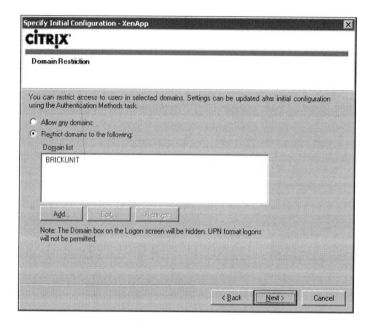

Here, he needs to choose the **Logon Screen Appearance**; the default option is **Minimal**, he decides to use the **Full** version for his lab.

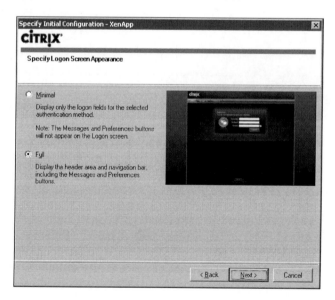

Now he needs to choose **Published Resource Type** supported by the site. Options are as follows:

- **Online:** Users access applications, content, and desktops hosted on remote servers. Users need a network connection to XenApp servers to access their resources.
- **Offline:** Users stream applications to their desktops and open them locally. Users need a network connection to log on to the site and start their applications. When the applications are running, the network connection is not required.
- **Dual mode:** Users access both online and offline applications, content, and desktops.

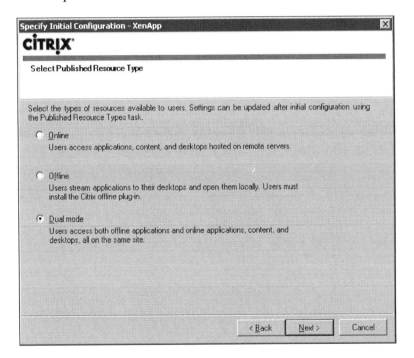

Installing XenApp 6

William clicks on the **Finish** button to complete the configuration.

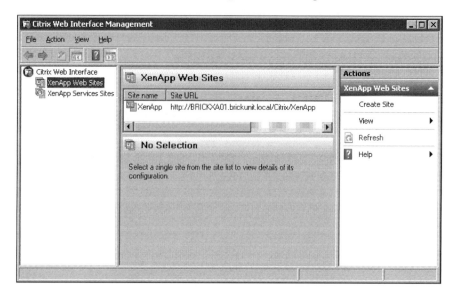

Creating a XenApp Services site

To create a new site, William needs to open the **Citrix Web Interface Management** console, clicks on **XenApp Services Site**, and then he clicks on **Create Site** on the right panel.

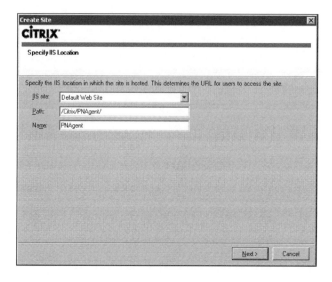

He clicks on the **Next** button until the site is successfully created.

Chapter 3

He needs to enter the **Farm name** and the name of at least one XenApp server running the XML service. In small or medium production environments, it is recommended to have two or more XML servers. In large farms, Citrix recommends at least two or more dedicated XML servers. Check if the XML service port is the right one for your environment (usually the XML port is 80 or 8080).

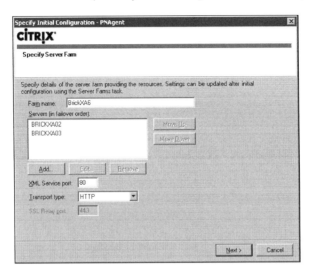

Now, he need to choose published resource types supported by the site. The options are the same as that of a XenApp website.

He clicks on the **Finish** button to complete the configuration.

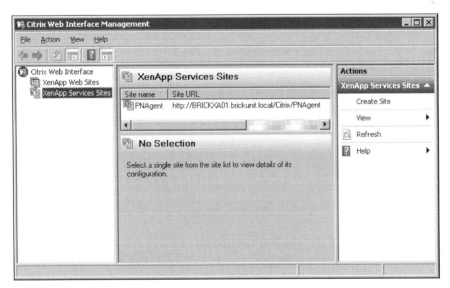

[71]

Configuring Remote Desktop licensing

The last step to finish the setup of the pilot Citrix farm is configuration of the Remote Desktop licensing.

We need to install the Remote Desktop Licensing Role Service, activate a Remote Desktop license server, and install Remote Desktop Services client access licenses (CAL) on a Windows Server 2008 or Windows Server 2008 R2 on our Active Directory Domain or test server, if we are testing the product on one single test server.

To install the Remote Desktop Licensing Role Service and install Remote Desktop license, contact your Active Directory administrator or follow the instructions available at http://xenapp6.musumeci.com.ar.

When you log in to XenApp servers before the Remote Desktop licenses are configured, you will see a balloon in the Windows taskbar, similar to the one shown in the following screenshot. The grace period for a Remote Desktop license setup is 120 days.

To specify the Remote Desktop licensing mode on XenApp Servers, we need to use the **Remote Desktop Session Host Configuration** console. To open the Remote Desktop Session Host Configuration, click **Start | Administrative Tools | Remote Desktop Services | Remote Desktop Session Host Configuration**.

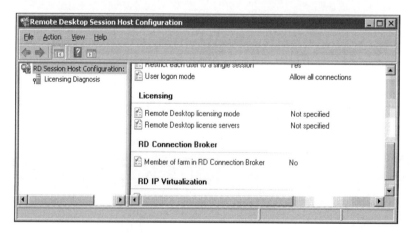

Under **Licensing**, double-click on the **Remote Desktop** licensing mode.

Select either **Per Device** or **Per User**, depending on your environment.

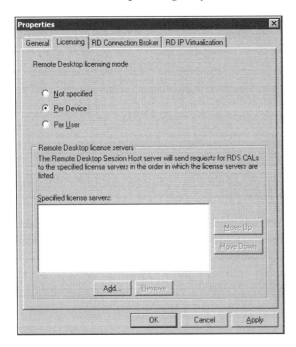

Click on the **Add** button, select decided license servers, and click on the **OK** button.

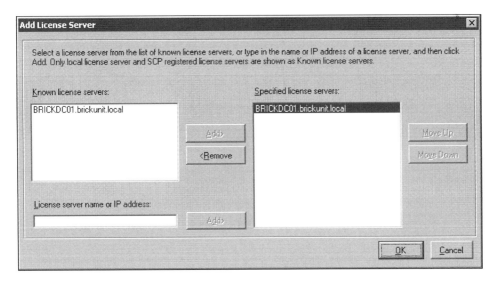

Installing XenApp 6

Licensing configuration is now complete. The resulting window will look like the one shown in the following screenshot:

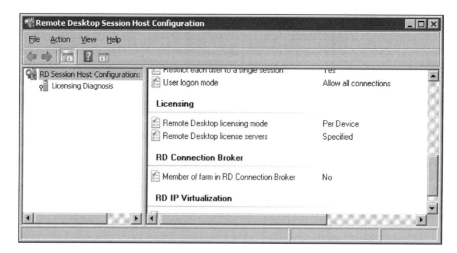

Configuring Remote Desktop licensing mode by using Group Policy

To specify the Remote Desktop licensing mode by using Group Policy (GPO), enable the **Set the Remote Desktop licensing mode** GPO.

This GPO setting is located under **Computer Configuration | Policies | Administrative Templates | Windows Components | Remote Desktop Services | Remote Desktop Session Host | Licensing**.

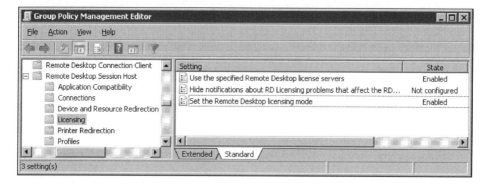

Please note that the GPO setting will overwrite the setting configured in the Remote Desktop Session Host Configuration.

To configure the GPO setting in Active Directory, we can use the Group Policy Management Console (GPMC) or the Local Group Policy Editor to configure the GPO setting locally on our XenApp server or workgroup. Using an Active Directory GPO is the preferred method to configure Remote Desktop licensing.

This is the end of our deployment plan. Now we are ready to start with our pilot plan.

Managing XenApp farms

We can manage our Citrix XenApp 6 farm from our desktop machine or management server installing the Citrix Delivery Services management console.

To start the setup, we need to open the DVD or mount the .ISO file (if we are using a Virtual Machine or a remote console) and run the file autorun.exe in the root of the disk.

1. After autorun.exe has been executed, the Citrix XenApp installation menu is displayed.
2. Select the **Manually Install** components.
3. Select **Common Components** and then **Management Consoles** on the next window.

4. Click on the **Next** button to launch the setup.
5. Click on the **Next** button to continue.
6. Click on the **Finish** button to complete the Setup.

Summary

In this chapter, we learned how to install and configure XenApp 6 and related components. Specifically:

- Installing and configuring Citrix Licensing Server
- Installing and configuring Citrix Web Interface
- Installing and configuring XenApp servers using the Wizard-based Server Role Manager
- Configuring Remote Desktop Licensing (formerly known as Terminal Server Licensing) using the Remote Desktop Session Host Configuration console and Active Directory Group Policy
- Installing the Citrix Delivery Services management console on non-Citrix servers

In the next chapter, we will discuss how to use the Citrix management console to manage our Citrix farms and provide access to other administrators to access all or some specific administration features.

Using Management Tools

The last chapter was a very hands on chapter. We set up a Citrix data store based on Microsoft SQL Server 2008 and talked about different data store options.

We configured Remote Desktop Licensing (formerly known as Terminal Server Licensing) using Remote Desktop Session Host Configuration console and Active Directory Group Policy.

We learned how to install different Citrix XenApp 6 components, and particularly the XenApp 6 license server and web interface server and discussed how to configure these three XenApp roles using the Wizard-based Server Configuration Tool.

Finally, we learned how to install the Citrix Delivery Services Management Console on non-Citrix servers or administration servers/desktops.

Now, we are going to help William Empire from Brick Unit Construction to manage Citrix components using Citrix Managements Tools, and in particular, we will work with the following:

- Citrix Delivery Services Console
- License Administration Console
- Citrix Web Interface Management Console
- Citrix SSL Relay Configuration tool
- Shadow taskbar
- SpeedScreen Latency Reduction Manager
- Managing Citrix administrators accounts

Using Management Tools

Management Consoles

Citrix offers a complete set of tools for managing servers, farms, published resources, and connections.

Citrix Delivery Services Console

The **Citrix Delivery Services Console**, formerly known as **Citrix Access Management Console**, is a tool that integrates into the Microsoft Management Console (MMC) and enables us to execute management tasks.

Using Citrix Delivery Services Console, we can set up and monitor servers, server farms, published resources and sessions, configure policies, printers, and application access.

We can manage load balancing, troubleshoot alerts, diagnose problems in our farms, view hotfix information for our Citrix products, and track administrative changes.

Now, let us look at what happens when William opens his Citrix Delivery Services Console for the very first time.

To open the console, he clicks on **Start | All Programs | Citrix | Management Consoles | Citrix Delivery Services Console**.

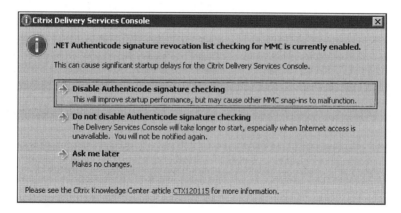

A pop-up window appears if .NET Authenticode signature for MMC console is enabled. He chooses **Disable Authenticode signature checking** as Citrix recommends it to improve startup performance.

In this screen, he needs to choose **XenApp** on products and components and click on the **Next** button. He can add more components later from the console by clicking on **XenApp** and then using the option **Configure and run discovery** in the **Actions** pane from the Citrix Delivery Services Console:

Chapter 4

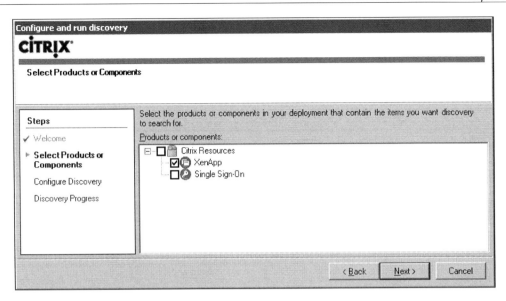

Now, he needs to add at least one XenApp 6 server. He can use the **Add Local Computer** button to add the current server or use the **Add** button to add a different server and click on the **Next** button to continue.

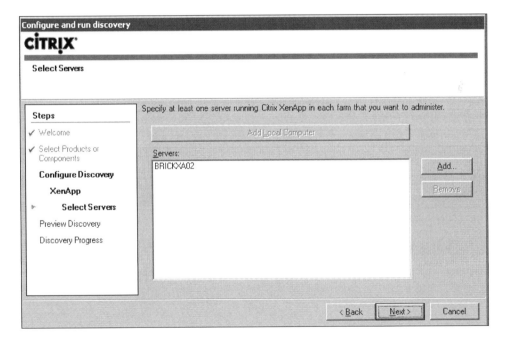

The console is ready to use as soon as the discovery is successful.

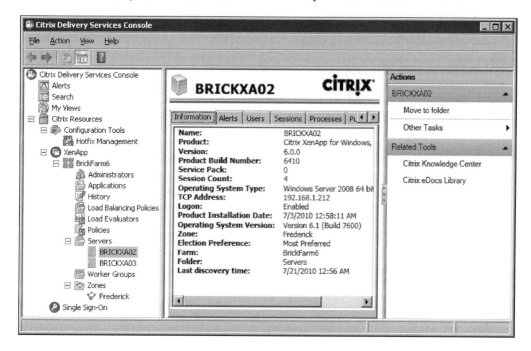

License Administration Console

This console is used to add, manage, and track Citrix licenses using a web browser.

A web browser can be used to open the console on a remote server using one of the following URL options:

`http://license-server-name:port` or `http://brickxa01:8082`

`http://license-server-IP-address:port` or `http://192.168.1.202:8082`

where:

- **License-server-name** is the name of our license server.
- **License-server-IP-Address** is the IP address of our license server.
- **Port** is the port number for the console's Web service. The default web service port for the console is **8082**.

In order to open the **License Administration Console**, on the machine on which it is installed, click on the **Start | All Programs | Citrix | Management Consoles | License Administration Console**.

Chapter 4

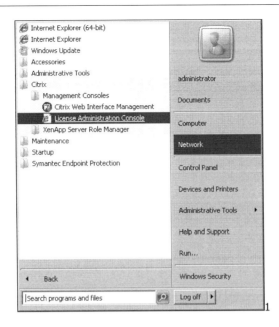

This is the default view when we open **Citrix License Administration Console**.

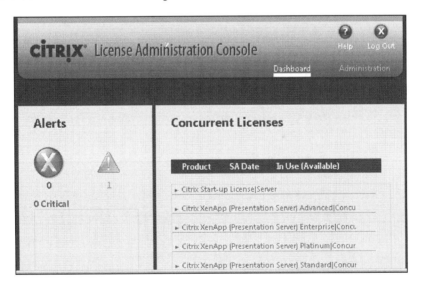

The console includes two areas to view and manage licenses: **Dashboard** and **Administration**. We can switch between both views using links at the top-right area of the console.

We can use the **Dashboard** to monitor licenses, license activity, and alerts.

[81]

Using Management Tools

Use the **Administration** area to view system information, add and administer licenses, configure users and alerts, log license management activities, secure the console server, and more.

To log in to the console, we need to click on the **Administration** area, enter our username (default is **admin**), password, and choose **Display Language** (optional).

The **System Information** tab provides very useful information like **Release Version** and **Host Name**. The host name is used when we need to assign Citrix licenses.

> The host name is case-sensitive.

For more information on how to install Citrix licenses, please refer to *Chapter 3, Installing XenApp 6*.

The **User Configuration** tab is where we can add or manage users. Now let us help William to create a new account for himself. He needs to click on the **New User** icon to create a new user for himself.

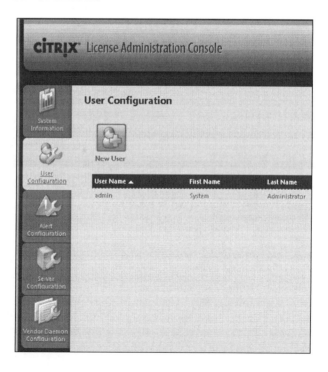

Chapter 4

In the **New User** screen, he needs to enter **User Name**, **First Name**, **Last Name**, and **Password**. Also, he needs to choose the role between **User** and **Administrator**. He will choose **Administrator**, so he can install and manage licenses. The **User** role is useful to check the configuration of the license server or to check the available licenses.

The following screenshot shows the list of users, including the new user created by William:

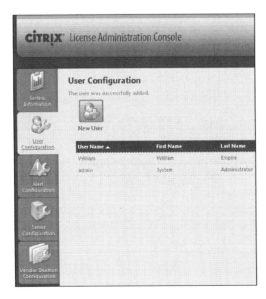

[83]

In the **Alert Configuration** tab, we can select the alerts we want to display on the dashboard and determine the threshold to trigger the alert.

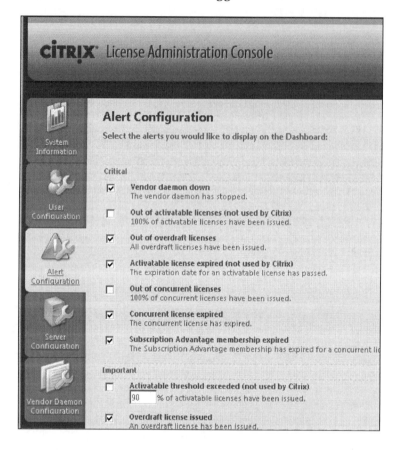

The **Server Configuration** tab helps us to change the license port, enable HTTPS protocol, install web certificates, configure License Server Manager Port, change Log Level, and adjust User Interface settings.

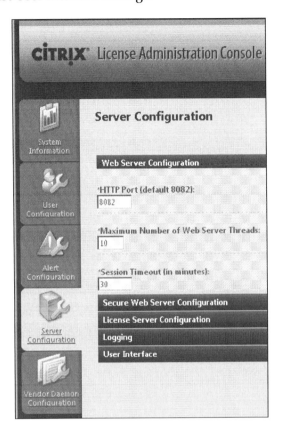

The **Vendor Daemon Configuration** tab is used to check the status of the Citrix License server. This is the first place we need to check, if we experience any license issues. The status must be **Running**.

This tab is the place we use to install and manage licenses. To install new licenses, we need to click on the **Import License** icon.

An alternative method to install licenses is to manually copy the `.LIC` file into the `C:\Program Files (x86)\Citrix\Licensing\MyFiles` folder and restart the Citrix Licensing service.

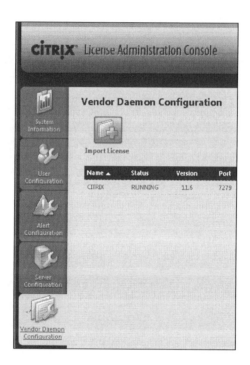

Citrix Web Interface Management console

The web interface provides users with access to XenApp applications and content. Users access their resources using a web browser or the Citrix Online Plug-in.

We have two options to configure web interface sites:

- We can create and configure web interface sites on Microsoft Internet Information Services (IIS) using the Citrix Web Interface Management console.
- We can manually edit the site configuration file `WebInterface.conf` to manage and administer web interface sites. Usually, this file is located on the `C:\inetpub\wwwroot\Citrix\<SiteName>\conf` folder, where `<SiteName>` is the name of the site. Restarting the IIS web server using `IISRESET` from the command line is recommended but not required. Please backup the file before making any changes on the web interface. Installing or upgrading a new version of web interface will overwrite changes.

Chapter 4

> Editing the .conf file and copying the file to multiple servers using a script is a common practice in environments with multiple or personalized web interface servers, but if our environment just involves one or two web interface servers, we would probably want to modify the site configuration from the console.

The following screenshot is a view of the **Citrix Web Interface Management** console. Using the **Actions** pane of the MMC console, we can **Create Site** or **Edit Settings** of the selected site.

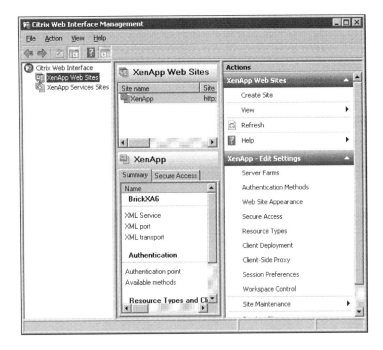

The **Server Farms** option on the **Edit Settings** pane helps us to set up XML Broker(s) and Citrix farm(s) accessible to the web interface.

The XML Broker (also referenced as XML service or XML server) and web interface work together to offer the users access to applications.

The web interface uses the XML Broker to display a list of applications based on the user's permissions. After a user receives applications and launches one of them, the XML Broker provides a list of servers in the farm that hosts this application. The XML Broker chooses one of them based on several rules and returns the address of this server to the web interface.

Using Management Tools

Choosing the appropriate XML Broker is critical for our farm. If we have one single XML Broker configured in the web interface and this server is down, users will be unable to launch any applications. We must consider having multiple or at least two XML Broker servers for redundancy.

In a small farm, with a few servers, the XML Broker is hosted on one or two servers used for multiple infrastructure functions. Also, sometimes for redundancy purposes, the least used XenApp application server is added as the XML Broker.

In a large farm, the XML Broker is usually configured on one or more dedicated servers, usually dedicated data collectors or most preferred servers to become data collector in the zone.

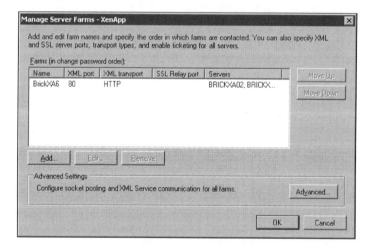

The **Authentication Methods** option on the **Edit Settings** pane is where we need to specify how users authenticate in the web interface. Authentication methods are explained in *Chapter 3, Installing XenApp 6*.

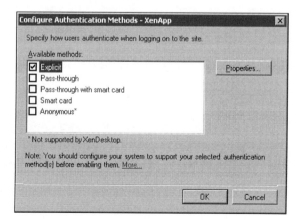

We use the **Secure Access** option on the **Edit Settings** pane to determine how users connect to a server farm. Access methods are explained as follows:

- **Direct**: Online Plug-in connects to the actual IP address of the XenApp server. This method is used when our users are located in a LAN or access our network using the Access Gateway Plug-in.
- **Alternate**: The Alternate method is similar to the Direct method, but users connect to an alternate IP address, defined on each XenApp server using the command ALTADDR, instead of the actual IP address of the XenApp server.
- **Translated**: The Translated method is similar to the Alternate method, except that the alternate address for each XenApp server is defined in the web interface configuration instead of using ALTADDR on each XenApp server.
- **Gateway direct**: The Gateway direct method is used for remote users accessing the LAN through Access Gateway (or Secure Access). The user connects to the URL of Access Gateway and the Online Plug-in initiates an SSL (Secure Sockets Layer) connection to the Access Gateway, which creates a connection to the actual address of the XenApp server. This method requires one or multiple STA (Secure Ticket Authority) server to validate incoming connections. This is the preferred method for users connecting through Access Gateway.
- **Gateway alternate**: The Gateway alternate method is similar to the Gateway direct method, except Access Gateway makes a connection to the alternate address, defined using the command ALTADDR of the XenApp server.
- **Gateway translated**: The Gateway translated method is similar to the Gateway alternate method, except Access Gateway makes a connection to the alternate address, defined in the web interface configuration of the XenApp server.

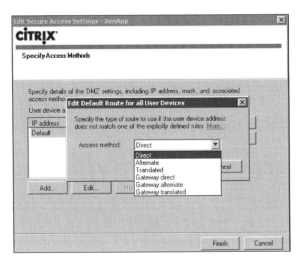

Using Management Tools

The **Resource Types** option on the **Edit Settings** pane sets up how users will access **Online** resources (applications, content, and desktops) through a web browser or the Citrix Online Plug-in. The **Offline** application feature enables users to stream applications to their desktops and open them locally and **Dual Mode** provides access to both options described before.

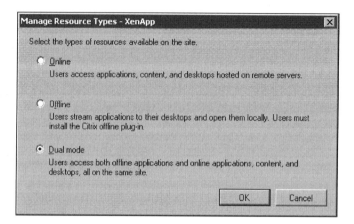

To access published resources (applications, content, and desktops), users must have, at least, either a supported Citrix receiver (also known as Citrix ICA Client or Plugin) or a supported web browser. We can use the **Client Deployment** task in the Web Interface Management Console to configure web-based client deployment. We can specify which Citrix clients are offered to users for download and installation.

Citrix recommends having the latest version of the plugin installed. For more information on how to install Citrix Receiver and Plugins, please refer to *Chapter 11, Receiver and Plugins Management*.

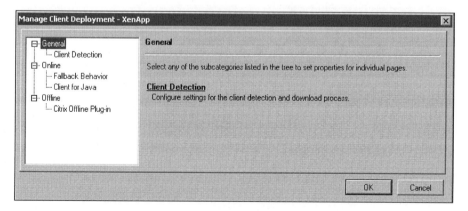

Chapter 4

We can use the **Client-side Proxy** task to configure whether Citrix plugins must communicate or not with the server running XenApp through the proxy server.

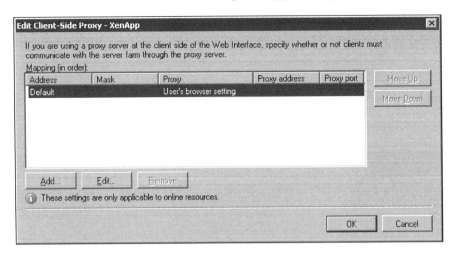

We can use the **Manage Session Preferences** task to specify the settings that users can change. We can also use this task to specify the time after which inactive users are logged off from the web interface, manage **User Customizations**, adjust **Connection Performance**, and **Display** settings. We can set up whether the web interface should override the plugin name in the case of published resources hosted on remote servers.

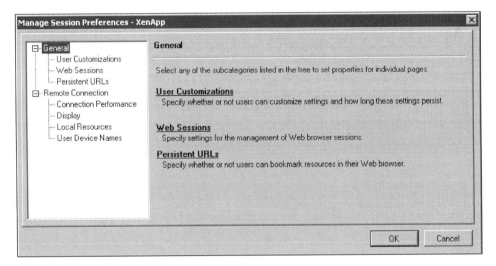

We can enable workspace control for XenApp Services sites using the **Workspace Control** task, which lets us configure automatic reconnection when users log on, configure the **Reconnect** button, and allows users of XenApp websites to log off from both the web interface and active sessions or from the web interface only.

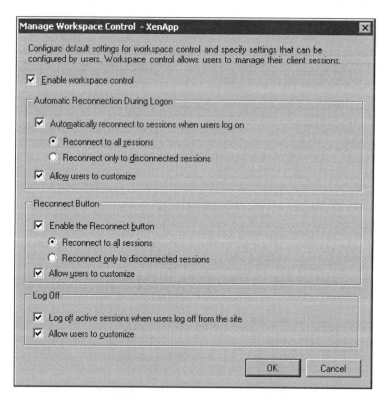

The **Site Maintenance** task opens a menu with the following four options:

- We need to use the **Manage IIS Hosting** task to change the location of our web interface site on MS IIS.
- **Repair Site** will repair the site and rebuild the original site content.
- **Uninstall Site** task removes sites. Uninstalling a site removes it from the system.
- The **Diagnostic Logging** task helps us to increase system security for error logging. We can suppress identical events from being logged recurrently and configure how many duplicate events are logged and how frequently.

Chapter 4

If we have created any images or custom scripts for our web interface site and we run the **Repair Site** task, all these customized files, including the `webinterface.conf`, are removed. All customized files are also removed when we use the **Manage IIS Hosting** task.

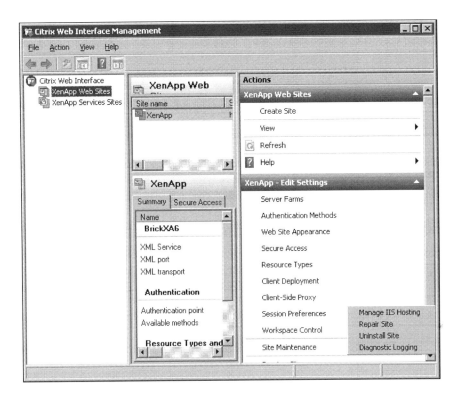

Other administration tools

Now we are going to talk about a few extra management tools included in XenApp 6 (and previous versions). These tools are rarely used, except for the Shadow taskbar, but can be useful for some specific deployments.

Citrix SSL Relay Configuration tool

We can use this tool to secure communication using SSL protocol between a server running the web interface and our farm.

[93]

Shadow taskbar

Shadowing allows administrators, or other users, to view and control other users' sessions remotely. Use the **Shadow** taskbar to shadow sessions and to switch among multiple shadowed sessions. We can shadow ICA sessions within the **Citrix Delivery Services Console** or **Citrix Access Management Console** too.

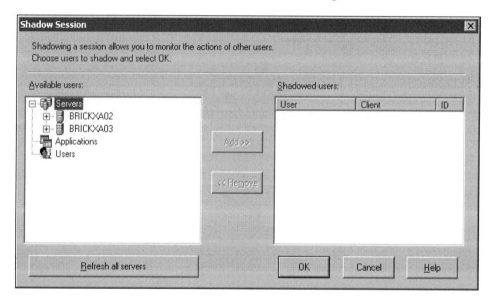

SpeedScreen Latency Reduction Manager

We can use this tool to configure local text echo and other features that improve the user experience on slow networks. **SpeedScreen Latency Reduction Manager** includes the following two technologies:

- **Local Text Echo** speeds up the display of the input text on the client machine on high latency networks
- **Mouse Click Feedback** provides visual feedback to a user updating the mouse pointer, to avoid user clicking the mouse several times

We can use the configuration wizard to configure latency reduction settings for the XenApp server or an application.

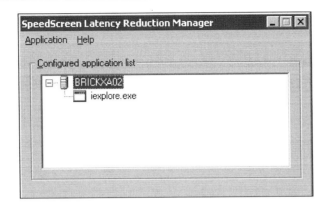

Managing Citrix administrators

Citrix provides a very simple (and powerful) approach to manage Citrix administrators. We can assign the Citrix administrator role to existing Active Directory accounts for both users and groups.

Add a Citrix administrator

Now we are going to help William Empire from Brick Unit Construction to assign full administrator permissions to his account.

From the **Start** menu, he selects **All Programs | Citrix | Management Consoles | Citrix Delivery Services Console**.

In the left pane, he needs to expand **Citrix Resources** and then **XenApp**, click on farm name, and then on the right pane, he needs to select **Action | Add administrator**.

Finally, he needs to click the **Add** button and select the desired user or user group account. In this case, he is going to add the wempire account as a Citrix administrator.

On the **Privileges** page, he needs to select the privilege level he wants to grant to his own user account. He has three options:

- **View Only**: Administrators can view all areas of XenApp farm but they cannot modify them
- **Full Administration**: Administrators can view and modify all areas of the XenApp farm and create and manage other administrator's accounts

Using Management Tools

- **Custom**: Administrators can view and/or modify almost all areas of the farm but they can't create and manage other administrator's accounts

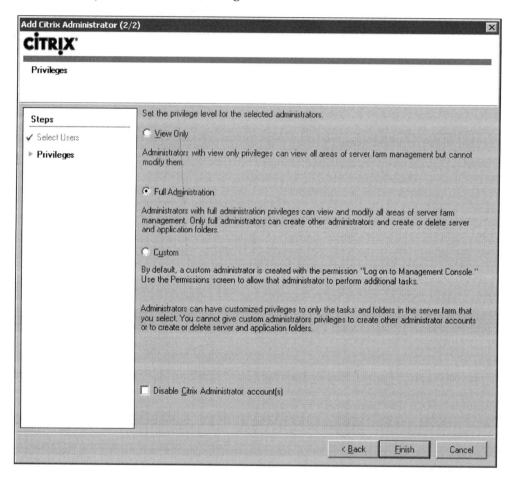

At this time, we are going to help William Empire to assign custom administrator permissions to the Helpdesk group account at Brick Unit.

First, he needs to choose the group account and in this case he is going to use Help Desk Brick Unit group account.

Chapter 4

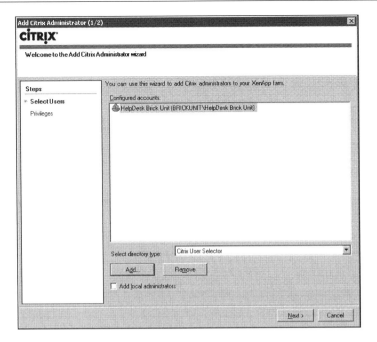

Then he needs to select the **Custom** privilege level.

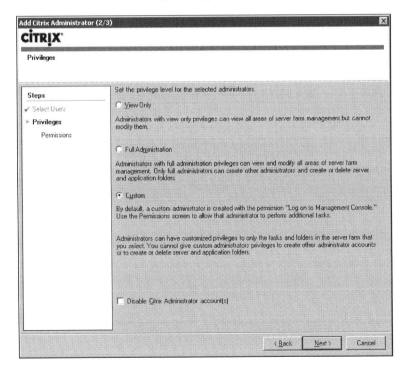

Using Management Tools

Finally, he can use granular tasks to set permissions.

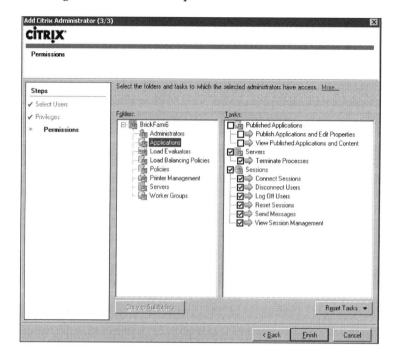

And here is the result: now we can see in the console accounts of both William and Helpdesk.

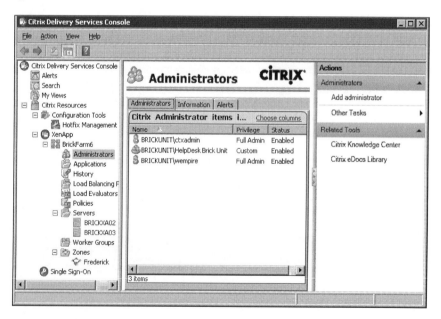

Disable a Citrix administrator

If we ever need to disable a Citrix administrator, for example, to temporarily remove access for an administrator but if we want to retain the account and settings, we need to select the administrator account whose privileges we want to disable.

On the **Actions** pane or **Action** menu, we click on the **Disable** button.

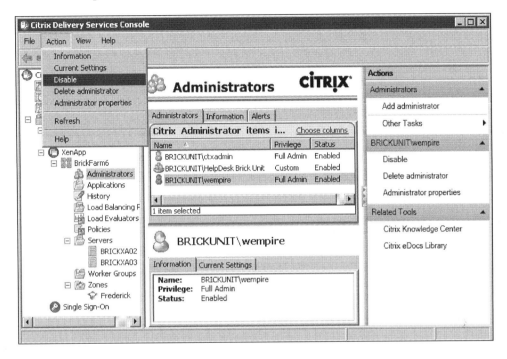

When an administrator account is disabled, the administrator icon appears in gray.

On the **Actions** pane or **Action** menu, we need to click on the **Enable** button to enable the account.

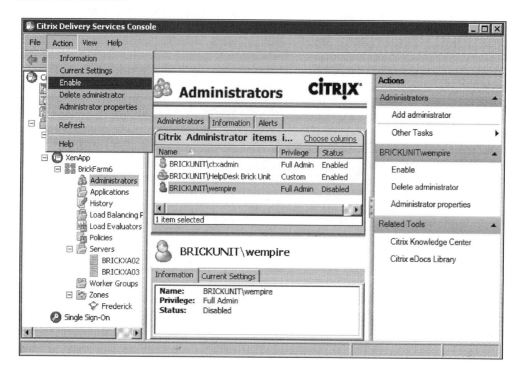

Modify administrator properties

First, we need to select the administrator account whose privileges we want to modify.

On the **Actions** pane or **Action** menu, we need to click on **Administrator properties**.

Then we need to select **Permissions**.

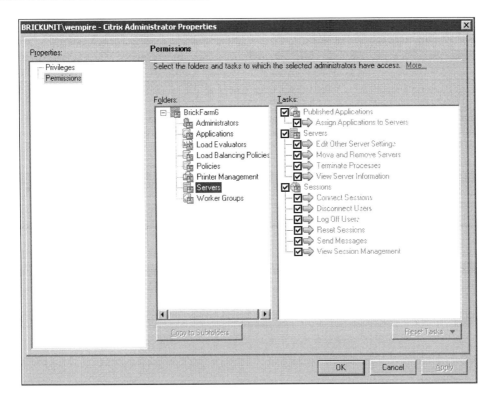

Summary

In this chapter, we have learned about different management tools provided by Citrix in XenApp 6. Specifically the following:

- Citrix Delivery Services Console, the main management console
- License Administration Console
- Citrix Web Interface Management Console
- Other management tools, including Citrix SSL Relay Configuration tool, Shadow taskbar, and SpeedScreen Latency Reduction Manager
- Creating and managing an administrator's accounts

In the next chapter, we will see how to use the Citrix management console to publish and manage applications on the farm.

5
Application Publishing

In the last chapter, we discussed about the Citrix management tools. In this chapter, we will use them to publish applications and resources so users can start using our Citrix farm.

In this chapter, we are going to learn:

- Choosing the best method to deliver applications
- Publishing a hosted application using the Publish Application wizard
- Publishing a streaming application using the Publish Application wizard
- Publishing a server desktop using the Publish Application wizard
- Publishing content using the Publish Application wizard
- Configuring content redirection

Publishing applications

Building a Citrix farm is an expensive solution, so we need to test all applications in a pilot environment to make sure all the applications can run on Remote Desktop Services (formerly known as Terminal Server) and on Citrix XenApp servers.

We need to decide on the appropriate application publishing method. Intensive testing of applications is critical for the success of Citrix farm deployment.

We can provide access to several types of published resources in XenApp to the users:

- Hosted applications are installed locally on servers running XenApp. When users access them, the published applications are executed on the servers, but appear to be running locally on client machines. Hosted applications only run when users are connected to XenApp servers.

Application Publishing

- Streamed applications are installed in application profiles and are stored on a file server in our App Hub, published using the XenApp publishing wizard, and delivered to any client desktop or server on demand. Streaming applications can run online or offline.

- Content: We can publish documents, data files such as Excel spreadsheets or Word documents, media files, web pages, and URLs.

- Server desktops: Users can access all of the resources available on the server. Usually, this feature is used for administrators, but is not a recommended practice for common users. In that case, we need to secure server desktops to prevent user access to sensitive areas of the operating system.

When we publish an application, configuration information for the application is stored in the Citrix data store of the server farm. This information includes the types of files that are associated with the application, which users can connect to the application, client-side session properties like window size and resolution, encryption level and audio settings, and more.

When delivered to users, published applications appear very similar to applications running locally on the client machine. This is the ultimate goal for Citrix: Provide a better-than-local experience to users.

Users start applications depending on the delivery options we configured in the publishing wizard and on the XenApp Plug-in they run on their client machine.

One best practice for application publishing is to use groups instead of users when we publish applications. For example, an application published to 300 users requires IMA to validate 300 objects. The same application published to a single group of 500 users requires IMA to validate only one object.

> Citrix defines the IMA (Independent Management Architecture) as a server-to-server infrastructure that provides robust, secure, and scalable tools for managing server farms of any size. Among other features, IMA enables centralized, platform-independent management, an ODBC-compliant data store, and management products that plug into a management console.
> http://community.citrix.com/display/edgesight/Report+Counters+Glossary

Choosing the best method to deliver applications

Selecting the appropriate delivery method for an application is the first step of publishing it. There is a big discussion around this subject. Some people prefer streaming applications and some people prefer hosted applications.

There is no magic formula to choose the appropriate way to publish an application; testing and more testing is the real way to figure it out.

I prefer to use hosted applications and if they don't work well, use streaming applications, but again this decision is related to the application, the size of the farm and type, and location of users. The following are some rules to help us decide the right way to publish an application:

- Patching and upgrade: Application streaming simplifies delivery by allowing us to setup and configure an application on one (or multiple) file server for delivery to client machines. To patch or upgrade the application, we make the updates only in the location where we stored the application. If we have a hosted application, we have more options to patch or upgrade the applications, depending on how many servers we have. If we have just a few servers, we can manually deploy updates, or use scripts to update them. If we have a medium to large farm, we can use Microsoft System Center Configuration Manager (SCCM), formerly known as Microsoft Systems Management Server (SMS) to deploy a patch or upgrade package, using Citrix Installation Manager or the preferred option included in the platinum license of XenApp 6: using the Provisioning Server to have a single image of the XenApp 6. For using Provisioning server, we need to update just the master image to update all servers.

- **Network connectivity** may be a big factor in our decision on whether to host or stream applications. If users are located in branch or are accessing applications remotely, hosted applications are the preferred option. Streaming applications are recommended if users are close to the server where the application's profiles are located. We can deploy streaming applications on multiple servers and Citrix will use the closest file server based on the IP address of the client machine.

- **Client machine type** is another aspect to help to decide the type of published resource. If we need to run a CPU-intensive application and we are using a Thin Client or very old computer, we need to choose hosted applications. Sometimes we can stream this CPU-intensive application to client machines to avoid overloading our XenApp servers, affecting other applications. If the client is a mobile user, we can use streaming applications, and the client can run the application offline.

- **Multiple versions** of the same software on the same server sometimes are not possible or extremely complex to setup on hosted applications. So, in this scenario, using streaming applications is the preferred option.
- **Application compatibility** is another factor in choosing streaming applications over hosted applications. For example, if we have multiple applications requiring different versions of Oracle clients, Crystal Reports, or any shared component.

There are more reasons, but again, most of these considerations will depend on our applications and the size of the environment, so we need to check how our clients are going to access our applications and test and re-test them.

Publishing a hosted application using the Publish Application wizard

William decided to deploy Microsoft Project 2010 on the farm. Project is one of the most important applications for Architects and Project Managers and is one of the first applications he wants to try on XenApp 6.

The first step is to install the applications for all users on XenApp 6 servers.

1. William needs to open a command prompt so that you are running it with Administrator privileges.
2. He then right-click on the command prompt on the **Start** menu and select **Run as Administrator**:

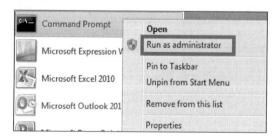

3. Another option is to execute the command prompt using the RUNAS command as administrator. For example, William will use the following command:

   `C:\>RUNAS /user:brickunit\wempire CMD`

4. Now that he is executing the command prompt as the administrator, he can run the following command in a command prompt:

   `C:\ >change user /install`

5. He will receive a message to confirm he is running Terminal Server on Install mode:

   `User session is ready to install applications.`

6. To see the terminal server mode, he needs to run the following command:

   `C:\ >change user /query`

7. Now he can run the setup of our application from the command prompt.

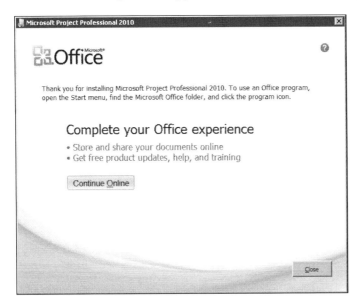

8. The setup of the Microsoft Project 2010 is complete. Now it's time to return the Terminal Server to execute mode. From the command prompt, he needs to type the following command:

   `C:\ >change user /execute`

Also, William can install applications using the option **Install Application on Remote Desktop Server** from the Control Panel.

In order to publish Microsoft Project 2010, he needs to open **Citrix Delivery Service Console**.

From the XenApp console, under the **XenApp** node, we need to expand the farm or server to which he wants to publish the application.

We need to select the **Applications** node.

Application Publishing

> We can use the **Actions** pane and choose **Create folder**. Name the folder for the application you are publishing. This step is optional if you have a few applications, but will be necessary to create folders to keep applications organized if we have dozens or hundreds of applications. These folders are visible only to Citrix administrators and not visible to standard users.

He needs to select the (optional) folder we created before and from the **Actions** pane choose **Publish application**.

In the Publish Application wizard, on the **Name** page, he needs to provide a **Display name** (maximum 256 characters) and **Application description**. The name appears on user devices when users access the application and on the console for the farm applications. XenApp supports application names that use Latin-1 and Unicode character sets, including characters used in Japanese, Chinese, and Korean.

On the **Type** page, he needs to specify the type of resource we want to publish and the delivery method. He has three types of resources to be published (server desktop, content, and application).

He needs to choose **Application**, then select **Accessed from a server** for **Application type**, and then choose **Installed application** to publish a hosted application.

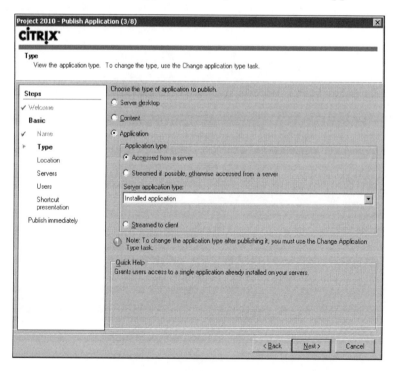

On the **Location** page, he needs to type or use the **Browse** button to set the command line and working directory (optional). When we publish the same application on multiple servers, we MUST install the application in the same path and the folder in all servers or the application will fail.

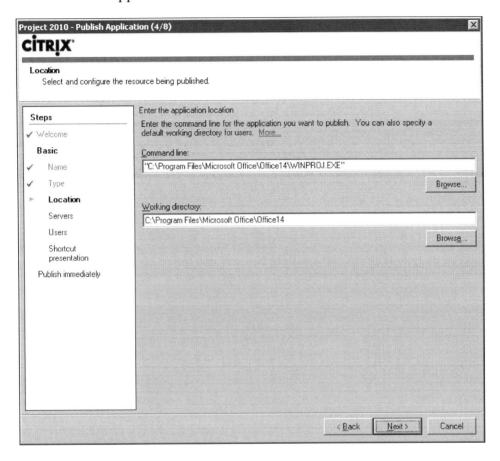

On the **Servers** page, William needs to add the individual servers or worker groups on which the published application runs.

Application Publishing

> To add a server to the list of servers for a published desktop or application (after publishing the application), drag-and-drop the server onto the published desktop or application in the left pane of the console. We can also drag-and-drop the published desktop or application onto the server.

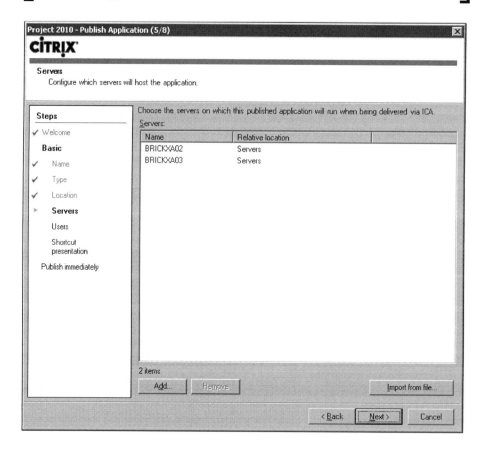

On the **Users** page, he needs to add users or groups who have access to the application and he can allow access only to configured user accounts or to anonymous users.

William assigned permissions to the **BU Project Managers** and **Domain Admin** groups.

Usually, it is a good practice in medium to large environment to create a Test Group and avoid using Domain Admins group for testing purposes.

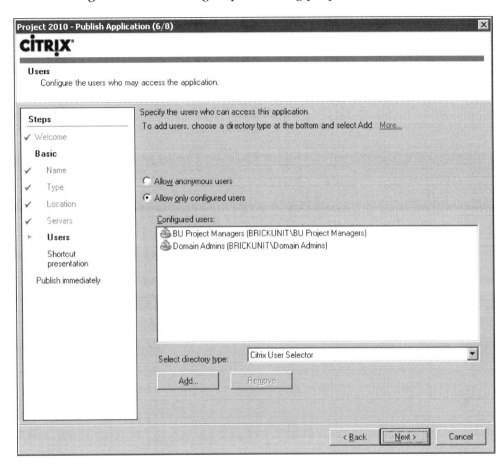

On the **Shortcut presentation** page, William selects the icon for the application and choose how the application is enumerated on the user device.

The client application folder is used when he needs to organize applications inside folders. This is a recommended practice, if we have a lot of applications.

Both **Add to the client's Start menu** and **Add shortcut to the client's desktop** options are used when client machines utilize the XenApp Plug-in to connect to the XenApp farm.

The console has a limit of 1,000 unique application icons. When that limit is exceeded, the console displays a generic icon for all new applications.

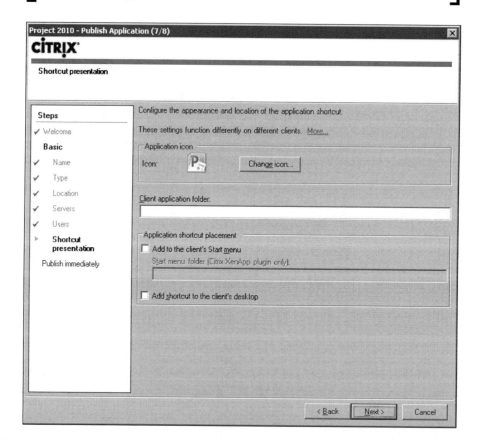

On the **Publishing immediately** page, he needs to select **Disable application initially**, if we want to prevent users from accessing the application. Later, he can manually enable it through application properties.

To view and select advanced options, he needs to check the **Configure advanced application settings now** option. Alternatively, he can modify the advanced settings using the application properties.

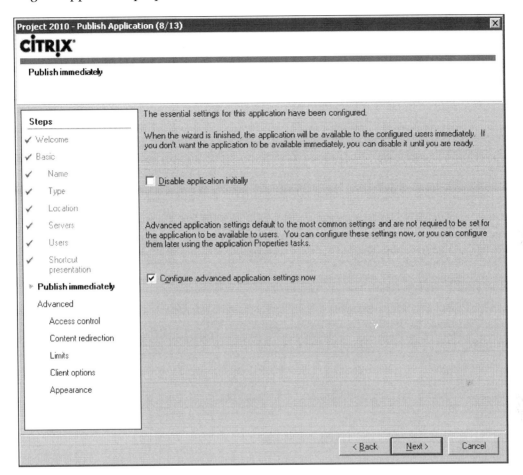

Application Publishing

On the optional **Access Control** page, William can configure the access to this application using Access Gateway Advanced Edition, the Citrix SSL VPN solution used to provide farm access to remote users.

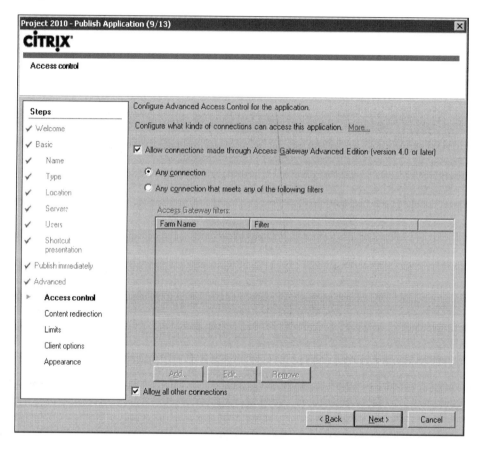

On the **Content redirection** page, he can configure the file types associated with his application. We will talk about content redirection at the end of this chapter.

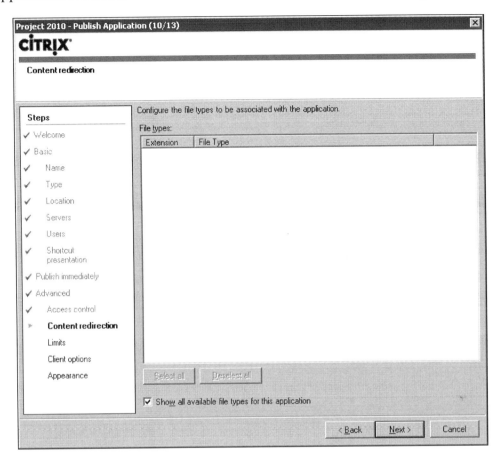

On the **Limit** page, he needs to configure application limits. William enables the **Limit instances allowed to run in server farm** checkbox and sets the **Maximum instances** option to **35**, because this is the amount of Microsoft Project licenses the company owns.

Application Publishing

William also enabled the checkbox **Allow only one instance of application for each user** to avoid one user using more than one license at the same time.

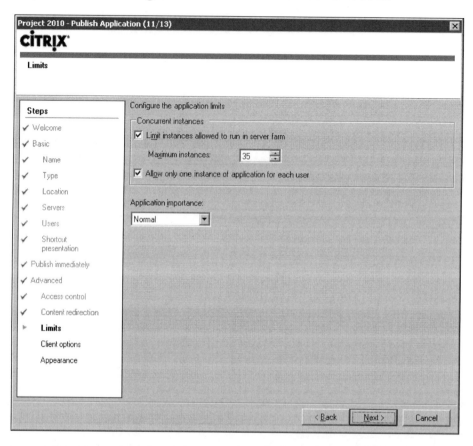

On the **Client options** page, he can configure multiple settings, like Client Audio, Connection encryption levels, and Printing.

Enabling the **Start this application without waiting for printing to be created option** improves the logon speed but sometimes can cause an issue, if a user has a lot of printers and user try to print before all printers are created.

Chapter 5

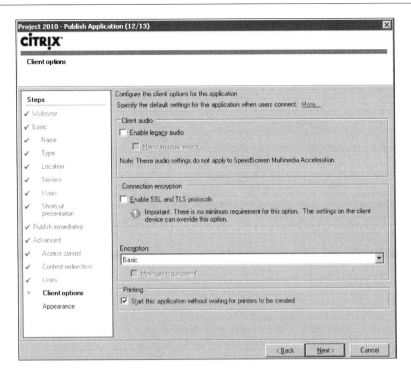

On the **Appearance** page, he can configure the visual setting of the application, like **Session window size**, color quality, and so on:

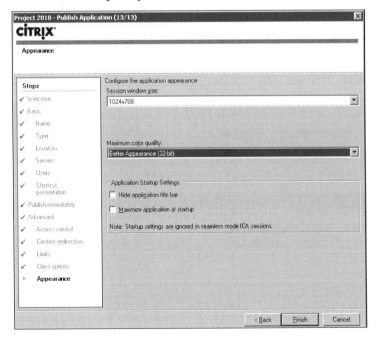

Application Publishing

When he finishes this wizard, the published hosted application (unless he disables it) is available for users.

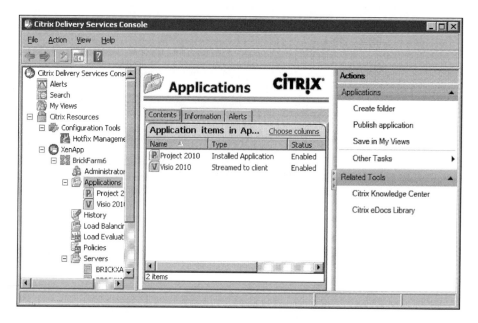

Also, he can use PowerShell to publish a hosted application. Detailed information to setup XenApp Commands on PowerShell can be found in *Chapter 12, Scripting Programming*.

```
New-XAApplication -BrowserName "Project 2010" -ApplicationType
"ServerInstalled" -DisplayName "Project 2010" -Enabled $true -
CommandLineExecutable "C:\Program Files\Microsoft Office\Office14\
Winproj.EXE" -WorkingDirectory "C:\Program Files\Microsoft Office\
Office14" -AnonymousConnectionsAllowed $false -AddToClientStartMenu
$true -InstanceLimit "-1" -WindowType "1024x768" -ColorDepth
"Colors256"
```

Publishing a streaming application using the Publish Application wizard

William decided to publish Microsoft Visio 2010 as a streaming application. This decision is based on the need of architects and project managers to take some notes and make diagrams, when they are visiting clients or construction sites, and they need to run Visio on their notebooks. The ability to run Visio in both online and offline mode is critical for both the groups.

Chapter 5

The first step is to profile Microsoft Visio 2010 and copy the application profile to the file server. We are going to cover how to install and configure streaming applications in detail in the next chapter.

When the application profile process is completed and the profile is copied to the file server, William needs to open the **Citrix Delivery Service Console**.

From the XenApp console, under the **XenApp** node, he needs to expand the farm or server to which he wants to publish the application.

He needs to select the **Applications** node and from the **Actions** pane he chooses **Publish application**.

In the **Publish Application** wizard, on the **Name** page, he needs to provide a **Display name** (maximum 256 characters) and **Application description**. The name appears on client machines when users access the application and on the console for the farm applications. XenApp supports application names that use Latin-1 and Unicode character sets, including characters used in Japanese, Chinese, and Korean.

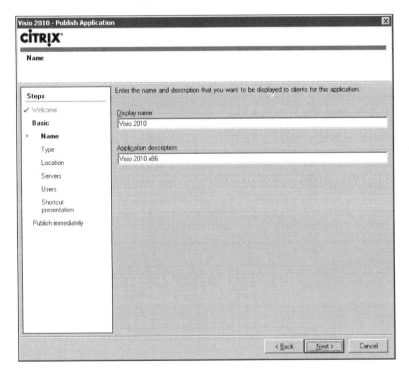

Application Publishing

On the **Type** page, William needs to specify the type of resource he wants to publish and the delivery method. He had three types of resources to be published (server desktop, content, and application).

He needs to choose **Streamed to client** to publish a streaming application. An alternative option is to choose **Streamed if possible, otherwise accessed from a server**, but this option will require installing (or streaming) the application on the XenApp server too.

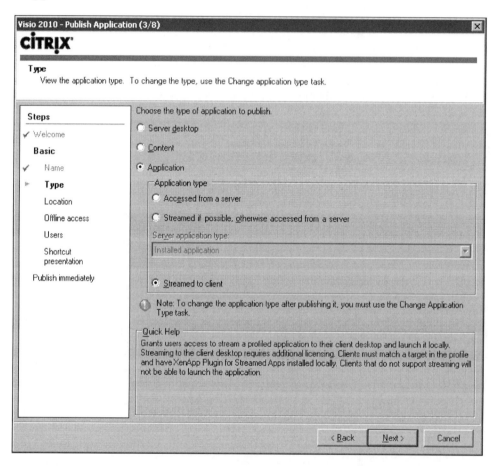

On the **Location** page, he needs to type or use the **Browse** button to set **Citrix streaming application profile address**, and then we need to choose the **Application to launch from the Citrix streaming application profile**. He can also set **Optional parameters** for the application.

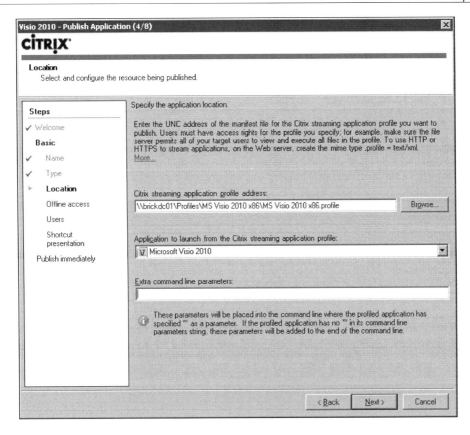

On the **Offline access** page, William can configure streamed applications for offline access.

The server fully caches applications enabled for offline access on client machines; the entire application is sent to client machines while the user is online so that the user can launch the application offline and have full functionality of the application. By default, applications are cached when a user logs on into the system.

When William clicks on the **Enable offline access** checkbox on the **Offline Access** page, he needs to configure the **Cache preference**:

- **Pre-cache application at login** caches the application when the user logs on (selected by default). However, concurrent logons may slow network traffic. Pre-caching is also possible using third-party tools, such as Microsoft System Center Configuration Manager (SCCM) or similar.
- **Cache application at launch time** caches the application when users launch it. Use this option if the number of users logging on at the same time (and pre-caching their applications) could overload the network.

Application Publishing

The offline access option requires the Citrix offline client to be installed on the client machine.

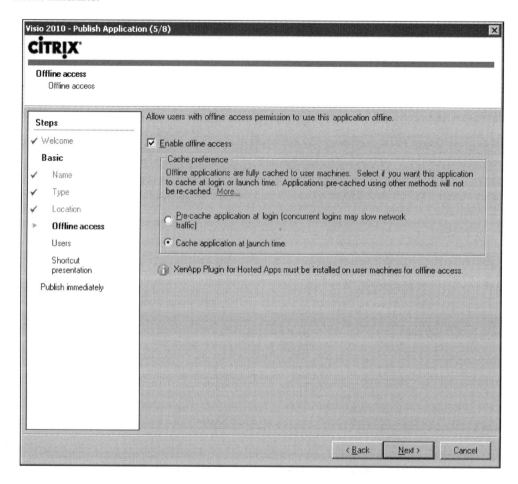

On the **Users** page, he needs to add users or groups who have access to the application and he can allow access only to configured user accounts or to anonymous users.

William assigned permissions to **BU Project Managers** and **Domain Admins** groups.

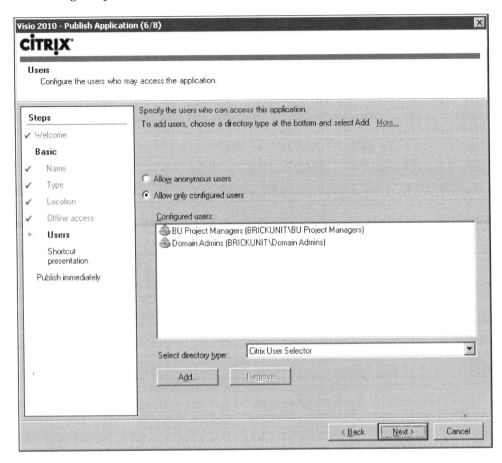

On the **Shortcut presentation** page, William selects the icon for the application and chooses how the application is enumerated on the client machine.

The client application folder is used when he needs to organize applications inside folders. This is a recommended practice, if we have a lot of applications.

The **Add to the client's Start menu** option creates a shortcut under the Programs folder of the local Start menu. If a folder structure is specified in the Start Menu Folder textbox, the folder structure is created within the local Programs folder. If no folder structure is specified, the application is available from the top level of the Start menu.

This option provides a real integration of the streamed application in the client machine and looks like the application is installed locally.

Application Publishing

The **Add shortcut to the client's desktop** option creates a shortcut to this application on the user's local desktop.

> The console has a limit of 1,000 unique application icons. When that limit is exceeded, the console displays a generic icon for all new applications.

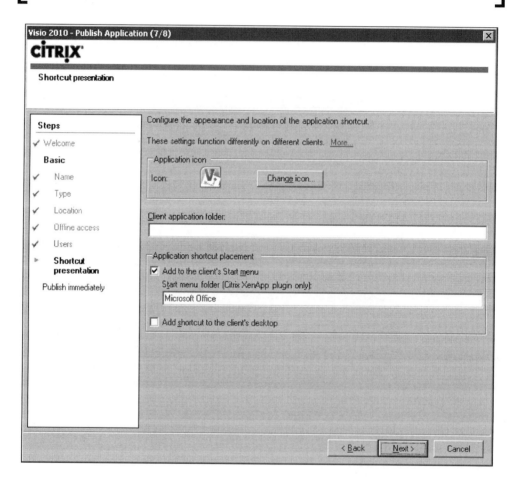

On the **Publishing immediately** page, he needs to select **Disable application initially**, if he wants to prevent users from accessing the application. Later, he can manually enable it through application properties.

To view and select advanced options, he needs to enable the **Configure advanced application settings now** option. Alternatively, he can modify the advanced settings using the application properties.

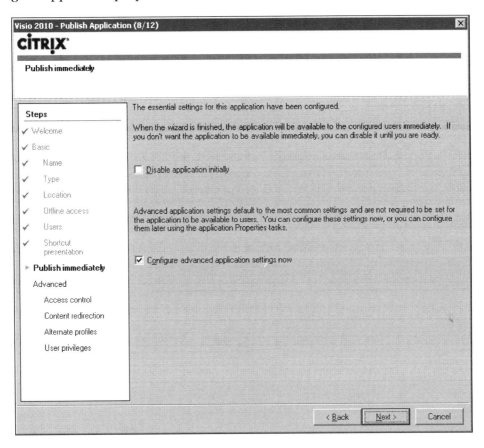

Application Publishing

On the optional **Access control** page, he can configure the access to this application using Access Gateway Advanced Edition, the Citrix SSL VPN solution used to provide access to the farm to remote users.

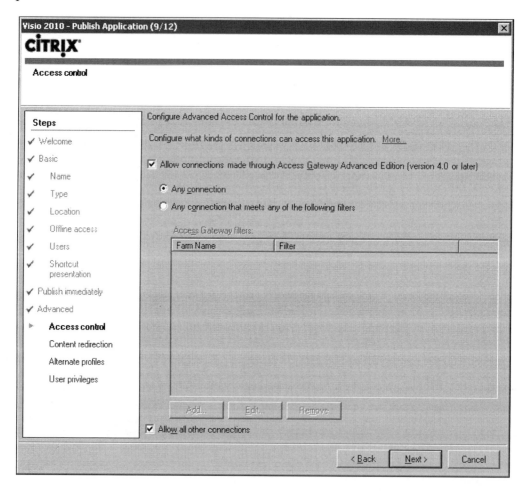

Chapter 5

On the **Content redirection** page, he can select the file types associated with our application.

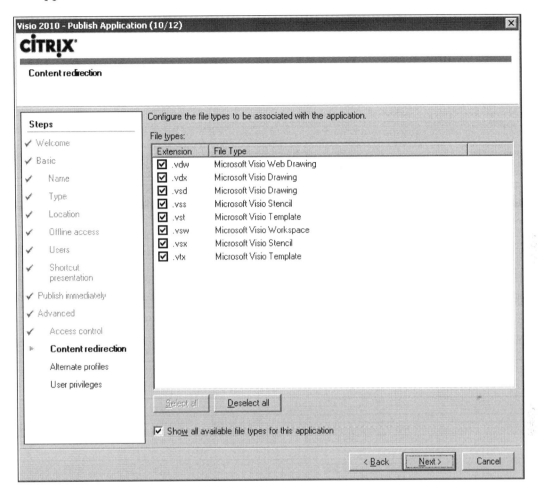

Application Publishing

On the **Alternate profiles** page, he can add an alternate profile for connections that come from specific IP addresses. For example, William can use an alternate profile to allow users in remote branches to access one published application using file servers on their location, increasing performance and reducing loading delays.

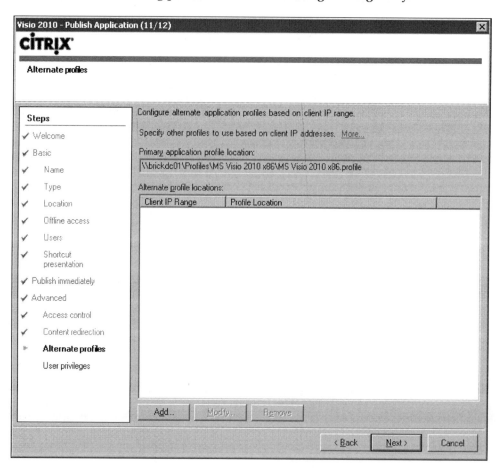

On the **User privileges** page, he can set up the level of privileges when the application runs on the client machine.

When the **Select Run application as a least-privileged user account** option (not selected by default) is enabled, all users, even those with an administrator account, run the application with normal user privileges.

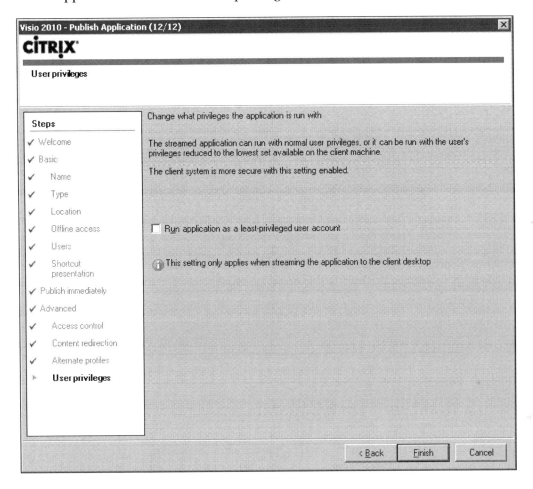

When he finishes this wizard, the published streamed application (unless he disables it) is available for users.

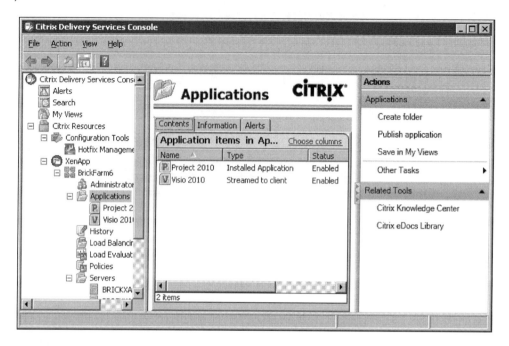

Publishing content using the Publish Application wizard

William will publish the **CtxAdmTools** website to administrators. CtxAdmTools is a popular site for free tools of Citrix, Microsoft, and VMware tools, featured on the Citrix community website.

To publish content, he needs to open **Citrix Delivery Service Console**.

From the XenApp console, under the **XenApp** node, he needs to expand the farm or server to which he wants to publish the content.

He needs to select the **Applications** node and from the **Actions** pane, he chooses **Publish application**.

In the **Publish Application** wizard, on the **Name** page, William needs to provide a **Display name** (maximum 256 characters) and **Application description**. The name appears on client machines when users access the application and on the console for the farm applications. XenApp supports application names that use Latin-1 and Unicode character sets, including characters used in Japanese, Chinese, and Korean.

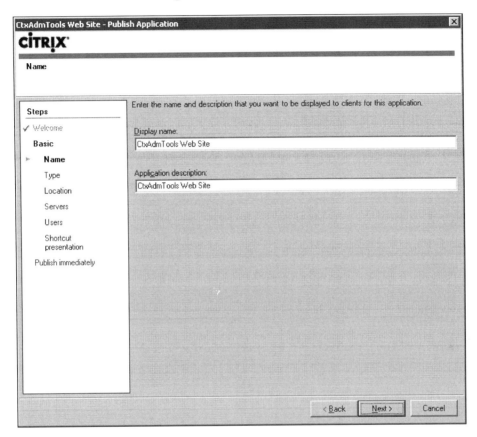

On the **Type** page, he needs to specify the type of resource he wants to publish and the delivery method. We have three types of resources to be published (server desktop, content, and application).

Application Publishing

William will choose the **Content** option to publish a website.

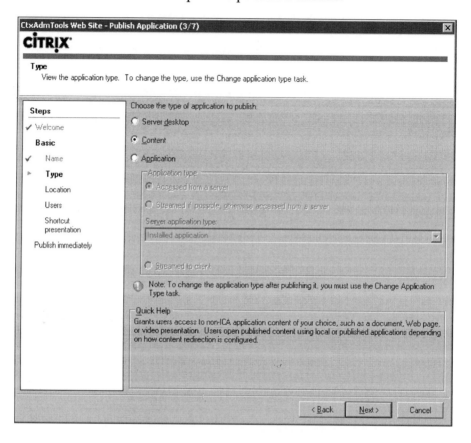

On the **Location** page, he needs to type or use the **Browse** button to set the path of the file or the URL of the resource, `http://ctxadmtools.musumeci.com.ar`.

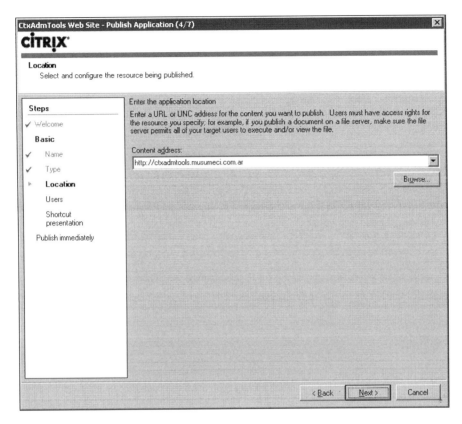

On the **Users** page, he needs to add users or groups who have access to the application. He uses the options to allow access only to the configured user accounts or to anonymous users.

Application Publishing

William assigned permissions to the **Domain Admins** groups because CtxAdmTools is a website for free Citrix, Microsoft, and VMware tools, and only administrators will access the site:

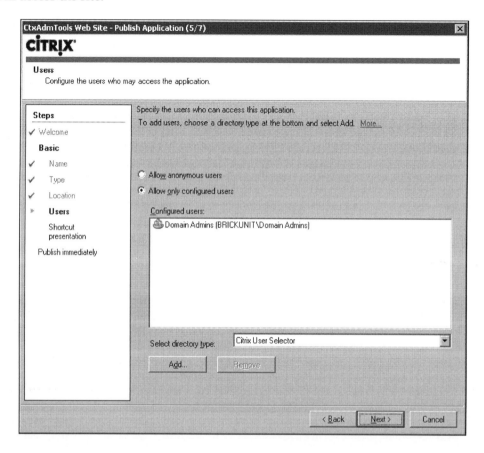

On the **Shortcut presentation** page, select the icon for the application and choose how the application is enumerated on the client machine.

The client application folder is used when we need to organize applications inside folders. This is a recommended practice, if we have a lot of applications.

Usually both **Add to the client's Start menu** and **Add shortcut to the client's desktop** are used when clients utilize the XenApp Plug-in to connect to the XenApp farm.

The console has a limit of 1,000 unique application icons. When that limit is exceeded, the console displays a generic icon for all new applications.

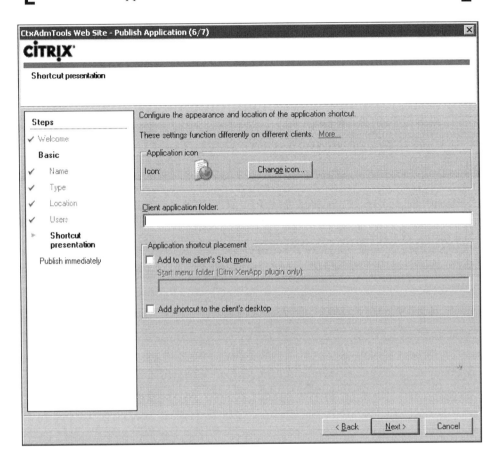

On the **Publishing immediately** page, he needs to select **Disable application initially**, if he wants to prevent users from accessing the application. Later, he can manually enable it through application properties.

Application Publishing

To view and select advanced options, he needs to enable the **Configure advanced application settings now** option. Alternatively, he can modify the advanced settings using the application properties:

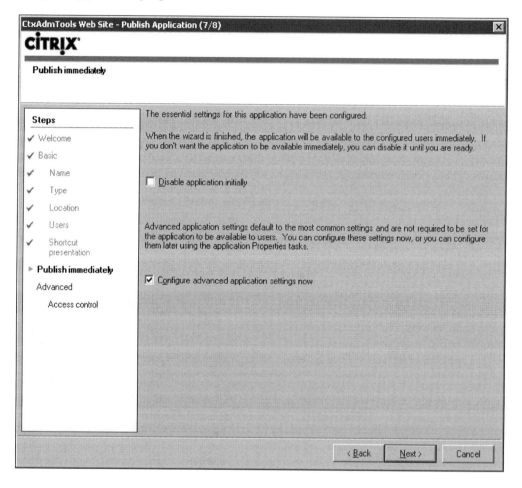

On the optional **Access control** page, he can configure access to this application using Access Gateway Advanced Edition, the Citrix SSL VPN solution used to provide access to the farm to remote users:

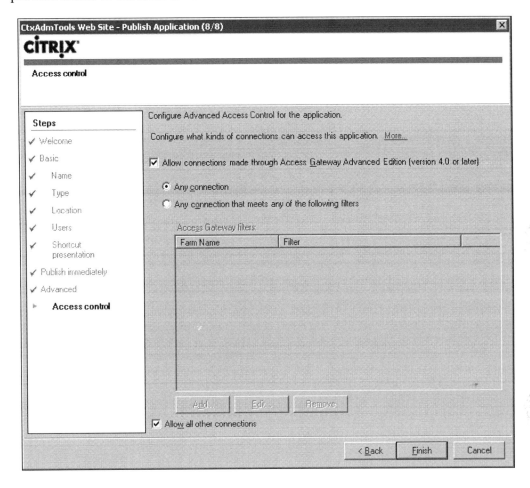

When he finishes this wizard, the published content (unless we disable it) is available for users:

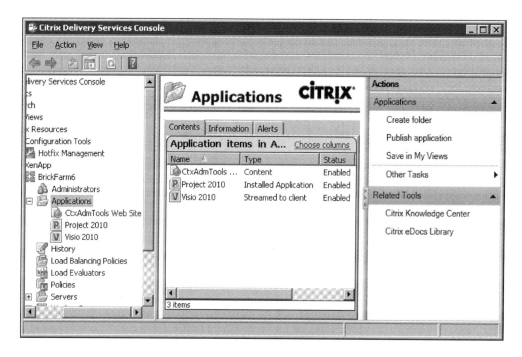

Publishing a server desktop using the Publish Application wizard

William will publish server desktops of Citrix servers to help administrators manage servers. To publish a server desktop, he needs to open the **Citrix Delivery Services Console**.

From the XenApp console, under the **XenApp** node, he needs to expand the farm or server to which he wants to publish the application.

He needs to select the **Applications** node.

 We can use the **Actions** pane and choose **Create folder**. Name the folder for the application we are publishing. This step is optional if we have a few applications, but will be necessary to create folders to keep applications organized, if we have dozens or hundreds of applications.

William needs to select the (optional) folder if he created one before; if not, just click on the root Applications node and from the **Actions** pane, he chooses **Publish application**.

In the **Publish Application** wizard, on the **Name** page, he needs to provide a **Display name** (maximum 256 characters) and **Application description**. The name appears on client machines when users access the application and on the console for the farm applications. XenApp supports application names that use Latin-1 and Unicode character sets, including characters used in Japanese, Chinese, and Korean.

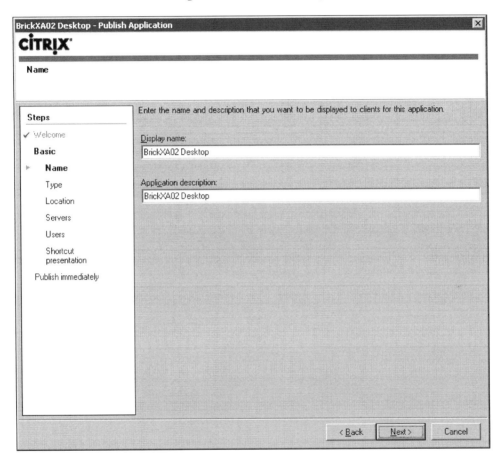

On the **Type** page, he needs to specify the type of resource he wants to publish and the delivery method. We have three types of resources to be published (server desktop, content, and application).

Application Publishing

William needs to choose **Server desktop**.

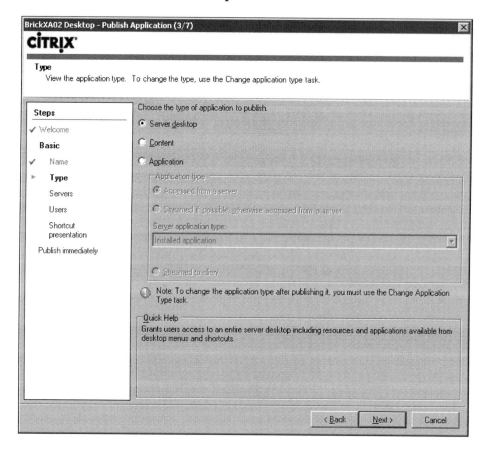

On the **Servers** page, he needs to add the individual servers or worker groups on which the published application runs.

Creating one published server desktop for each XenApp server for administration purposes is a common practice, in most of the environments.

To add a server to the list of servers for a published desktop or application (after publishing the application), drag-and-drop the server onto the published desktop or application in the left pane of the console. We can also drag-and-drop the published desktop or application onto the server.

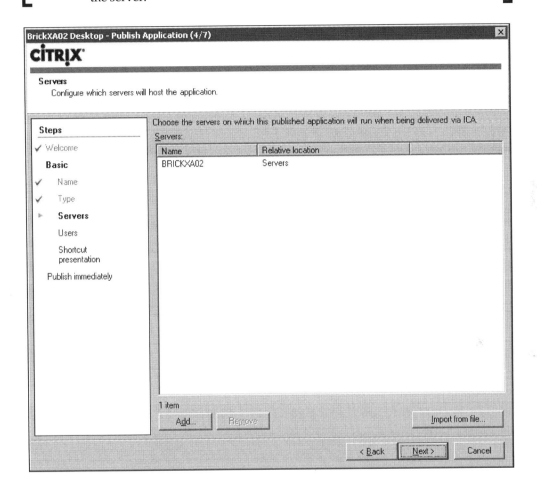

On the **Users** page, he needs to add users or groups who have access to the application. He uses the options to allow access only to configured user accounts or to anonymous users.

William assigned permissions to the **Domain Admins** group, because only administrators will access the server desktop.

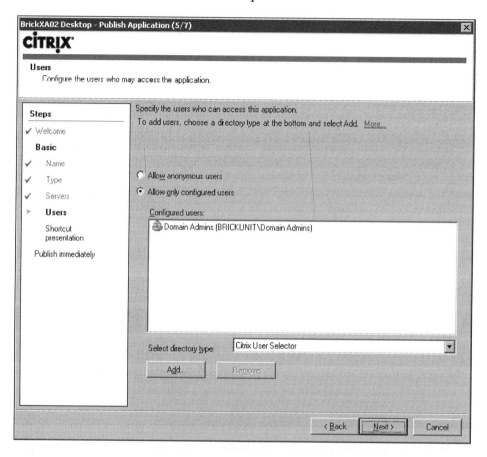

On the **Shortcut presentation** page, he selects the icon for the application and chooses how the application is enumerated on the user device.

The client application folder is used when he needs to organize applications inside folders. This is a recommended practice, if we have a lot of applications.

Usually both **Add to the client's Start menu** and **Add shortcut to the client's desktop** options are used when clients utilize the XenApp Plug-in to connect to XenApp farm.

> The console has a limit of 1,000 unique application icons. When that limit is exceeded, the console displays a generic icon for all new applications.

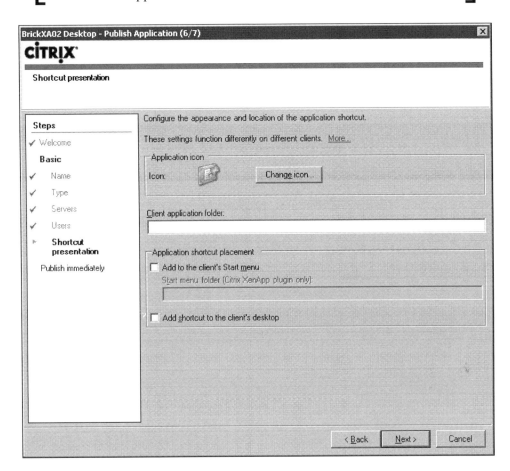

On the **Publishing immediately** page, he needs to select **Disable application initially**, if he wants to prevent users from accessing the application. Later, he can manually enable it through application properties.

Application Publishing

To view and select advanced options, William needs to enable the **Configure advanced application settings now** option. Alternatively, he can modify the advanced settings using the application properties.

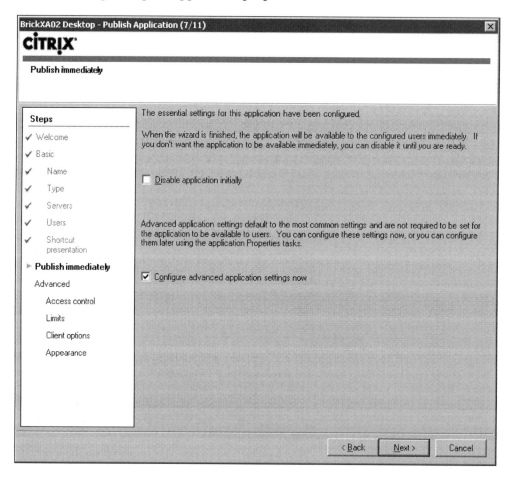

On the optional **Access control** page, he can configure the access to this application using Access Gateway Advanced Edition, the Citrix SSL VPN solution used to provide access to the farm to remote users.

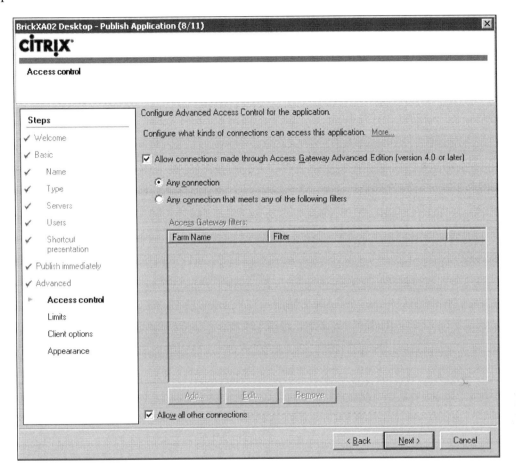

On the **Limit** page, he needs to configure application limits. William doesn't enable the **Limit instances allowed to run in server farm** checkbox and **Maximum instances** checkbox, because there is no need to limit the amount of simultaneous connections.

Application Publishing

William also keeps the checkbox **Allow only one instance of application for each user** disabled.

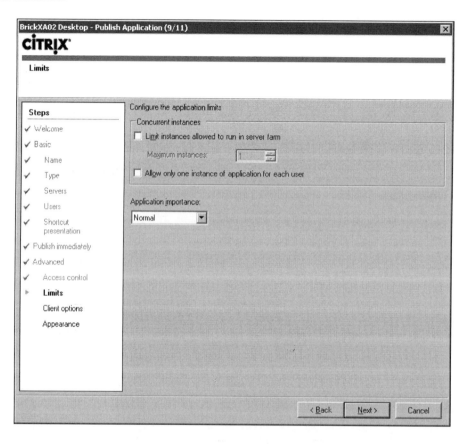

On the **Client options** page, he can configure multiple settings, like Client Audio, Connection encryption levels, and Printing.

Enabling the **Start this application without waiting for printing to be created** option improves the logon speed but sometimes can cause issues, if a user has a lot of printers and he tries to print before all printers are created.

Chapter 5

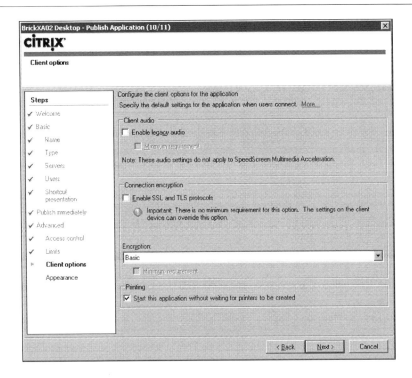

On the **Appearance** page, he can configure the visual setting of the application, like **Session window size**, color quality, and so on.

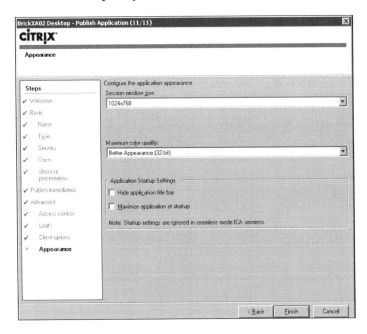

Application Publishing

When he finishes this wizard, the published desktop is available for users, unless we disabled it before.

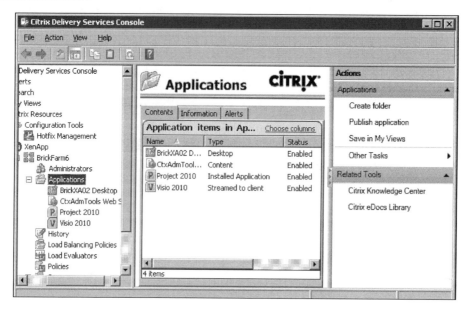

Configuring content redirection

The capability to redirect application and content launching from server to client or client to server is referred to as **content redirection**.

Content redirection allows us to manage whether users access information with applications published on servers or with applications running locally on client machines.

Enabling content redirection from server to client

When we enable server to client content redirection, the XenApp server intercepts embedded URLs and sends them to the client machine and the web browser, or multimedia players, on the client machine open these URLs. This feature reduces the usage on servers from processing these types of requests by redirecting application launching for supported URLs from the server to the local client machine. The browser locally installed on the client machine is used to navigate to the URL. Users cannot disable this feature. Accessing published content with local client desktops does not use XenApp resources or licenses because local viewer applications do not use XenApp sessions to display the published content.

For example, users can access a training website with a lot of graphics and sound in their client machines, without overloading servers. Multimedia sites, such as training sites with intensive graphics, usually run better on client machines.

> If the client machine fails to connect to a URL, the URL is redirected back to the server.

The following URL types are opened locally through client machines for Windows and Linux when this type of content redirection is enabled:

- HTTP (Hypertext Transfer Protocol)
- HTTPS (Secure Hypertext Transfer Protocol)
- RTSP (Real Player and QuickTime)
- RTSPU (Real Player and QuickTime)
- PNM (Legacy Real Player)
- MMS (Microsoft Media Format)

If content redirection from server to client is not working for some of the HTTPS links, we need to verify that the client machines has an appropriate certificate installed. If the appropriate certificate is not installed, the HTTP ping from the client machine to the URL fails and the URL is redirected back to the server.

Configuring content redirection from client to server

When we configure client to server content redirection, users running the XenApp Online Plug-in open all files of the associated type using applications published on the server. Content redirection from client to server is available only for users connecting with the XenApp Online Plug-in.

For example, Brick Unit Construction doesn't have enough licenses of Project 2010 for all client machines. However, occasionally, some users receive a project file attached in an e-mail. When users double-click project attachments on the e-mail application running locally, the attachment opens in a Project 2010 session that is published on the server.

Application Publishing

When we configure content redirection from client to server, context menu commands available from within Windows Explorer function differently than on client machines that do not use this feature. For example, if we right-click a file in Windows Explorer on a client machine with content redirection from client to server enabled for the file type, the Open command opens the file with the remote application on XenApp. For a streamed application, the file could be opened either on the client machine or on the XenApp server, depending on the delivery configuration.

Most commands on the Windows Explorer context menu are unaffected. Context menu items are generally defined by each application when installed.

Associating published applications with file types

When we publish applications, we associate the published item with certain file types present in the Windows registry on the server. We can associate published applications with file types initially from the Publish Application wizard.

To modify the file types, first select the application from the **Action** menu, select **Application properties**, and then select **Content redirection**.

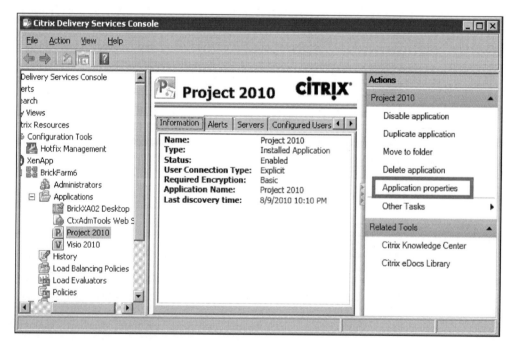

Enable the **Show all available file types for this application** checkbox and then select one or multiple file types.

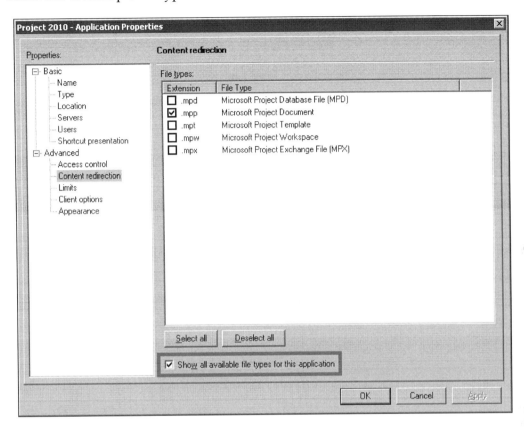

Updating file type associations

File types are associated with applications in a server's Windows registry. If we set up and then publish applications after installing XenApp 6, we need to update the file type associations in the Windows registry on the server.

To verify which file types are associated with a published application, select the application and then from the **Action** menu, select **Application properties** and then select **Content redirection**.

Use **Update file types** to associate these file types with the application in the XenApp farm's data store.

Application Publishing

 Updating the file type association data for a farm can take a long time. This time depends on the amount of servers, the number of streamed applications, and the availability of the streamed application file shares.

We need to update the file type associations in the data store if:

- We installed a new application but we have not published it yet.
- We plan to enable content redirection from client machine to the server or have users open published content using the application.
- The data store does not already contain the file type associations. If we updated the file types from the registries of other servers hosting the application, the data store already contains the associations.

If needed, update file types for the farm or for an individual server:

In the console, select a farm in the left pane and from the **Action** menu, select **Other Tasks** and then **Update file types**.

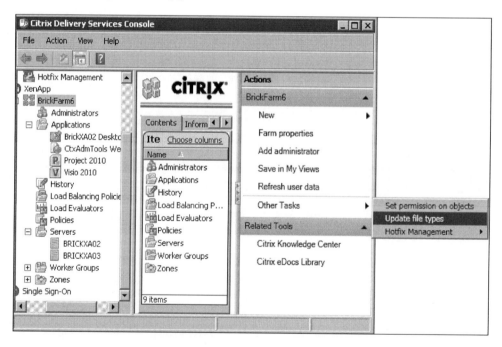

Select a server in the left pane and from the **Action** menu, select **Other Tasks** and then **Update file types from registry** option.

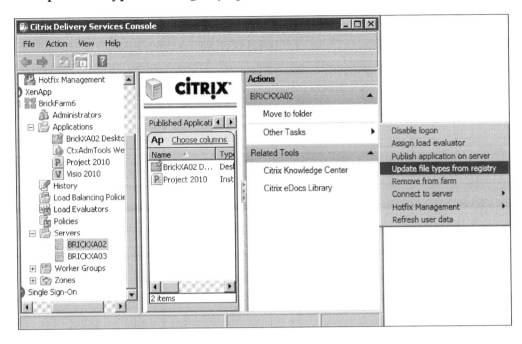

William to choose which file types are opened with a published application. When we publish an application, a list of available file types appears on the **Content redirection** page. This list is current only if the data store was updated with the file type associations for the application.

If he publishes applications to be hosted on more than XenApp server, he needs to update the file types on each server.

Enabling or Disabling content redirection

William needs to log in to the Citrix Web Interface server and then open the **Citrix Web Interface Management** console.

Application Publishing

He selects **XenApp Services Sites** and in the **Actions** pane, he clicks on **Server Farms**.

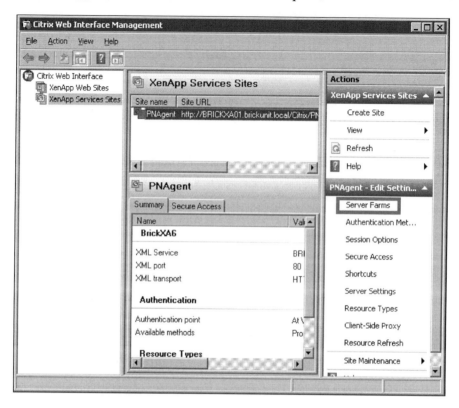

On the **Manage Server Farms** window, he needs to click on the **Advanced** button.

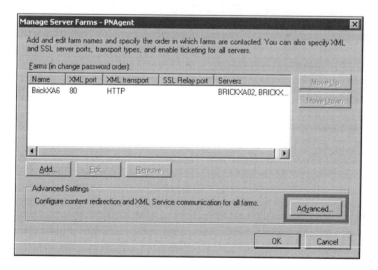

William can use the **Enable content redirection** checkbox to enable or disable content redirection.

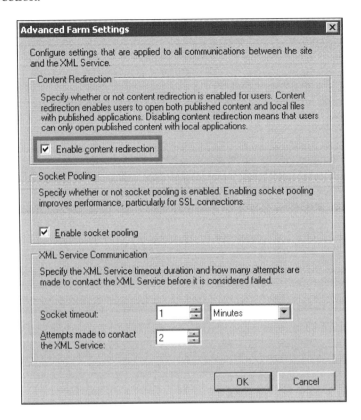

Summary

In this chapter, we learned how to publish different types of resources in XenApp. In particular:

- Hosted applications
- Streamed applications
- Content
- Server desktops

Also, we covered content redirection, from server to client and client to server, and we learned how to set up and update file type associations.

In the next chapter, we are going to learn how to install and configure streaming applications in detail.

6
Application Streaming

In the previous chapter, we learned how to publish different types of resources in XenApp. In particular, we installed and published a hosted and streamed applications and server desktops.

Also, we talked about content redirection, from server to client and client to server, and how to configure it and update file type associations.

In this chapter, we are going to cover the installation, configuration, and delivery of streaming applications. By the end of the chapter, you will have learned:

- Application streaming
- System requirements for application streaming
- Components for application streaming
- Choosing which plugins to use for application streaming
- How to profile Microsoft Office 2010
- Publishing Office 2010 on the Citrix farm

Application streaming

Application streaming simplifies application delivery to users by virtualizing applications on client machines. We can install and configure an application centrally and deliver it to any XenApp server or client machine on demand. One of the major features of application streaming is the ability to run multiple versions of an application on the same client, for example, we can run Office 2007 and Office 2010 on the same client machine.

Using streamed applications provides a lot of benefits, including:

1. The ability to install an application once on a profiler workstation and copy and replicate to fileservers within the company.
2. Use of streamed applications reduces patching complexity in large environments.
3. Updates to a streamed application don't require re-profiling applications.
4. All streamed applications run within isolated environments that keep the applications from interfering with others running on the same client machine.
5. Application files can be cached on the client machine to allow faster access the next time the application is launched.
6. A wide range of target environments can host streamed applications. Specifically, supported versions include Windows XP Professional, Windows Server 2003 and 2008, Windows Vista, and Windows 7.
7. We can configure XenApp to stream software to client machines or run the application on the client machine from a XenApp server.
8. Streamed applications that can be accessed through the server appear next to other applications that the user is familiar with, either within the web interface, Citrix Plugins, or on the desktop; thus giving a consistent end-user experience. The user does not have to know where and how the application is executing.
9. When a streamed application is configured and delivered, applications can be accessed even when the user is offline. The only requirement is the Citrix Offline Plug-in is installed on the client machine.
10. Streamed applications can easily be delivered to a XenApp farm. When publishing applications in a server farm, choose to virtualize applications from XenApp. Instead of installing applications on our farm servers, we can stream them to XenApp from a central file share in our App Hub. Update the application in the central location and we update the application on all the farm servers.
11. Streamed applications allow easy disaster recovery because the application and data are not lost if the profiles can be easily backed up, and servers and client machines can be replaced easily.

System requirements for application streaming

The Citrix Offline Plug-in and the streaming profiler are supported on the following Microsoft operating systems:

- Microsoft Windows XP Home and Professional editions, and 64-bit, with the last service pack
- Microsoft Windows Vista (Home, Business, Enterprise, and Ultimate editions), 32-bit and 64-bit editions, with Service Pack 1
- Microsoft Windows 7, 32-bit and 64-bit (Enterprise, Professional, Ultimate)
- Microsoft Windows Server 2003 R2, 32-bit and 64-bit editions
- Microsoft Windows Server 2008, 32-bit and 64-bit editions
- Microsoft Windows Server 2008 R2

The current Citrix Offline Plug-in supports Citrix Receiver versions 1.0, 1.1, 1.2, and 2.0.

We need to have a dedicated machine, usually called a profiler workstation. The profiler workstation must provide an environment that is as close to our users' environment as possible, such as the same or similar operating system and platform (x86, x64).

We need to install the application on the profiler workstation on the same disk partition of client machines. Don't install applications on the D drive, if client machines only have a C drive.

The profiler workstation should also include standard programs that are a part of the company image, such as an antivirus program or hotfixes. Same User Account Control setting is also recommended.

> Important: Do not install the Citrix Offline Plug-in on the profiler workstation.

To stream Microsoft Office 2007 or 2010 programs or to stream profiles enabled for inter-isolation communication, install .NET Framework 2.0 (3.0 or 3.5 optional). Without .NET Framework, streaming will fail.

Citrix defines inter-isolation communication as a feature that links individual profiles, so applications in separate profiles can communicate with each other when they are launched on the client machine. Also, this feature can be used if a streamed application fails because it needs data from another streamed application, but cannot detect it because both are running in isolation environments.

When we create a profile enabled for inter-isolation communication, applications launched on the client machine can interact with other applications, but applications stay isolated from the system and from other isolated applications.

Install the profiler in a path with single-byte characters only. Double-byte characters in the installation path are not supported. For example, Japanese, Korean, and Chinese.

The client device must meet the following requirements:

- A network connection to the server farm always, or the first time, when Offline access is enabled.
- A supported browser like Microsoft Internet Explorer 6.0, 7.0, or 8.0.
- Uninstall any previous version of the Streaming Client and Program Neighborhood Agent on the client machine.
- Install the most recent version of the online and offline plugins. Citrix recommends using Citrix Receiver on the client machine to manage Citrix plugins.
- To stream applications to client machines, install both the Citrix Offline Plug-in and Online Plug-in on the client machines.
- To stream applications to a server, install the online plugin or Web plugin on the client machine.
- To stream Microsoft Office 2007 or 2010 programs or to stream profiles enabled for inter-isolation communication, we need to install .NET Framework 2.0 on the client machine (3.0 or 3.5 is optional).
- The Offline Plug-in is not required, unless you are planning to run offline streamed applications.

If streaming from a web interface site, we need to add the site to the list of trusted sites. We can use a GPO to add the web interface site to the list of trusted sites.

The Group Policy setting can be found at the following location:

Computer Configuration | Administrative Templates | Windows Components | Internet Explorer | Security Zones: Use only machine settings

Components for application streaming

Citrix provides multiple components that support virtualization on the client machine, including the XenApp server, Citrix licensing, streaming profiler workstation, file servers, web interface, and Citrix Plugins. These components can be separated into four different categories as follows:

- **Licensing**: The licensing component includes the license server and License Management Console. We use the License Management Console to manage licensing. To install Citrix licensing, please refer to *Chapter 3, Installing XenApp 6*.

   For detailed information about licensing, read through *Application Streaming Licensing Explained* at http://support.citrix.com/article/CTX112636

- **Administration (server farm)**: Consists of the following components:
  - XenApp servers
  - IMA database
  - Web Interface servers
  - The Delivery Services Console, used to configure, manage, and publish applications on the farm

- **Citrix streaming profiler**: Citrix streaming profiler is used to create and manage streaming application profiles. The streaming profiler is an independent application that enables us to profile Windows applications, web applications, browser plugins, files, folders, and registry settings that can be streamed to user machines and/or servers.

  We can profile one application to one or more targets (operating systems) within an application profile; this creates a single profile that can be used for multiple user platforms.

- **Citrix plugins**: The Citrix Offline Plug-in (formerly known as the Streaming Client) is used to stream applications to the client machine and provide offline access to applications. We need to install both Citrix Offline Plug-in and Online Plug-in on client machines to support dual-mode streaming. When a user clicks on a published application in a web interface site, the plugin finds the correct target in the profile in the App Hub, sets up the isolation environment on the user machine, and then streams the application from the profile location to the safety of the isolation environment set up on the client machine.

Choosing which plugin to use for application streaming

The plugins that our users must install on their client machines are determined by the method of streaming:

- Streamed to client desktops: When streaming applications directly to client desktops, some of the application files are cached locally and the applications run using the resources of the client machine.

    We need to install both Citrix Online and Offline Plug-ins on client machines: `CitrixOnlinePluginFull.exe` and `CitrixOfflinePlugin.exe`. This enables us to:
    - Provide dual-mode streaming. When we select **Streamed if possible, otherwise accessed from a server** and **Streamed to server**, if streaming to the client machine fails, applications automatically stream to a XenApp server and then launch using the online plugin.
    - Enumerate published applications located on the **Start** menu and create shortcuts on the desktop of the client machine.
    - Configure applications and users for offline access. This is because the entire application is fully cached on the client machine. Users can use the application for the time specified in the offline license, even if they are disconnected from the network.

- Accessed from a server: The profile is streamed from the App Hub to the XenApp server, where the Citrix Offline Plug-in is installed by default. The Offline Plug-in is not required on the client machine and the application runs on the client machine using the Online Plug-in or Web Plug-in.

    When we publish applications as **Accessed from a server** and **Streamed to server**, users will access the applications using the Citrix Online Plug-in or Web Plug-in. This method does not support desktop integration or offline access to applications.

We have two versions of Citrix Online Plug-in:

- We need to install `CitrixOnlinePluginFull.exe` to stream applications to XenApp servers and launch them with the online plugin, or launch applications from a web interface site using a web browser. This file provides the full online plugin feature set.
- We need to install `CitrixOnlinePluginWeb.exe` to stream applications to XenApp servers and launch them from the Web Interface. This file provides a limited online plugin.

Profiling Microsoft Office 2010

William Empire is the IT Manager of Brick Unit Construction. William decided to stream Office 2010 from XenApp servers to client machines. We will help him profile Office 2010 and then publish it to all users in Brick Unit Construction.

The following process of configuring and profiling Office 2010 is based on the 32-bit version of Office 2010 (64-bit applications are not supported by Citrix Profiler 6.0)

William will use a KMS server to activate Office 2010 licenses. MAK license activation currently is not supported by Citrix.

> Latest Microsoft products such as Windows 7, Windows Server 2008 R2, Windows Vista, Windows Server 2008, and Microsoft Office 2010, use a new type of product activation called Volume Activation (VA). To activate these operating systems or applications with VA, we can use either a Multiple Activation Key (MAK) or Key Management Service (KMS), requiring a KMS server.

For more information on KMS server setup and configuration for Office 2010, please visit http://xenapp6.musumeci.com.ar.

Once the KMS server is installed and configured, the next step is installing a profiler workstation.

Installing a profiler workstation

The profiler workstation is a dedicated (and clean) machine to profile applications. This machine should have the same or similar operating system (such as Windows 7 and Windows Vista) as the one we are going to stream to. If we need to stream the application to both 32-bit and 64-bit client machines, we have to profile the application on two different machines, one for 32-bit and the for other 64-bit. We cannot profile a package on a 32-bit operating system and stream the profile to a 64-bit operating system and vice versa.

William will start the profiling process installing the latest version of streaming profiler on the profiler workstation. The minimum version required to profile Office 2010 is the version 6.0. Previous versions of the profiler don't support streaming of services.

His preferred option is to use a virtual machine for the Profiler Workstation machine. So he can take a snapshot before making any changes and easily rollover any modifications in seconds.

Operating systems earlier than Microsoft Windows Vista require some Microsoft hotfixes. He needs to install the following hotfixes on the profiling computer and client machines:

- For Microsoft Windows XP SP3, we need to install hotfix KB978835, available at http://support.microsoft.com/kb/978835.
- For Microsoft Windows XP x64 and Microsoft Windows Server 2003 x64: KB973573 available at http://support.microsoft.com/kb/973573.
- MSXML 6: This file installs Microsoft Core XML Services (MSXML) 6.0 Service Pack 1 in the profile. MSXML6 is included in Windows 7 and Windows 2008 R2.
- MSVCR80.DLL: Search for the file MSVCR80.DLL and keep a copy of the last version of this file in a folder.
- To profile and stream Microsoft Office applications to Windows Server 2003, William needs to install the Windows Data Execution Prevention (DEP) hotfix on the server and in the profiler workstation. This hotfix is available for download at http://support.microsoft.com/kb/931534.

The streaming profiler can be installed from the XenApp DVD or downloaded from the Citrix website. Always check the Citrix website for the latest version.

Installing the Citrix streaming profiler is really simple; William needs to run the .EXE file, follow the Installation Wizard, and reboot the machine.

1. He will see the following window when he launches the setup of the Citrix streaming profiler:

2. He clicks on the **Next** button and then he types the appropriate program folder name. Then he clicks on the **Install** button.
3. Finally, he clicks on the **Finish** button to complete the setup.

Customizing the Office 2010 installation

William starts the process mounting the Microsoft Office 2010 DVD on the profiler workstation and copies the installation files to the local drive.

Then he opens a command prompt, navigates to the Microsoft Office 2010 installation directory, and types:

`setup /admin`

The `/admin` switch starts the Microsoft Office Customization Tool that allows him to pre-configure the installation options in order to perform an unattended installation. All customized settings are stored in an `.MSP` file that must be saved in the `Updates` subfolder in the Microsoft Office 2010 installation directory.

He selects the **Create a new Setup customization file for the following product** option and then clicks on the **OK** button:

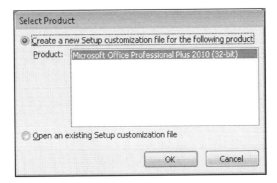

Under **Setup, Install location and organization name**, he needs to enter the organization name. Also, he can change the default installation path, if he wants.

Under **Setup, Licensing and user interface**:

1. William selects **Use KMS client key** (default) and enables the **I accept the terms in the License Agreement** checkbox.
2. Then he selects **Basic** for **Display Level** and enables the **Suppress modal** checkbox for a silent installation. (We could also keep the **Full** option (default), useful for a test installation.)

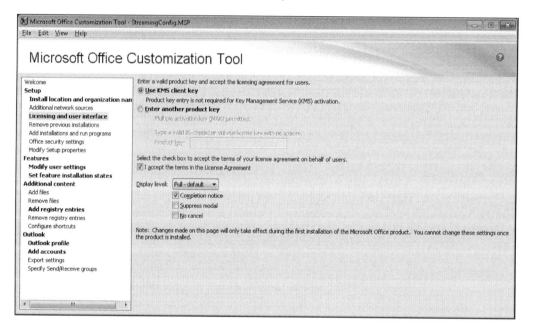

Under **Features | Modify user settings** he must:

- Expand Microsoft Office 2010 and click **Global Options**
- Select **Enabled** in the **Use ClearType** option

Under **Features | Modify user settings**:

- He expands **Privacy** and chooses **Trust Center**
- Then he selects **Enabled** in the **Disable Opt-in Wizard on first run** option

Under **Features | Set feature installation states**:

- He clicks the drop-down menu for **Microsoft Office**, selects **Run all from My Computer**, and then he unchecks specific features or products that he won't need:

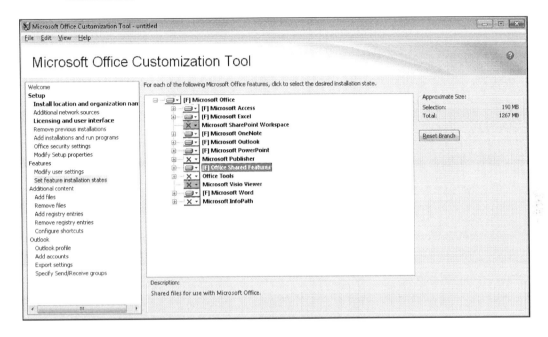

Under **Additional Content**, select **Add registry entries**.

Add the following registry entries to prevent pop-up windows, disable first-run dialogs, and set the KMS server name and port.

> Warning: This section, method, or task contains steps that tell you how to modify the registry. However, serious problems might occur if you modify the registry incorrectly. Therefore, make sure that you follow these steps carefully. For added protection, back up the registry before you modify it.

Disabling the Office Welcome Screen

This registry prevents the Office Welcome Screen from asking for the user information:

Root: HKEY_CURRENT_USER

Data type: REG_DWORD

Key: Software\Microsoft\Office\14.0\Common\General

Value name: ShownOptIn

Value data: 00000001

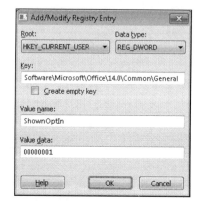

Disabling some Office popups

This registry key prevents some Outlook windows from being shown:

Root: HKEY_CURRENT_USER

Data type: REG_SZ

Key: Software\Microsoft\Office\14.0\Outlook\Option\General

Value name: PONT_STRING

Value data: 60

Chapter 6

Setting the KMS server name (32-bit target device)

This registry key sets the KMS server name on 32-bit machines:

Root: HKEY_LOCALMACHINE

Data type: REG_SZ

Key: Software\Microsoft\OfficeSoftwareProtectionPlatform

Value name: KeyManagementServiceName

Value data: Name or IP Address of KMS License Server

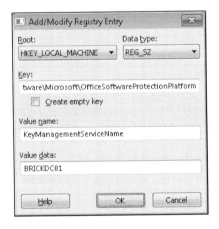

Setting the KMS server name (64-bit target device)

This registry key sets the KMS server name on 64-bit machines:

Root: HKEY_LOCALMACHINE

Data type: REG_SZ

Key: Software\Wow6432Node\Microsoft\OfficeSoftwareProtectionPlatform

Value name: KeyManagementServiceName

Value data: Name or IP Address of KMS License Server

Setting the KMS port number (64-bit target device)

This registry key sets the KMS port number on 64-bit machines:

Root: HKEY_LOCALMACHINE

Data type: REG_SZ

Key: Software\Wow6432Node\Microsoft\OfficeSoftwareProtectionPlatform

Value name: KeyManagementServicePort

Value data: 1688

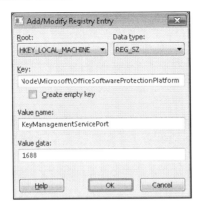

Setting the KMS port number (32-bit target device)

This registry key sets the KMS port number on 32-bit machines:

Root: HKEY_LOCALMACHINE

Data type: REG_SZ

Key: Software\Microsoft\OfficeSoftwareProtectionPlatform

Value name: KeyManagementServicePort

Value data: 1688

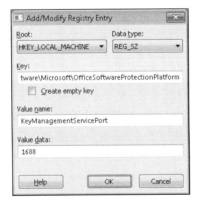

Application Streaming

The following window will show all registry keys added by William to the Office Setup:

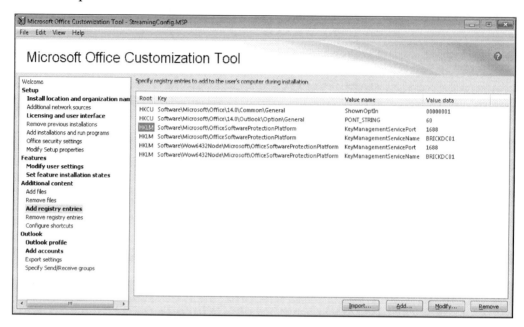

Under **Outlook | Outlook Profile**, he sets up Microsoft Exchange accounts.

He selects **Modify Profile**:

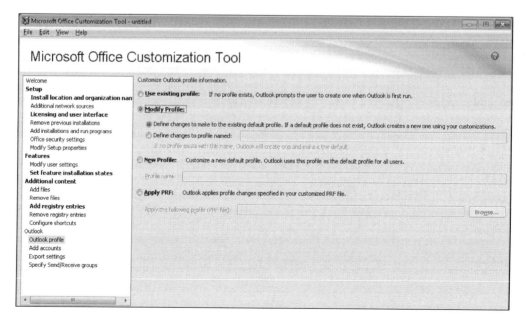

Then, William clicks on **Add accounts**.

Select **Customize additional Outlook profile and account information**.

Click **Add**.

He selects **Exchange** to set up a Microsoft Exchange Server account:

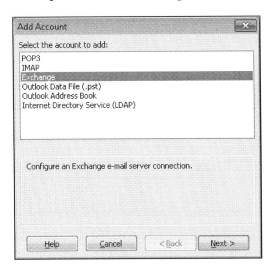

Then he enters an **Account Name**, and he leaves **User Name** as `%username%` and enters the Exchange server name.

The **More Settings** button includes alternative options such as **Cached Mode**.

Save the customization file:

- He clicks on **File** in the menu bar, and selects **Save**
- He browses to the `Updates` folder in the `Microsoft Office 2010` installation directory and enter a filename like `StreamingConfig` when saving it

Profiling Microsoft Office 2010

William completed the customization of Microsoft Office 2010. Now, he must open the Citrix streaming profiler and start profiling the application setup.

Application Streaming

He Clicks on the **New Profile** button, and at the Wizard introduction notification, he clicks on the **Next** button:

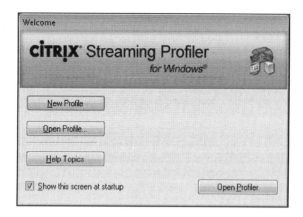

In the next window, William enters a name for the profile (**Office2010**) and clicks the **Next** button:

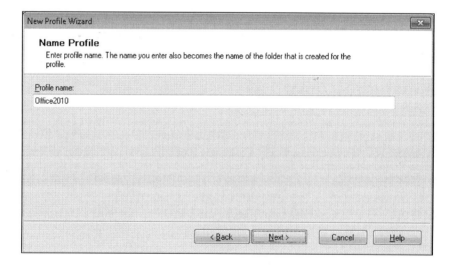

William accepts the default target operating system and target language.

The target machine must be run on a compatible operating system and processor architecture (32-bit or 64-bit) of the operating system, so, if we create a profile or an application on a 32-bit operating system, we can stream this application only to a similar 32-bit operating system.

After he selects all the required operating systems, he clicks on the **Next** button to continue:

Chapter 6

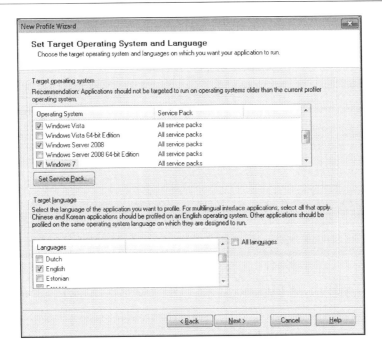

Now, he chooses **Advanced Install** and then clicks on the **Next** button.

This is an optional step required if we are running Windows 2000 Service Pack 4, Windows Server 2003 Service Pack 1, or Windows XP Service Pack 2. We need to install Microsoft XML support before Microsoft Office 2010.

1. Download the MSXML6 package to a folder in the profiler workstation.
2. Select **Run install program or command line script** and then click on the **Next** button.
3. Browse for the previously downloaded file (`msxml6_x86.msi`) and then click on the **Next** button.
4. Click **Launch Installer**.
5. Click on the **Finish** button when the installation completes.
6. At the **Select Next Step** dialog, select **Perform additional installations** and then click on the **Next** button.

Now William installs Microsoft Office 2010:

He needs to select **Advanced Install** and in the **Select Install Option** screen, he clicks on the **Next** button.

Then he selects **Run install program or command line script** and clicks on the **Next** button.

[175]

Application Streaming

William browses to the Microsoft Office 2010 installation folder, selects `setup.exe` file, and then clicks on the **Next** button:

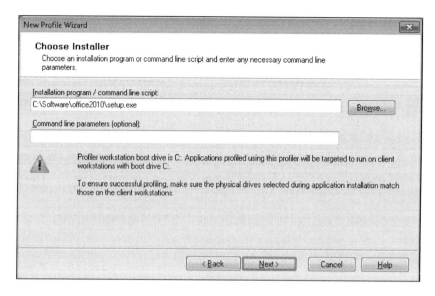

In the **Run Installer** screen, he clicks on the **Launch Installer** button.

Once the Microsoft Office 2010 setup process starts, he clicks on the **Install Now** button to continue.

When the Office 2010 installation is complete, he needs to click the **Next** button to run the installer.

Now, a virtual reboot is required to complete the setup:

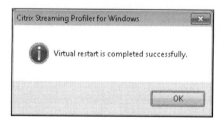

Now, he needs to install additional required files:

He selects **Perform additional installations** and then clicks on the **Next** button:

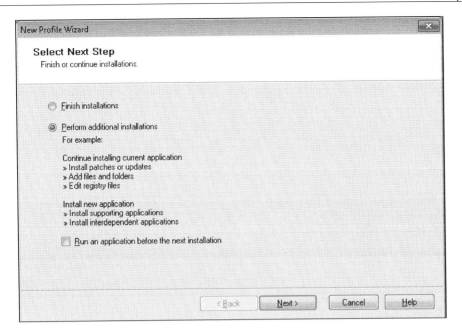

William clicks **Select files and folders** and then he clicks the **Next** button.

The following four files are to be added to the package:

- `MSVCR80.DLL` (Required by Microsoft C Runtime Library and Visual Studio). Located in several places.
    - 32-bit target copy to `C:\Program Files\Microsoft Office\Office14`
    - 64-bit target copy to `C:\Program Files (x86)\Microsoft Office\Office14`
- `CMD.EXE` (Windows Command Prompt).
    - Located at `C:\Windows\system32 folder`
    - 32-bit target copy to `C:\Windows\system32`
    - 64-bit target copy to `C:\Windows\SysWOW64`
- `CONTROL.EXE` (Windows Control Panel).
    - Located in `C:\Windows\system32 folder`
    - 32-bit target copy to `C:\Windows\system32`
    - 64-bit target copy to `C:\Windows\SysWOW64`

Application Streaming

- `MLCFG32.CPL` (Required setup Exchange accounts in Outlook).
    - Located in folder `c:\ctxpackager\<Target>\device\c\Program Files\Microsoft Office\Office14v`
    - 32-bit target copy to `C:\Windows\system32`
    - 64-bit target copy to `C:\Windows\SysWOW64`

For each of these files above, he needs to:

1. Browse for the file on the left-hand pane.
2. Select the target folder on the right-hand pane.
3. Click the green arrow icon to copy the file.

Then he clicks on the **Next** button to return to the **Select Next Step** screen:

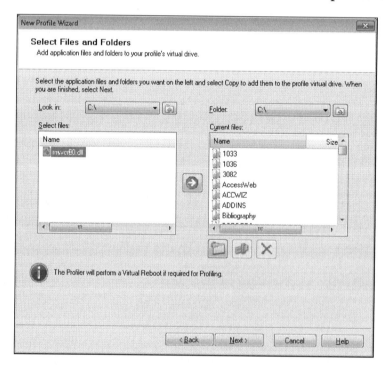

On the **Select Install Method** page, he chooses the **Continue with none of the above** option and then he clicks on the **Next** button.

On the **Run Application** screen, he needs to keep the **Application Not Run** option for all applications and clicks on the **Next** button:

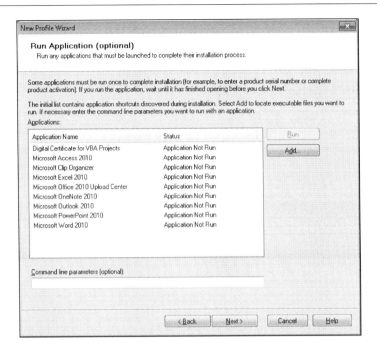

Here is the list of applications William can publish using the Citrix Delivery Services Console. He can add or delete applications, if he needs to. He decided to add one extra application, the **Outlook Profile Editor**:

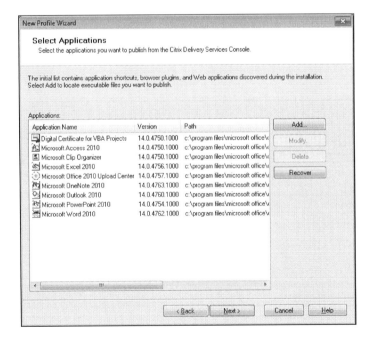

Application Streaming

On the **Select Applications** screen, he clicks on the **Add** button, and then he enters the information as shown in the following screenshot:

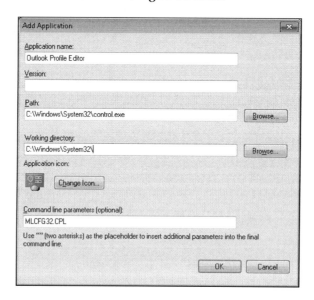

He chooses the **Do not sign profile** option and then clicks on the **Next** button.

 If you need to sign the profile, please read the document CTX110304 at http://support.citrix.com/article/CTX110304

He clicks the **Terminate All** button to end all running processes (like OSPPSVC.exe):

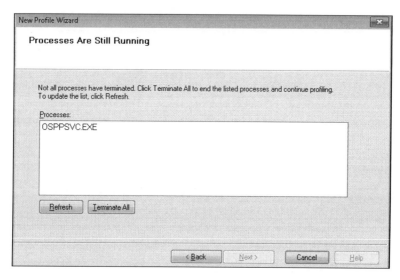

The profiling process is almost complete; William needs to click on the **Finish** button to generate the profile.

The following steps are optional, but will be necessary if we receive an error.

One common error we can receive is related to security permissions. So sometimes we need to reset the permissions of all files inside the profile, using the following process:

1. Open the Windows Explorer, select the `CtxPackager` folder.
2. Right-click over this folder and select **Properties**.
3. Click on the **Security** tab and then on the **Advanced** button.
4. Click on the **Owner** tab, then the **Edit** button.
5. Enable the **Replace owner on subcontainers and objects** checkbox.

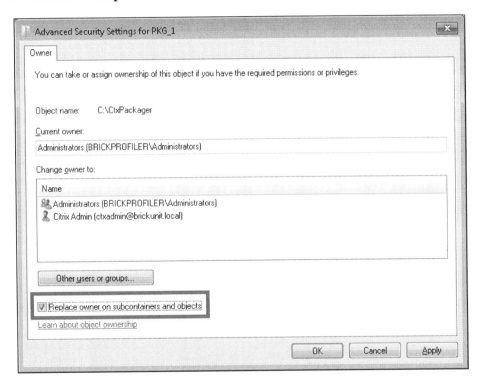

Now, he clicks on the **Finish** button to complete the process!

Application Streaming

Once the profile is created, William needs to set services to start automatically:

1. Expand the profile.
2. Right-click the target name.
3. Browse to **Properties**.
4. Click **Services**.
5. Click **Modify for each service** and change the **Start Type** to **Automatic**:

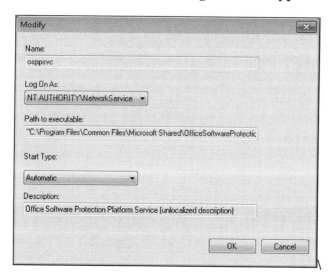

Here, the screen shows us that both services are changed to **Automatic**:

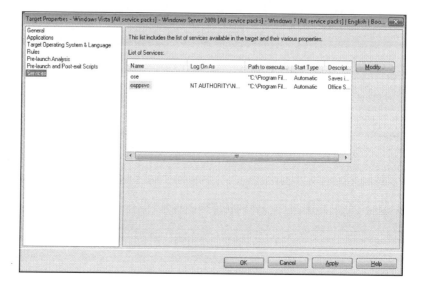

After that, William saves the profile to the network file:

1. He clicks on **File | Save As**.
2. He enters or browses to the file share where profiles will be stored.
3. He clicks on the **Save** button:

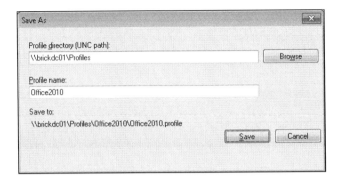

Publishing Office 2010 on the farm

William is now ready to publish Microsoft Office 2010 applications in the XenApp farm using the Citrix Delivery Services Console. For detailed information about the Application Publishing process, please refer to *Chapter 5, Application Publishing*.

William needs to open the Citrix Delivery Services Console.

From the XenApp console, under the XenApp node, he needs to expand the expand the XenApp farm or server to which he wants to publish the application.

After that, he needs to select the Applications node, and from the **Actions** pane, he chooses **Publish application**.

Application Streaming

He types the name of the application, **Excel 2010** in the **Display name** and **Application description**:

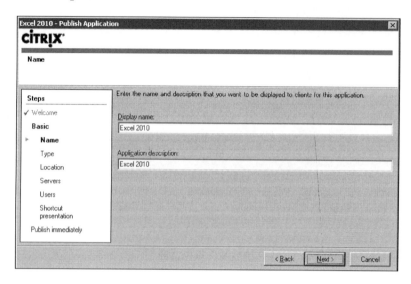

On the **Type** page, he needs to specify the type of resource he wants to publish and the delivery method. He chooses **Application** and **Streamed to client** to publish a streaming application:

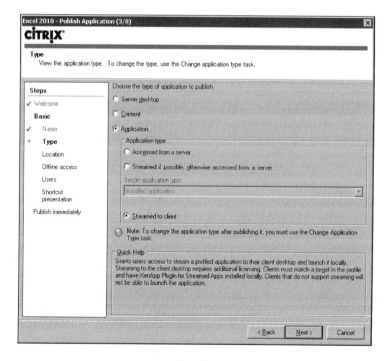

On the **Location** page, William needs to type or use the **Browse** button to set **Citrix streaming application profile address**, this is generally UNC of the file share, and then he needs to choose **Microsoft Excel 2010** from the **Application to launch from the Citrix streaming application profile** pull down. He can also set **Optional parameters** for the application.

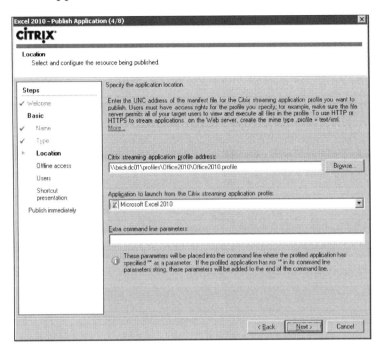

On the **Offline access** page, he can configure streamed applications for offline access.

The server fully caches applications enabled for offline access on client machines; the entire application is sent to user devices while the user is online so that the user can launch the application offline and have full functionality of the application. By default, applications are cached when a user logs on.

When he clicks on the **Enable offline access** checkbox on the **Offline Access** page, he needs to configure the **Cache preference**:

- Pre-cache application at login: Caches the application when the user logs on (selected by default). However, concurrent logons may slow network traffic. Pre-caching is also possible using third-party tools, such as Microsoft System Center Configuration Manager (SCCM) or similar.

- Cache application at launch time: Caches the application when users launch it. We can use this option if, if the number of users logging on at the same time (and pre-caching their applications) could overload the network.

Application Streaming

The offline access option requires the Citrix Offline Plug-in to be installed on the client machine.

On the **Users** page, he needs to add users or groups who have access to the application and he can allow allow access to anonymous users or specified groups selecting **Allow only configured users** and add users or groups using the **Add** button.

William assigned permissions to the **Domain Users** group:

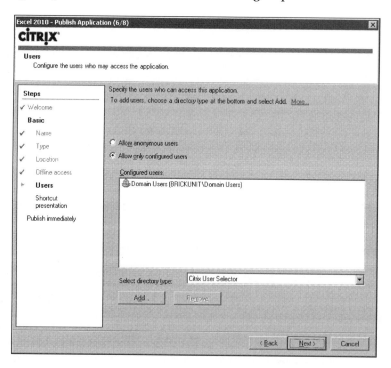

On the **Shortcut** presentation page, he can choose the icon for the application using the **Change icon** button.

The **Client application folder** is used when we need to organize applications inside folders. This is a recommended practice, if we have a lot of applications. William will keep it blank to display all applications together.

The **Add to the client's Start menu** option creates a shortcut under the Programs folder of the local **Start** menu. If a folder structure is specified in the **Start Menu Folder** textbox, the folder structure is created within the local Programs folder. If no folder structure is specified, the application is available from the top level of the **Start** menu.

This option provides a real integration of the streamed application in the client machine and looks like the application is installed locally.

The **Add shortcut to the client's desktop** option creates a shortcut to this application on the client machine.

On the **Publishing immediately** page, William needs to select **Disable application initially**, if he wants to prevent users from accessing the application. Later, he can manually enable it through application properties.

To view and select advanced options, William needs to enable the **Configure advanced application settings now** checkbox. Alternatively, he can modify the advanced settings using the application properties later. It is recommended to uncheck **Enable Legacy Audio option** in this step:

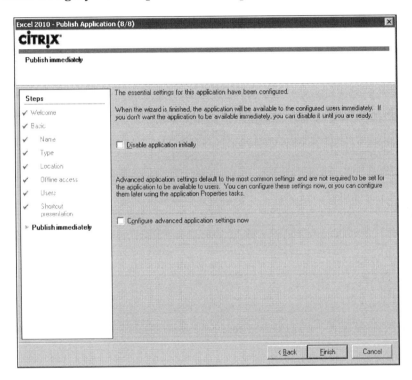

Specifying trusted servers for streamed services and profiles

The last step before users can start using Office 2010 on the Citrix farm is set up in all client devices or servers, if we are going to stream applications to servers, a registry key with the Applications Hubs names.

Application Streaming

 In Citrix application streaming, the "Application Hub" is the place where streaming profiles are stored. The streaming profiler writes content to the Application Hub and the streaming client pulls content from the Application Hub at runtime. An Application Hub is the file server or web server where we stored our streaming application's profiles. The Application Hub supports all kinds of protocols and services like SMB, CIFS, Samba, Novell, HTTP, HTTPS, Apache, or IIS.

To ensure that client machines run only approved services, William needs to edit the registry on client machines to enable a whitelist of approved server locations.

On the client machine, he creates the following registry location (the same for 32-bit and 64-bit systems), using `regedit.exe` or `regedt32.exe`:

Key: **HKEY_LOCAL_MACHINE\SOFTWARE\Citrix\Rade**

Value: **AppHubWhiteList**

Type: **REG_SZ**

Then he adds the server names (or local filesystem folder) in the registry value in a semicolon (;) delimited format, without spaces before or after the semicolon.

If the application has been streamed from a web location (also called HTTP streaming), the server name must be prefixed with HTTP (or HTTPS) in the `AppHubWhiteList` registry entry. Also, there is a clear distinction between HTTP and HTTPS servers.

If our profile location `\\BRICKdc01\Profiles\Office2010\Office2010.profile`, then the AppHubWhiteList must contain BRICKDC01 or the IP Address of BRICKDC01:

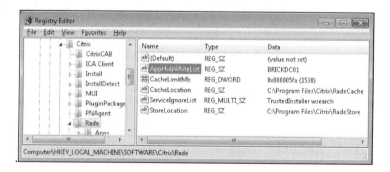

Also, we can use Active Directory GPO to set up the AppHubWhiteList registry key.

Summary

In this chapter, we learned about application streaming. In particular, we talked about:

- System requirements for application streaming
- Components for application streaming
- Choosing plugins to use for application streaming

Then we learned how to profile Microsoft Office 2010:

- Install a profiler workstation
- Customizing the Office 2010 installation
- Profiling Microsoft Office 2010
- Publish Office 2010 on the Citrix farm
- Specifying trusted servers for streamed services and profiles (AppHubWhiteList)

In the next chapter, we will discuss about Citrix policies; in particular, we are going to learn about:

- Working with Citrix policies
- Creating and applying Citrix policies
- Troubleshooting policies

7
Managing Policies

In the last chapter, we learned about application streaming, including system requirements and components for application streaming, choosing plugins to use for application streaming, and profiling Microsoft Office 2010.

Now we are going to discuss Citrix policies, and in particular, we are going to cover the following in this chapter:

- Understanding Citrix policies
- Using the Group Policy Management Console, Citrix Delivery Services Console, and Local Group Policy Editor to manage Citrix Policies
- How to create, manage, and apply Citrix policies
- Troubleshooting Citrix policies

Understanding Citrix policies

In the Active Directory, a Group Policy contains two categories (also called nodes): **Computer Configuration** and **User Configuration** settings.

- The Computer Configuration node contains policy settings applied to computers, XenApp servers, when we use GPO to manage servers
- The User Configuration node contains settings applied to users accessing the machine, the XenApp server in our case, regardless of where they log on

Citrix policies also have same categories: computer and user.

- Computer policy settings in Citrix applied to XenApp servers. When the server is rebooted, these policies are applied to the server.
- User policy settings are used for the duration of the session and are applied to user sessions. Policy settings changes can also take effect when XenApp re-evaluates policies every 90 minutes.

Managing Policies

Citrix policies are the preferred way to manage session settings or user access and the most effective method of controlling connection, security, and bandwidth settings on XenApp farms.

We can create and assign Citrix policies to users, groups, machines, or connection types and each policy can contain one or several settings. Using policies allows us to turn on/off settings like:

- ICA session settings, like Auto Client Reconnect, Keep Alive, Session Reliability, or Multimedia configuration
- Licensing configuration, like license server hostname or port
- Mapping of local drivers, printer, and ports
- Server settings, like Connections Settings, Reboot Behavior, Memory/CPU Management
- Shadowing options and permissions

Working with Citrix policies

A policy is basically a collection of settings or rules. Citrix policies include the user, server, and environment settings that will affect XenApp sessions when the policy is enforced. Policy settings can be enabled, disabled, or not configured.

For some policy settings, we can enter a value or we can choose a value from a list when we add the setting to a policy.

We can set some policies to one of the following conditions to enable or permit a policy setting: **Enabled** or **Allowed** and we can use **Disabled** or **Prohibited** to turn off or disallow a policy setting.

Also, we can limit configuration of the setting by selecting **Use default value**. Selecting this option disables configuration of the setting and allows only the setting's default value to be used when the policy is enforced.

If we create more than one policy in our environment, we need to prioritize the policies. The best way to track applied settings is to run a **Resulting Set of Policies Logging report** from the Group Policy Management Console or the **Citrix Policy Modeling Wizard**.

These reports will show all Citrix settings configured via a policy, and which Group Policy Object, including the farm GPO, has actually won the merging calculation. We are going to talk about this in detail later.

Usually, Citrix policies will override the same or similar settings applied to the farm, specific XenApp servers, or on the client machine, except for the **highest encryption setting** and the most **restrictive shadowing** setting, which always overrides other rules or settings.

Best practices for creating Citrix policies

The following is a list of recommendations when configuring policy settings:

- Reduce the amount of policies: Avoid creating multiple policies for different groups of users. Create one policy and apply filters to it.
- Disable unused policies: Unused policies waste processing resources. If we are using Active Directory Group Policies, we can disable the unused part of the policy (Computer or User part).
- Assign policies to groups: If we assign policies to groups rather than a user, management is easy and can reduce processing time.
- Remote Desktop Session Host Configuration settings are similar to Citrix policy settings in a few ways. We need to avoid using Remote Desktop Session Host Configuration to reduce overlapping of settings.

> We can use Remote Desktop Session Host Configuration (formerly known as Terminal Services Configuration on Windows Server 2003) to configure settings for new connections, modify the settings of existing connections, and delete connections. We can configure settings on a per connection basis or for the server as a whole.

Guidelines for working with policies

The process for configuring policies is as follows:

- Create and give a name to the policy: We need to create and provide a name for the new policy.
- Configure policy settings: We need to choose if we are going to create a User Configuration or Computer Configuration policy and then set the policies.
- Apply the policy to connections using filters: Using filters we can choose to apply the policy to a specific group of users or computers.
- Prioritize the policy: In the final (and optional) step, we will assign priority so that policies will override or take precedence over other policies.

Working with management consoles

In previous versions of Citrix XenApp, Citrix Presentation Server and Citrix MetaFrame policies were stored on the IMA and we managed Citrix policies from the Citrix Management Console.

Starting with XenApp 6, policies are stored on the Active Directory and we can manage Citrix policies through the Group Policy Management Console or Local Group Policy Editor in Windows or the Delivery Services Console in XenApp servers. Choosing the right console depends on our network environment and permissions.

Using the Group Policy Management Console

The Group Policy Management Console (shown in the following screenshot) allows us to view or create Active Directory policies. It also enables us to view the resulting policies applied to users or computers, which is very useful for troubleshooting (more about this is discussed later).

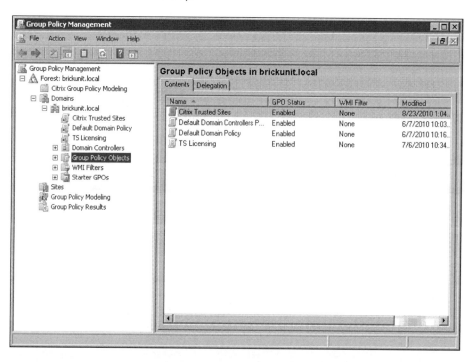

If our network environment is based on the Active Directory and we have the appropriate permissions to manage Group Policies (GPO), using the Group Policy Management Console to create policies for our farm is the preferred option.

Chapter 7

The main reason to use the Group Policy Management Console over the Citrix Delivery Service Console is because Active Directory GPOs take precedence over the farm GPO (also known as IMA GPO).

Using the Delivery Services Console

The Citrix Delivery Services Console (shown in the following screenshot), formerly known as the Citrix Access Management Console, is a tool that integrates into the Microsoft Management Console (MMC) and enables us to execute management tasks, including creating and viewing Citrix Policies. Detailed information about this console is covered in *Chapter 4, Using Management Tools*.

If we don't have permissions to manage the Active Directory of our company or if our environment doesn't use the Active Directory, we need to use the Citrix Delivery Services Console to create policies for our farm. Policies are stored in a farm GPO in the Citrix data store.

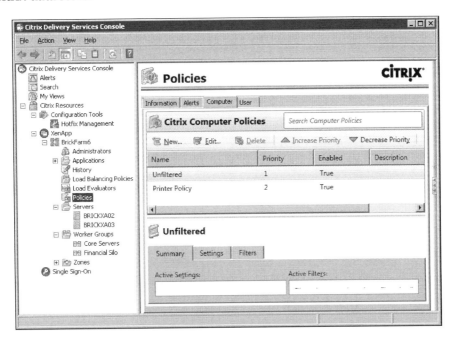

In the **Citrix Delivery Services Console**, we can view the policies configuration by clicking the **Policies** node, then select either the **Computer** or **User** tabs in the middle pane.

[195]

Managing Policies

When we click one of these two tabs, three more tabs will be displayed, as shown in the following screenshot.

- **Summary**: Shows the settings and filters configured for the selected policy
- **Settings**: Shows available and configured settings by category for the selected policy
- **Filters:** Shows the available and configured filters applied to the selected policy

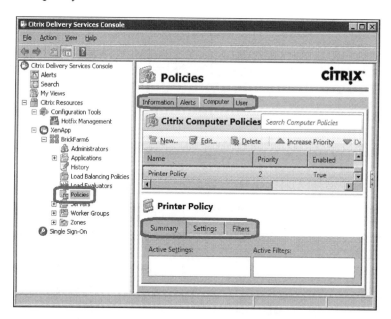

Using the Local Group Policy Editor

If we don't want to use the Citrix Delivery Services Console, we don't have permissions to modify or create a GPO in the Active Directory, or we don't have an Active Directory domain (a NetWare network or workgroup, for example), we have another option. We can create a local GPO using the Local Group Policy Editor (shown in the following screenshot).

If we type GPEDIT.MSC, from **Start** | **Run**, the Local Group Policy Editor will open. We can modify the local policy of a single server, so it is useful to create or edit a policy in one or maybe a couple of servers, for example, silos or test servers, but it is not useful for medium to large farms. The Local Group Policy will affect everyone who logs onto this machine—including users accessing via Citrix and administrators.

Chapter 7

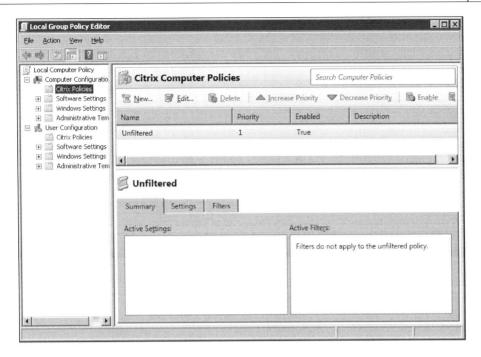

We can access policies and their settings in the Local Group Policy Editor, by clicking the **Citrix Policies** node under **User Configuration** or the **Computer Configuration** in the tree pane, located on the left.

 Active Directory Group policies take precedence over farm GPO; and farm GPO takes precedence over Local Group policies.

Managing Policies

Creating Citrix policies

William Empire from Brick Unit Construction is planning to use Citrix policies to manage the XenApp farm. He needs to decide which group of users, servers, or machines he wants to affect, before he creates the policy.

Because Brick Unit Construction network infrastructure uses Active Directory, he can use existing Active Directory OU structure to create the Citrix policies.

Commonly, policies are based on geographic location (HQ, remote sites, and so on), connection type (local or remote users), user role (IT, financial, and so on), and client machines (laptops, thin clients, and so on.)

Creating a policy using consoles

From the **Citrix Delivery Services Console**, he selects the **Policies** node on the left pane and then selects the **Computer** or **User** tab and clicks **New**. These policies are stored on the IMA datastore.

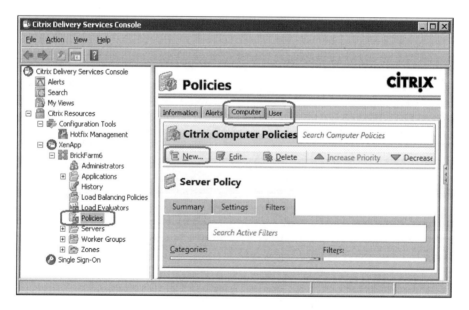

William also can use the **Local Group Policy Editor** to create or modify local policies. He needs to select the **Computer Configuration** or **User Configuration** node, then **Citrix Policies**. He clicks the **New** option to add a new policy. As we mentioned before, the policy is stored in local machine policy and can be used to add specific policies to a few servers.

Chapter 7

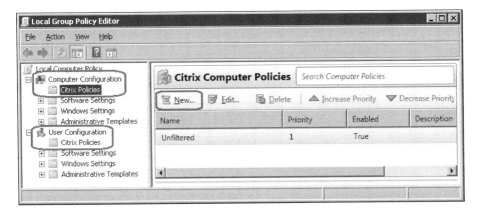

The last and preferred console is the **Group Policy Management Console**. William needs to select the container for the policy, Group Policy Objects, in this case. He right-clicks over the container and selects **New**. Finally, he gives the new GPO a name and clicks the **OK** button.

Starting in this step, the following process is common to all consoles.

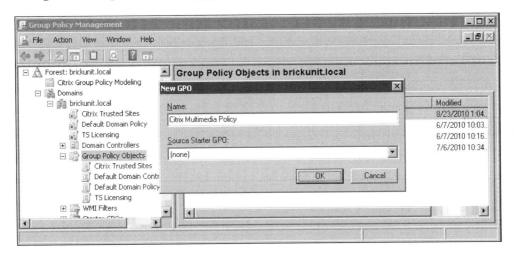

[199]

Managing Policies

After he gives the policy a name, he needs to select the **Computer Configuration** or **User Configuration** node, and then under **Policies**, clicks **Citrix Policies**. Next, he clicks **New** to add a new policy.

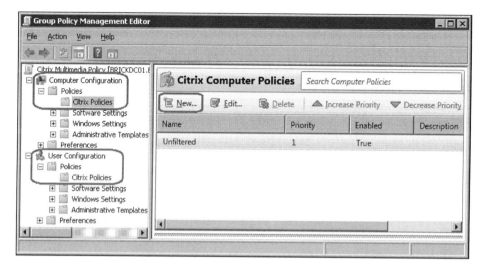

After the **New Policy** wizard appears, William adds a **Name** and **Description**, and clicks the **Next** button. In this example, he is going to create a policy to manage multimedia policies.

He needs to choose the policy settings he wants to setup. In this case, he will enable the **HDX MediaStream Multimedia Acceleration** using the **Add** button.

Chapter 7

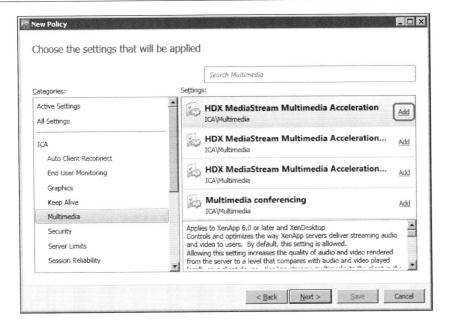

He chooses the **Allowed** option to enable HDX MediaStream Multimedia Acceleration.

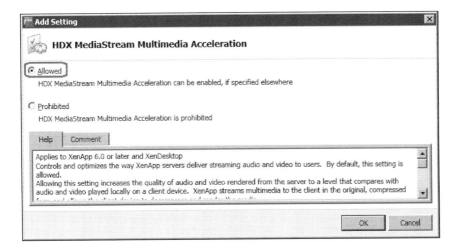

Managing Policies

Then he needs to choose the filters he wants to apply to the policy. Here, he applies the multimedia policy to the **Training Devices** worker group, so all users using XenApp Servers in the training room (members of the **Training Devices** worker group) will improve the multimedia performance.

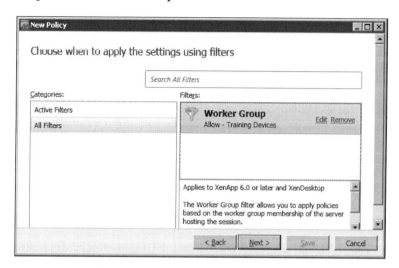

In the final step, William selects the **Enable this policy** checkbox to leave the policy enabled; enabling the policy allows it to be applied immediately to users logging on to the farm. Also, he can clear the **Enable this policy** checkbox to disable the policy; disabling the policy prevents it from being applied.

 XenApp installs the Citrix Group policy engine, when the Citrix Delivery Services console is installed (on a XenApp 6 server or standalone machine). The Citrix group engine provides integration between Active Directory group policies and Citrix policies.

Applying policies to sessions

When William creates a policy, their settings are applied to sessions. By default, the policy is applied to all sessions, if no filter is added.

He can use filters to apply a policy to a target group (users, groups, or computers, for example).

When a user logs in to the farm, XenApp recognizes the policies that match the filters for the connection and applies them based on the priority ranking of the policy.

Some filters depend on whether we are applying a Computer or a User policy. The following list shows the available filters:

- **Access control**: The policy is applied based on a connection Citrix Secure Gateway. This filter applies only to User policies.
- **Client IP address**: The policy is applied based on the client's IP address (IPv4 or IPv6 address) used to connect to the XenApp farm. This filter applies only to User policies.
- **Client name**: The policy is applied based on the name of the client machine used to connect to the XenApp farm. This filter applies only to User policies.
- **User**: The policy is applied based on the user or group membership of the user. This policy can apply to local or Active Directory users. This filter applies only to User policies.
- **Worker group**: The policy is applied based on the worker group membership of the XenApp server hosting the session. This filter applies to either User policies or Computer policies.

[Disabled policy settings take precedence over a lower-ranked setting that is enabled and policy settings that are not configured are ignored.]

Unfiltered policies

By default, XenApp provides Unfiltered policies for Computer and User policy settings. The settings added to this policy apply to all connections.

William will use the Group Policy Management Console to manage Citrix policies, and settings heading to the Unfiltered policy are applied to all farm servers and connections that are within the scope of the Group Policy Objects (GPOs) that contain the policy.

If he uses the Citrix Delivery Services Console to manage Citrix policies, settings we add to the Unfiltered policy are applied to all servers and connections in the farm.

Managing Policies

Now we are going to help William apply policies. He creates a test policy which he will apply to his account so that he can test it. From the policy wizard, he needs to select the **User** filter and click the **Add** button.

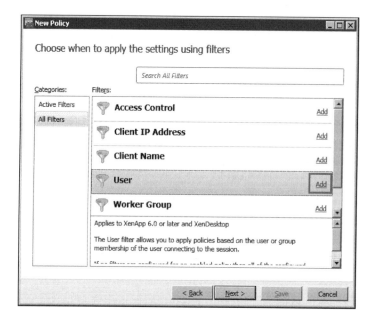

From the **New User Filter** dialog box, he selects his account and clicks the **Add** button.

Now, he can see all filters applied to the policy.

Chapter 7

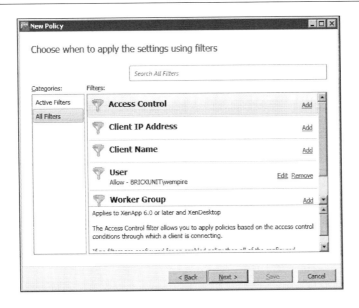

The policy is applied the next time William logs on to the XenApp farm.

Using multiple policies

We can use multiple policies to provide access to users based on their job functions, geographic locations, or connection types.

For example, William can create a policy that prevents remote users from mapping printers and local hard drives.

However, there is a group of project managers at Brick Unit Construction who are working from home and need access to their local drives and printers. So, William can create another policy and assign it to this group. Then he needs to prioritize the two policies to control which one takes precedence.

After William creates both policies, he needs to change the priority of policies.

From the console tree, he chooses to view Citrix Computer Policies or Citrix User Policies.

He created two policies: One called "Block Mapping Local Disks and Printers" is applied to all remote users. The second one, called "Enable Mapping Local Disks and Printers Project Manager", is applied to the project manager group.

From the middle pane, he selects the policy he wants to prioritize.

He needs to click the **Increase Priority** or **Decrease Priority** buttons until the policy has the preferred rank. He needs to give more priority to the project manager policy.

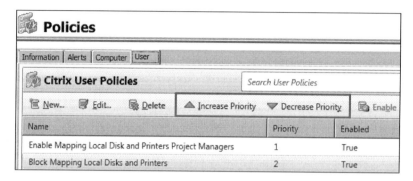

In general, policies override similar settings configured for the entire XenApp farm, for specific servers, or on the client machine. The exception is security. The highest encryption setting in our environment, including the operating system and the most restrictive shadowing setting, always overrides other settings and policies.

Troubleshooting policies

Occasionally, a connection does not respond as expected because multiple policies are applied to the session. If a higher priority policy also applies to a session, it can override the settings we configured in the original policy. As we saw before, we can determine how the final policy settings are merged for a connection by calculating the **Resultant Set of Policy**.

We can calculate the Resultant Set of Policy in the following ways:

- We can use the Citrix Policy Modeling Wizard to simulate a connection scenario and discern how Citrix policies might be applied.
- We can use Group Policy Results to produce a report describing the Citrix policies in effect for a given user and server.
- We can launch both tools from the Group Policy Management Console in Windows. If our XenApp environment doesn't use the Active Directory, we can launch the Citrix Group Policy Modeling Wizard from the **Actions** pane of the Citrix Delivery Services Console.

Using the Citrix Policy Modeling Wizard

The Citrix Group Policy Modeling Wizard generates a report of Citrix policies applied to a particular environment such as domain controller, users, Citrix policy filter evidence values, and simulated environment settings such as slow network connection.

> Results of the wizard will be based on the user account we use and where we run it.

If we are logged on to the server with a domain account and our environment includes Active Directory, the wizard result will include Active Directory GPOs. If we run the wizard from the Citrix Delivery Services Console, the farm GPO is included in the result too. However, if we are logged on to the server as a local user account and run the wizard from the Citrix Delivery Services Console, the wizard calculates the Resultant Set of Policy using only the farm GPO.

Simulate connection scenarios with Citrix policies

Depending on our XenApp environment, we can use the Citrix Group Policy Modeling Wizard from the Citrix Delivery Services Console or the Microsoft Group Policy Management Console.

From the Citrix Delivery Services Console, we need to click the **Policies** node in the console tree and then click **Run the modeling wizard** from the **Actions** pane.

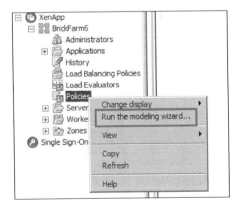

Managing Policies

Now we are going to help William run the Citrix Group Policy Modeling Wizard from the Group Policy Management Console. He needs to right-click the **Citrix Group Policy Modeling** node in the console tree and then select **Citrix Group Policy Modeling Wizard**.

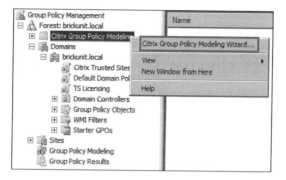

The wizard starts with the welcome page. He then clicks on the **Next** button. He follows the wizard and selects the domain controller; users, computers, environment settings, and Citrix filter criteria he wants to use in the simulation.

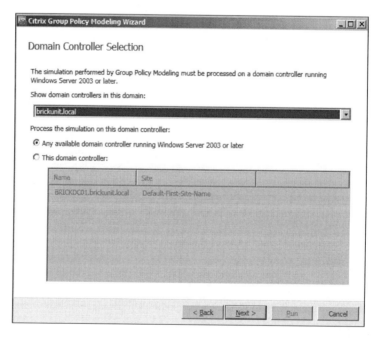

He selects his user and selects the computer container.

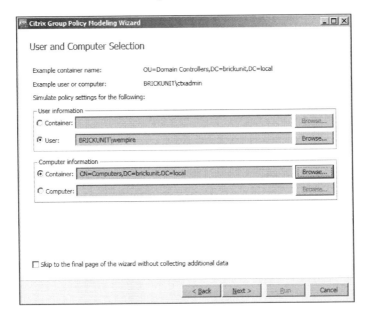

In the **Advanced Simulation Options** page, he keeps the default options.

In the **Alternate Active Directory Paths** page, he selects OU for the User location.

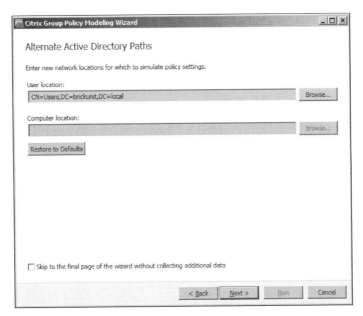

Managing Policies

In the **Filter Evidence Selections** page, he enters the **Client IP address**.

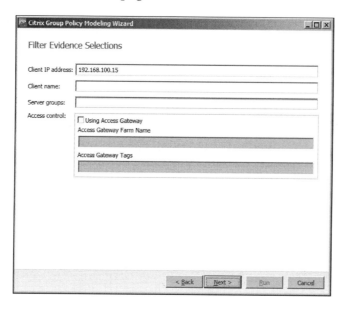

In the **Summary of Selections** page, William clicks on the **Run** button.

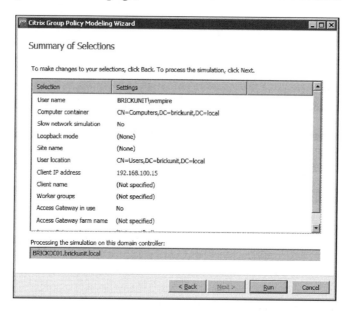

When he clicks on the **Close** button, the wizard produces a report of the modeling results. In the Citrix Delivery Services Console, the report appears as a node in the console tree, underneath the Policies node. The **Modeling Results** tab in the middle pane displays the report, grouping effective Citrix policy settings under the **User Configuration** and **Computer Configuration** headings.

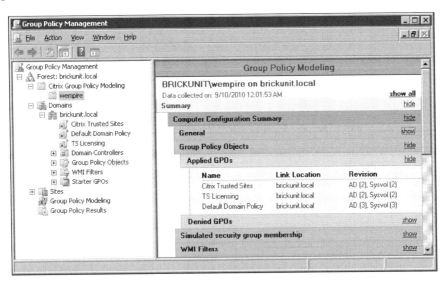

Citrix settings precedence over Windows settings

In a XenApp environment, Citrix settings override the same settings configured in an Active Directory policy or using Remote Desktop Session Host Configuration. This applies to settings that are related to Remote Desktop Protocol (RDP) client connection settings such as desktop wallpaper, menu animation, and so on.

Exceptions to this rule are settings for encryption and shadowing where the most restrictive settings are configured by Remote Desktop Session Host Configuration, Active Directory settings, application configuration, and Citrix settings applies.

Searching policies and settings

From the Citrix Delivery Services Console, we can search the policies and their settings and filters. Now we are going to help William Empire from Brick Unit Construction to search policies.

Managing Policies

All searches find items by name as he types the policy name. He can perform searches from the following places:

- For searching policies, he can use the search box over the list of Citrix policies:

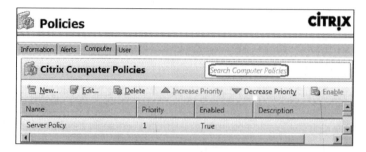

- William can use the search tool on the **Settings** tab to search policy settings. He types license and all policies matching the word license are displayed.

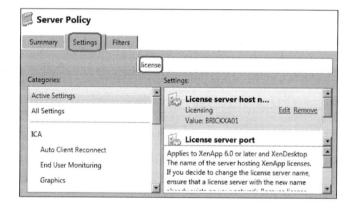

- For searching filters, he can use the search tool on the **Filters** tab.

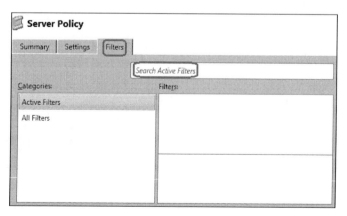

When managing policies through the Delivery Services Console, we need to avoid making frequent changes. It can adversely impact server performance. When we modify a policy, the XenApp server synchronizes its copy of the farm Group Policy Object (GPO) with the data store, propagating the change to other servers in the farm.

For example, if we make changes to five policies, the server synchronizes the farm GPO five times. In a large farm with multiple policies, this frequent synchronization can result in delayed server responses to user requests.

To ensure server performance is not impacted by needed policy changes, arrange to make these changes during off-peak usage periods.

Importing and migrating existing policies

We can use the **Citrix XenApp 6 Migration Tool** to migrate settings (including Citrix policies) from XenApp 5.0 farms to XenApp 6.0 farms.

The **Citrix XenApp 6 Migration Tool** is available for download at `http://support.citrix.com/article/CTX125471`.

We can migrate our Citrix policies from farm GPOs to Active Directory GPOs using a PowerShell script available at `http://community.citrix.com/x/GQDPC`.

Summary

In this chapter, we have learned about managing policies on XenApp 6. Specifically:

- Understanding Citrix policies
- Using the Group Policy Management Console, Citrix Delivery Services Console, and Local Group Policy Editor to manage Citrix policies
- Creating, managing, applying, and troubleshooting Citrix policies

In the next chapter, we are going to talk about printing in a XenApp environment.

8
Printing in XenApp Environments

In the last chapter, we learned about Citrix policies, how to create, manage, apply, and troubleshoot policies, using the Group Policy Management Console, Citrix Delivery Services Console, and Local Group Policy Editor.

In this chapter, we are going to learn about printing in XenApp environments. This chapter will cover:

- Windows and Citrix XenApp printing concepts
- Assigning network printers to users using Citrix policies
- Managing printer drivers
- Using the Citrix universal printer
- Implementing printers
- Printing for mobile users
- XenApp printing optimization pack

Windows printing concepts

The following is a list of basic printing concepts and components in the Windows environment.

We can print from our machine to a locally attached printer connected on USB or LPT port or we can print from a network printer that is managed by a print server.

- **Printing device**: A printing device is the physical printer (the hardware device) to which we send print jobs.
- **Printers:** This is the software representation of a printing device. Computers store information about printers, so they can find and interact with printing devices.

- **Printer driver:** Printer driver is the software program that lets the computer communicate with the printing device. The driver converts the information to be printed to a language that the printing device can understand and process appropriately.
- **Print job:** When a user sends a document to print, the data sent to the printer is known as a print job. Print jobs are queued to the printer in a specific sequence, controlled by the print spooler.
- **Print spooler:** This Windows service manages printer objects, coordinates drivers, helps us install new printers, manages the scheduling of print jobs, and determines where print jobs are processed. The print spooler also determines if the printer prints each page as it receives it or if the printer waits until it receives all pages to print the job.
- **Print queue:** The print queue keeps a list of the print jobs waiting to be printed in a specified order. The spooler maintains this list for each printer in the computer.
- **Print server:** Print server usually is a dedicated Windows server, hosting shared printers and managing the communications between client machines and printers. Also, print servers provide print drivers to client devices and keep print jobs in a print queue until the printer can print them. A print server acts like a remote print spooler.
- **Network printer:** A printer object connected to a wired or wireless network, usually accessed through a network print server.

Print job spooling

Spooling is the process of sending data to a spool. A spool can be a printer spool (the memory of the printer) or a document saved on the disk of a printer server, before being sent to the printer.

Print jobs can be spooled either remotely or locally. Typically, print jobs sent to locally attached printers are spooled locally, and jobs sent to network printers are spooled remotely. Where print jobs are spooled is where print jobs are processed. The processing location can generate or reduce the network traffic and affect the time of processing and resources used on the device machine or print server.

The Windows machine processes the job when print jobs are spooled locally. The application creates a spooled print job. The local print spooler uses the printer driver to process the print job and sends the print job to the printing device (the physical printer). In a Windows environment, printer drivers and settings are stored on the client machine itself.

When print jobs are spooled remotely, a Windows print server processes the print job.

A typical printing process for spooled print jobs is as follows:

- For local spooling, the application tells the local spooler to create a print job and an associated spool file on the local machine, or the application tells the remote spooler to create a print job and an associated spool file on the print server for remote spooling.
- On the local machine, Windows sends the application's drawing commands to the local spool file (local printing) or the remote spool file (remote spooling).
- Windows sends writing commands until the job is completely spooled.
- The local spooler or the remote spooler processes the print job with the print driver. This process is known as **rendering**.
- For local printing, the local spooler delivers the rendered data to the printing device (usually a local printer); or for remote printing, the print server delivers the rendered data to the printing device (usually a network printer).

When the client machine doesn't have enough resources available, such as thin clients, remote spooling is the best option because the print job is processed on the print server, causing little overhead on the client machine.

Unlike remote spooling, local spooling does not use the network servers like a print server. If the print jobs are spooled remotely across the WAN, and users are facing latency issues, local printing is the recommended option for this scenario.

Printing on Citrix XenApp

The XenApp printing works on top of the Windows printing environment, so the first step is to configure the printers in the Windows environment. When users log in to a XenApp session, XenApp will create the appropriate printers. Printer drivers must be installed on the XenApp server.

Most XenApp printing functions are configured through the following Citrix policy categories:

- **Bandwidth:** This category contains settings to limit the bandwidth allocated to printers
- **Printing | Client Printers:** These settings affect the client redirected printers and printing using the client printing pathway
- **Printing | Drivers:** These settings control driver management

- **Printing | Universal Printing**: These settings configure universal printers and drivers

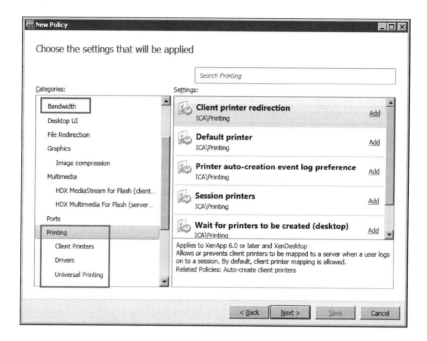

Printing settings are evaluated once the user logs on and stay the same throughout the session. Any new printers added to a policy or a client machine during a session do not appear in the session until the user logs off.

Please note that Citrix policies always take precedence over Windows policies in a XenApp environment.

Printing pathway

The printing pathway is a very important concept in XenApp 6; it includes the path by which print jobs are routed and the location where print jobs are spooled. Both aspects of this concept are very important because routing affects network traffic, and spooling affects utilization of local resources (CPU, memory, and disk space) on the client machine that processes the job.

In XenApp, print jobs can use two different printing pathways:

- Client printing pathway
- Network printing pathway

The **client printing pathway** refers to print jobs that are routed, using the ICA protocol, through the client machine to the printer and spooled on the Citrix Online Plug-in. The printer can be connected directly to the client machine or located in a print server.

When we use the client printing pathway, a virtual printer is constructed in the session that redirects to the printer object on the client machine, and then the client machine sends the print job to the printer. These jobs are spooled locally on the XenApp server. There are two different configurations of the client printing pathway: one for printers attached directly to the client machine (client local printing) and another for network printers (client network printing).

When the **network printing pathway** is used to print jobs that are routed from the XenApp server hosting the user's session to a print server and spooled remotely; there are two different configurations of the network printing pathway: one for network printers connected to the printer server (server network printing) and another for printers attached directly to XenApp (server network printing).

Client local printing

First, we need to install and configure the printer and printer driver on the client machine. Then we need to install and configure the printer driver on the XenApp server or enable the universal driver.

In client local printing, the print job spools from the XenApp server to the client machine and then to the printer installed on the client machine. An example of this environment is a remote user working from home or a small office without network printers.

This is the process when a print job is spooled in the client local printing environment:

- The published application tells the local spooler, on the XenApp server, where the application is located to create a print job and an associated spool file
- On the XenApp server, Windows writes the application's drawing commands to the local spool file until the job is completely spooled
- The local spooler processes the job using the printer driver in a process known as rendering
- The rendered data is delivered to the client machine through the ICA protocol

- The client machine sends the print data to the locally attached printer on the client machine

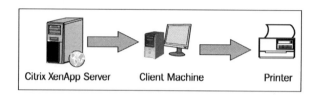

Client network printing

The process is almost the same to the client local printing device, but instead of sending the job to the printer attached to the client machine, the job is sent to the printer server.

Following is the process when a print job is spooled in the client network printing environment:

- The published application tells the local spooler on the XenApp server where the application is located to create a print job and an associated spool file
- The XenApp server sends the print job to the client machine for processing
- The client machine processes the spooled job and sends it to the print server for processing
- The print server then sends the print job to the appropriate network printer

Configuring the client printing pathway for network printing is useful for low bandwidth connections such as WANs. Also, the ICA connection provides traffic compression and we can limit traffic or restrict bandwidth assigned for print jobs.

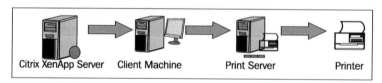

Server network printing

In a server network printing environment, the XenApp server sends the print job to the network print server and then to the printer.

To configure network printers, we need the printer drivers on the servers running XenApp. Then we can assign printers to users using the session printers policy. We can filter the policy by access control, client IP address, client name, server, or users and groups. For example, we can create a rule to assign a specific printer to all users in a specific floor of a building, based on the IP address of the client machine.

When a print job is spooled remotely, it uses the following process:

- The application on the XenApp server tells the remote spooler to create a print job and an associated spool file
- The Windows print provider sends the spool file to the print server
- The print server processes the spool file
- The print server sends the print job to the appropriate network printer

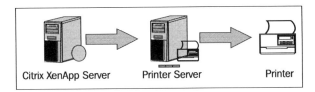

Assigning network printers to users

Automatic printer creation can fail for session printers or network printers on a client machine, usually because the right drivers are not installed automatically by Windows. Often, this is caused by a policy setting preventing auto-installation or because they are manufacturer drivers. We can resolve this problem by installing the corresponding drivers to our XenApp servers manually or using a script if we have multiple print drivers. Later, we will learn how to work with print drivers on XenApp.

Now we are going to help William Empire from Brick Unit Construction to set up a session printer, used to assign a specific printer using Citrix policies.

Adding session printers settings to a Citrix policy

William opens the Group Policy Management Console, chooses **Group Policy Objects** | **Create or edit a Citrix policy** | **User Configuration** | **Citrix Policies** | **Printing** | **Client Printer and Session printers**, and adds a network printer using one of the following methods:

- He types the **Printer UNC path** using the format \\servername\printername.

- He uses the **Browse** button to browse for printers on a specific server. He can also type the server name using the format \\servername and click **Browse**:

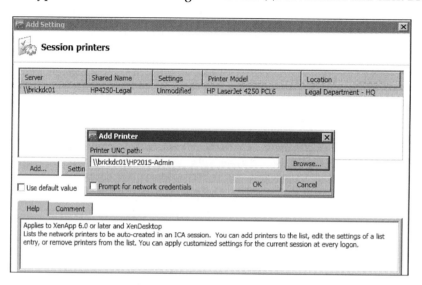

 The server merges all enabled session printer settings for all applied policies, starting from the highest to lowest priorities. When a printer is configured in multiple policies, the custom default settings are taken from only the highest priority policy object in which that printer is configured.

Setting a default printer for a session

After adding a few printers to the session printer policy, William needs to specify a default printer, using the Citrix policy setting **Printing | Default printer** from the settings page, from the **Choose client's default printer** drop-down list, and he chooses one of the following:

- **One printer created by a session printer rule:** Sets the default printer to an existing session printer.
- **Set default printer to the client's main printer:** Sets the default printer to the client's current default printer, if the client's main printer is mapped.

- **Do not adjust the user's default printer**: Uses the current Remote Desktop Services or Windows user profile setting for the default printer. Note that the default printer is not saved in the profile and it does not change according to other session or client machine properties:

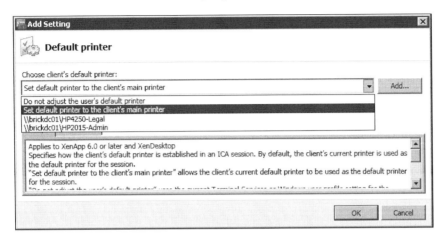

Also, he can use the last option to present users with the nearest printer through profile settings (this functionality, known as Proximity Printing, is explained later).

Finally, he applies the policy to a group of users (or other filtered objects).

Modifying settings of session printers

William can modify default printer settings like paper size, copy count, print quality, and orientation.

On the **Session printers** settings page, he selects the name of the printer for which he wants to modify the settings and clicks the **Settings** button.

He checks the **Apply customized settings** checkbox and then changes the required settings.

He needs to select the **Apply customized settings at every logon** checkbox to ensure that these settings are restored in future sessions (even if users modify them):

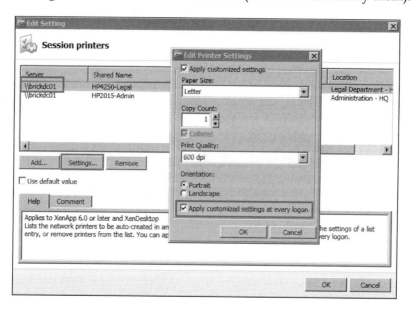

After clicking on the **OK** button, the settings value in the list of printers on the session printers page changes to **Modified**.

Server local printers

Server local printers are printers installed locally on the XenApp server. Server local printers are shared printers that are connected to a XenApp server.

This option is not popular in medium to large enterprise environments, because they require managing printers and drivers on XenApp servers and printing jobs can cause an overhead on the servers, but it is a good option for small XenApp environments without print servers.

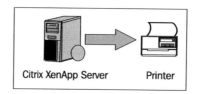

To use a locally attached printer as a server local printer in a XenApp farm, the printer must be shared; otherwise XenApp does not recognize it.

Configuring server local printers

To let our users print from a printer installed locally on the XenApp server, William needs to share it as follows:

On the server where the printer is physically connected, in **Control Panel | Hardware | Devices and Printers**, he right-clicks the printer he wants to share.

Choose Printer Properties.

In the **Sharing** tab, he enables these two checkboxes:

- **Share this printer**
- **Render print jobs on client computers**

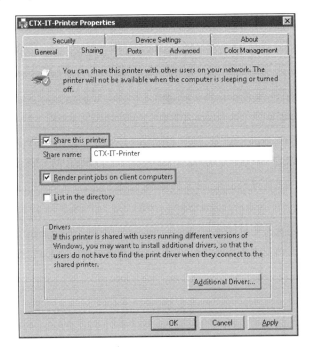

Sharing the printer allows creation of the printer when a session on that XenApp server is launched.

Managing printer drivers

Because users in a XenApp environment do not have a persistent workspace, drivers cannot be stored on the client machine. To print, XenApp must find the correct driver on the client machine or the XenApp server.

The printer driver on the XenApp server and the driver used by the client machine must match exactly. If not, printing fails.

Missing drivers can prevent users from printing successfully. If a non-native or manufacturer printer driver has multiple or inconsistent names across our farm, a session might not be able to find the right driver and a user's job may fail to print.

Printing to a client printer with a defective driver can cause a fatal system error on a server. Number one cause of issues and blue screens on XenApp servers are printer drivers.

XenApp servers do not download any drivers, including printer drivers, from the print server. We need to install the correct device-specific printer driver for the XenApp server's operating system, for both version and architecture (32 or 64-bit).

Advise: Test your printer drivers and do not install any non-native or manufacturer printer driver if you don't need it. If a defective driver is replicated throughout a server farm, it is a difficult and time consuming task to remove it from every XenApp server and always check the printer's manufacturer websites before any printer purchase.

> Download CtxCertifyPrinters from http://ctxadmtools.musumeci.com.ar. This FREE tool will scan your servers or Citrix Farm for non-native or manufacturer drivers and export the results to an Excel file.

Controlling printer driver automatic installation

Managing printer drivers is critical for a successful printing experience. When XenApp autocreates printers, it determines if their corresponding drivers are missing. By default, XenApp installs any missing printer drivers from the Windows native printer driver set. If a problematic printer driver is installed automatically, it can cause issues.

We can either prevent printer drivers from being installed automatically, or, if we want to have them installed automatically, we can control what drivers are installed on XenApp servers by specifying the drivers on a compatibility list.

When users log on:

- The XenApp server checks the client machine printer driver compatibility list before it sets up the client printers
- If a printer driver is on the list of drivers that are not allowed, XenApp does not set up the printer unless the **Universal Printing** feature is enabled
- When the compatibility list prevents setup of a client printer, XenApp writes a message in the server's Event log

To prevent drivers from being installed automatically, William can configure the Citrix policy setting **Automatic Installation of in-box printer drivers**, available at **Printing | Drivers**.

The **Enabled** option allows Windows native drivers to automatically install on the XenApp server. Disabling this setting prevents the automatic installation of printer drivers:

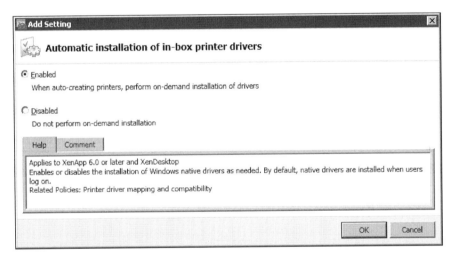

Modifying the printer driver compatibility list

William can configure the Citrix policy setting **Printing | Drivers | Printer driver mapping and compatibility** to specify whether printers can be created with specific drivers or not, or with universal printer drivers. He can use this setting to add driver mapping, edit an existing mapping, remove a mapping, or change the order of driver entries in the list.

- **Allow** option enables the use of printer driver
- **Do not create** option blocks the printer driver

- **Create with universal driver only** option forces the printer to use the universal driver
- **Replace with** option allows you to use a different print driver

Here, William will force printers using the HP LaserJet 1320 (driver famous for causing a lot of print issues on XenApp) to use the universal driver:

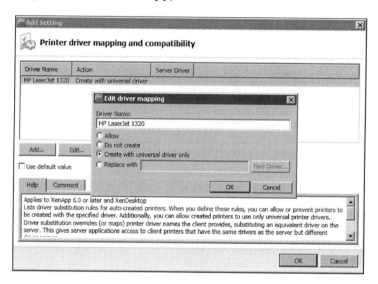

If client machines and XenApp servers use the same drivers but with a different name, for example, "HP LaserJet P2055" on client machines and "HP LaserJet P2055DN" on XenApp, XenApp may not recognize the drivers causing printer autocreation failures.

William can resolve this issue by mapping the printer driver name on the client machine to a similar driver on the XenApp server.

Here William will map the **HP LaserJet 4250 PCL5** driver on client machines to **HP LaserJet 4250 PCL6** on XenApp servers. Unlike previous versions of Windows, Microsoft provides only a certified PCL6 driver for the popular HP LaserJet 4250 printer on Windows Server 2008 R2:

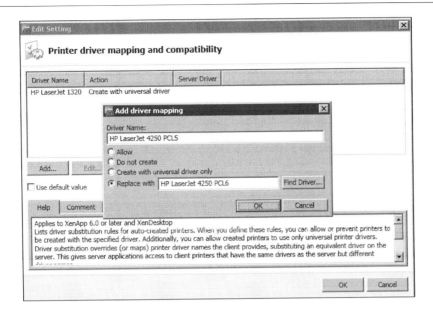

 We can use wildcards in print driver mapping. For example, William can force all HP printers to use a specific driver by specifying HP* in the driver name.

Replicating print drivers in XenApp

XenApp 5 and previous versions allow print driver replication in the Citrix Management Console. However, in XenApp 6, this feature has been replaced by PowerShell commands and other methods in the Windows operating system.

In XenApp, we replicate print drivers with the following PowerShell commands:

- `Get-XAPrinterDriver`: Retrieves farm printer drivers
- `Start-XAPrinterDriverReplication`: Replicates printer drivers
- `Update-XAPrinterDriver`: Updates printer driver information

 More information about using PowerShell commands to replicate printer drivers is available at CTX126125 at `http://support.citrix.com/article/CTX126125`.

In Windows Server 2008 R2, the printer driver replication can be managed using **Print Management Administrative Tool** (`printmanagement.msc`) or `PrintBrmUI.exe` to export and import print drivers and printing settings.

Printing in XenApp Environments

Optionally, `PrintBrm.EXE` can also be used to create scripts to export and import print drivers.

`PrintBrm.EXE` is located in the `%systemroot%\System32\Spool\Tools` folder.

Installing the Print Management Console is required to access the console or PrintBrm tools. To install the feature, open **Server Manager | Add Features | Remote Server Administration Tools | Role Administration Tools | Print and Document Services Tools**.

Using the Citrix Universal Printer

The Citrix Universal Printer is a generic printer created at the beginning of sessions that can be used with almost any printer. Using a single print driver simplifies the deployment of a XenApp farm.

The Citrix Universal Printer name doesn't change when users reconnect; this is good because changing printer names can cause issues on some applications.

When the Citrix Universal Printer is enabled, an extra printer is created in each session with the name Citrix UNIVERSAL Printer in the session number of session.

Using Citrix Universal printers provides two benefits:

- Reduce print management complexity
- Increase the speed of starting a session

Often, Citrix Universal printing can't work in our environment, for example:

- A few printers models are incompatible with the Citrix Universal driver
- Some users require access to advanced printer options which are not available, for example, duplexing
- The Citrix Universal Printer and printer driver solution require the Citrix Online Plug-in or the Citrix Offline Plug-in
- If the users are using the Citrix Offline Plug-in and streaming applications to the client machine, or not connecting through the ICA channel, the Citrix Universal Printer doesn't work in this scenario

When we talk about the Citrix Universal Printer, we find that XenApp provides:

- **Citrix Universal Printer:** This is the generic printer object that replaces the printers during users' sessions. This printer can be used with almost any printer model.

- **Citrix Universal Printer Drivers:** These Windows-native Printer drivers are generic drivers that work with almost any printer and even with non-Windows clients. Citrix-created Universal printer drivers consist of the Citrix XPS Universal Printer driver and the EMF-based Citrix Universal Printer Driver. We will talk about this later.

We can use the Citrix Universal Printer Driver in the following ways:

- Auto-Created Citrix Universal Printer with a Citrix Universal Printer Driver: When the session starts, just one Citrix Universal Printer is auto-created. The session uses the Citrix Universal Printer Driver to communicate with the driver on the client machine and the print job is processed locally.
- Auto-Created Device Printers, Auto-Created Citrix Universal Printer with a Citrix Universal Printer Driver: When the session starts, both the Citrix Universal Printer and local printers are auto-created using the Citrix Universal Printer Driver.
- Auto-Created Device Printer with Citrix Universal Printer Driver: Local printers are auto-created using the Citrix Universal printer driver and the print job is processed locally.

The Citrix Universal Printer Driver provides a lot of benefits, but we need to TEST it with each printer in our environment. Sometimes it might be better to use a device-specific driver or another Universal Printer solution like HP Universal Printer Driver, because the driver might be able to optimize print jobs for the printer or create smaller print jobs.

> Citrix Universal Printer is available in the Presentation Server 4.0 to XenApp 6. Supported clients included: Citrix Presentation Server Client, Version 9.x or 10.x, Citrix XenApp Plug-in 11.x or later, Citrix Online Plug-in 12.x or later, Citrix XenApp Plug-in for Streamed Apps, and Citrix Offline Plug-in.

Now we will walk William through all settings used to configure the Universal Printing using the **Printing | Universal Printing** policy settings. This policy includes multiple rules:

- **Auto-create generic universal printer:** This rule enables or disables the auto-creation of the Citrix Universal Printer. By default, generic universal printers are not auto-created.
- **Universal driver priority:** This rule specifies the order in which XenApp tries to use universal printer drivers, starting with the first entry in the list. He can add, edit, or remove drivers and change the order of the drivers in the list.

- **Universal printing**: This rule specifies when to use universal printing.
- **Universal printing preview preference**: This rule specifies whether to use the print preview function for auto-created or generic universal printers.

 These four options are available when we install XenApp 6.0 RTM. After we install the XenApp Printing Optimization Pack, more options are available. We are going to talk about new settings available in the XenApp Printing Optimization Pack, at the end of this chapter.

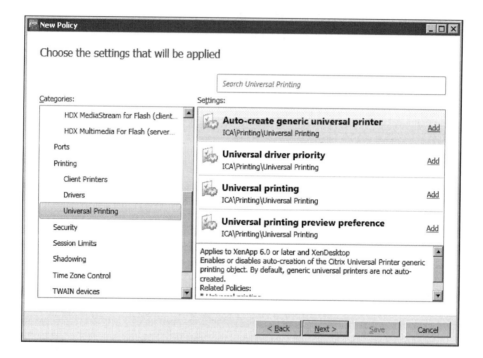

Setting up an auto-create generic universal printer

By default, Universal Printers are not auto-created. William can use this setting to enable or disable auto-creation of the Citrix Universal Printer.

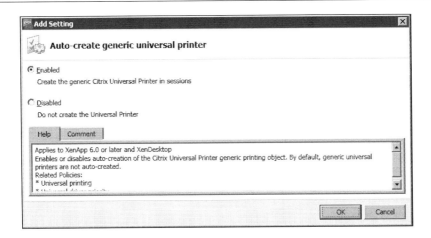

Setting up universal driver priority

There are several different Universal Print Drivers, but the two more popular versions are:

- Citrix Universal Printer driver (EMF-based)
- Citrix XPS (XML Paper Specification) Universal Printer Driver

Now William will change the order in which UPD drivers are used, assigning XPS as a preferred option. He needs to modify the Citrix policy setting **Printing | Universal Printer | Universal driver priority** and move XPS to the top of the list.

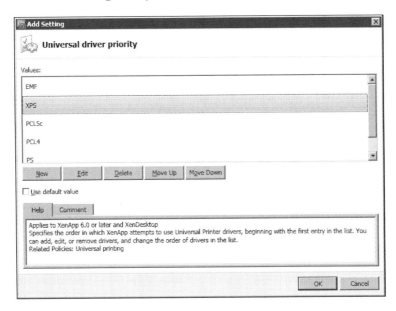

Printing in XenApp Environments

There are several versions of the Citrix Universal Print Driver:

- EMF (Enhanced Metafile Format): EMF is the default and preferred option, because it provides several benefits including the reduction of the size of some print jobs, faster printing, reduction of load on the server, and printing delays on high latency connections
- XML Paper Specification: XML Paper Specification (XPS) is a platform-independent printing language and is a new feature in Windows server 2008
- PCL5c: This printer command language is based on the HP Color LaserJet 4500 PCL 5 driver
- PCL4: This printer command language is based on the HP LaserJet Series II driver
- PS (PostScript): PS is based on the HP Color LaserJet 4500 PS driver

Here we can see the Citrix Universal Printer Drivers listed in the **Print Management** MMC snap-in:

- **Citrix Universal Printer**, which is the EMF driver
- **Citrix XPS Universal Printer**
- **HP Color LaserJet 2800 PS** (Citrix PS Universal Printer Driver)

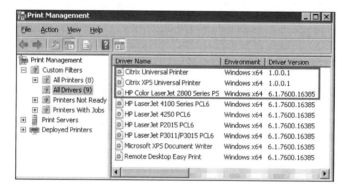

Configuring the Universal Printer Driver on sessions

We can configure the Universal printing Citrix policy setting by choosing one of the following:

- **Use only printer model specific drivers:** Client printer uses only the native drivers that are auto-created at logon. The client printer cannot be auto-created, if the native driver of the printer is unavailable on the XenApp server.
- **Use universal printing only:** Client printer uses the Universal Printer Driver only.
- **Use universal printing only if requested driver is unavailable:** The client printer uses native drivers if they are available. If they are not available on the XenApp server, the client printer uses the universal driver, based on Universal driver priority policy setting.
- **Use printer model specific drivers only if universal printing is unavailable:** The client printer uses the Universal Printer Driver. If the driver is not available on the XenApp server, the client printer is created with the native printer driver.

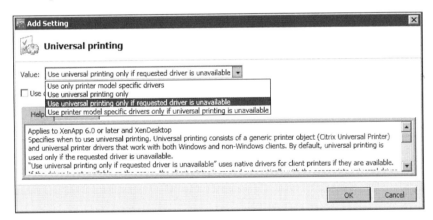

Configuring only a universal printer driver will not improve session start time (printers on the client device are still enumerated and auto-created at the beginning of sessions), but, configuring a universal printer driver does improve printer driver performance.

Setting up universal printing preview preference

This setting allows William to enable or disable the print preview function for the auto-created and/or generic universal printers. This option is disabled.

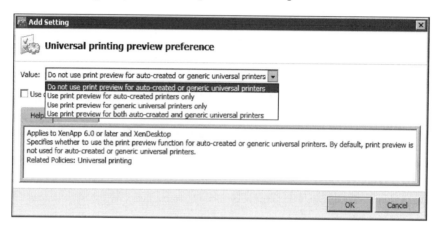

Change the default settings on the Universal Printer

We can change the default settings for the Citrix Universal Printer, including settings for paper size, paper width, print quality, color, duplex, and the number of copies. We can override the default settings of the Citrix Universal Printer and modify these settings manually using the following registry key:

HKEY_LOCAL_MACHINE\SOFTWARE\Citrix\Print\UPDDevmode

More information on the default settings is available at http://support.citrix.com/article/CTX113148.

Implementing Printers

Another important concept on XenApp printer deployment is Printer Provisioning. This is the process by which XenApp makes printers available in a session. We can find two types of printer provisioning:

- Static: When we connect to a server's local printer in a session, printers are provisioned once and always created in the sessions with the same properties.

- **Dynamic:** When our users start a session, printers are created dynamically. Two of the most common methods of dynamic printer provisioning are Auto-creation, where printers are created automatically based on Citrix policies and User Provisioning, where users self-provision their printers.

Because static printer provisioning is pretty easy to understand, we are going to talk about dynamic provisioning.

Auto-creation

The auto-creation printer policy allows us to configure whether printers are automatically created within a user session or not, and allows us to configure which types of printers are automatically created.

By default, XenApp makes printers available in sessions by creating all printers configured on the client machine automatically, including locally attached and network printers. When the user closes the session, all printers for that session are deleted.

When the user logs in, the auto-creation feature creates a list of printers, their print drivers will be installed, and all printers in this list will be available.

XenApp can auto-create redirects client printers in two ways:

- By creating a one-to-one match with printers on the client machine
- By creating one Citrix Universal Printer which represents all printers on the client machine

In several environments, especially medium and large ones, it is a common (and good) practice to auto-create only the default printer. Auto-creating a smaller number of printers creates less overhead on the XenApp server and reduces CPU utilization.

However, in small environments or locations where users need to print to several local printers, we may want to leave the default auto-creation setting so that all printers are created on logon.

Auto-creating client machine printers

At the start of a session, XenApp auto-creates all printers on the client machine by default. We can manage what types of printers are provisioned to users or prevent auto-creation entirely using the Auto-create client printers policy (explained below).

When configuring policies for printer auto-creation, we need to check if:

- User accounts are not shared
- Users are not members of local power user or administrators group on the client machine
- Microsoft native or fully tested drivers only are used
- Users have write access on the XenApp server to the folder `%systemroot%\system32\spool`

Auto-creating network printers

By default, any network printer on the client machine is created automatically at the beginning of a session.

The preferred method to create network printers is using the session printers on Citrix policies, rather than auto-create all the network printers available in the client machine.

Session printers are easy to manage and apply to several users using Citrix policies. They are very useful if we want to assign printers to users located on the same floor of one building or in a branch office using the IP address of client machines, for example.

Configuring printer auto-creation settings

Now William will use the **Auto-create client printers** policy to configure the way printers are created automatically at the beginning of sessions. By default, XenApp creates all printers on the client machine.

To change the printer auto-creation policy, William needs to configure the **Printing | Client Printers | Auto-Create Client Printers** policy, using one of the following settings:

- **Do not auto-create client printers:** Printers in the client machine are not mapped
- **Auto-create the client's default printer only:** Only the client machine's default printer is auto-created in the session
- **Auto-create local (non-network) client printers only:** Only locally attached (non-network) printers are auto-created in the session
- **Auto-create all client printers:** Both local and network printers connected to the client machine are auto-created in the session

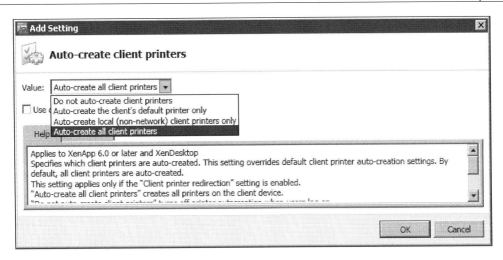

Configuring legacy client printer support

The **Client printer names** policy enables the use of legacy client printer names. This setting allows us to preserve backward compatibility for users or groups using Citrix MetaFrame 3.0 or earlier.

We need to use the setting **Legacy printer names** option from the **Printing | Client Printers | Client Printer Names** policy to auto-create client printers with legacy printer names and Standard printer names to use the default name based on Terminal Server.

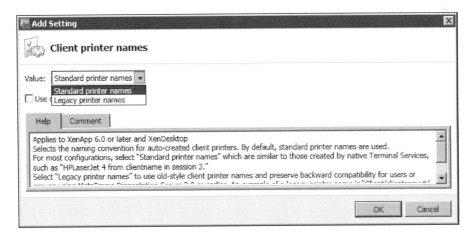

User provisioning

We can also allow users to add printers to their sessions on their own. Users can map client printers that are not auto-created by a policy manually in a user session through the Windows Add Printer wizard on the server (in their sessions). If users have thin clients or cannot access their client devices, they can self-provision by running the ICA Client Printer Configuration tool (PrintCfg.exe).

We need to publish PrintCfg.exe or the Add Printer wizard on our farm to allow users to self-provision their own printers or after a user adds a printer using either of these methods, XenApp retains the printer information for future sessions from that client machine. Client printers created using this process are called **retained printers**.

Publishing the Windows Add Printer wizard

Now, we help William to publish the Add Printer wizard.

He creates the following folder at the root level of one of the XenApp server's drives, C:\Printers.{2227A280-3AEA-1069-A2DE-08002B30309D}, where C represents a drive on the XenApp server; then when he presses Enter, the folder icon changes to a printer icon.

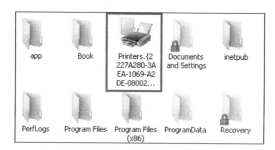

Then he needs to create a published application with the following properties:

c:\windows\explorer.exe C:\Printers.{2227A280-3AEA-1069-A2DE-08002B30309D}

in the command line and the path where explorer.exe is located as a working directory.

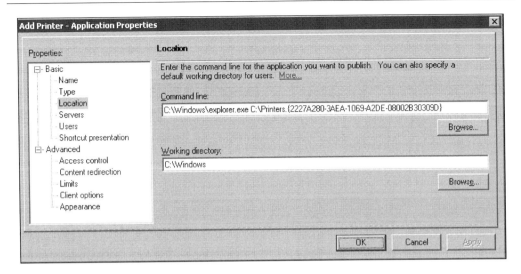

Publishing the ICA Client Printer Configuration tool

To publish the ICA Client Printer Configuration tool, William needs to follow the instructions for publishing an application using the Publish Application wizard (explained in *Chapter 5, Application Publishing*).

On the **Location** page, he needs to enter the path for the ICA Client Printer Configuration tool (`printcfg.exe`) on the XenApp server.

By default, the tool is located in `C:\Program Files (x86)\Citrix\system32\printcfg.exe`.

Storing users' printer properties

After publishing any of the tools, William wants to keep the user printer's settings. To retain the user printer properties, he needs to configure the **Printing | Client Printers | Printer Properties Retention** policy by choosing from the following settings:

- **Held in profile only if not saved on client:** This is the default option and allows XenApp to determine the method. It tries to store printer properties on the client machine if available, or if not, in the user profile. This option increases logon time and uses extra bandwidth to check. Usually, this version is used for backward compatibility with prior versions of XenApp.

- **Retained in user profile only:** This option reduces logon time and network traffic, but only works if a Remote Desktop Services roaming profile is used. Recommended if the users use legacy plugins like MetaFrame Presentation Server Client 8.x or earlier.
- **Saved on the client device only**: This option stores printer properties only on the client machine. This is the preferred option if the users use Remote Desktop Services mandatory profile or roaming profile.
- **Do not retain printer properties:** Does not retain printer properties.

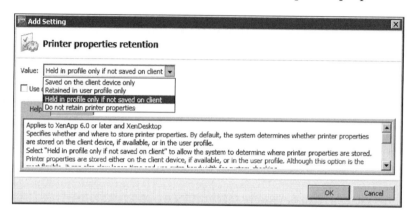

As we mentioned earlier, XenApp attempts to store printing settings on the client machine. If the client does not support this operation, XenApp stores printing properties in the user profile for that specific user.

Sessions from non-Windows XenApp plugins or even older Windows XenApp plugins use the user profiles on the server for properties retention.

We can use the Printer Properties Retention policy rule to force properties to be saved on either the client machine or on the XenApp server.

If the users have trouble saving printer information, we need to check items in the following list and sometimes reconfigure how XenApp stores user printing preferences:

- Client version: Users must be running Citrix Presentation Server Client 9.x and higher to store user-modified printer properties on the client machine. Not all XenApp plugins allow users to store printer properties on a client machine.
- Type of Windows user profile: If we are using a mandatory profile and we want to retain the user's printer properties, we must store the properties on the client machine.

- Type of users: If we have remote or mobile users using roaming profiles, we need to save the printer properties to the user's profile and not the client machine.

> A mandatory user profile is a special type of preconfigured roaming user profile that we can use to specify settings for users. With mandatory user profiles, a user can modify his or her desktop, but the changes are not saved when the user logs off. The next time the user logs on, the mandatory user profile created by us is downloaded.

If none of these factors apply to us or we don't have any issues, Citrix recommends no change where the printer properties are stored and keeps the default setting, which saves the printer properties on the client machine and is the easiest way to guarantee consistent printing properties.

If we want to keep changes to the printer settings the users make locally outside of a session or offline with locally attached printers, we need to modify the registry key in the client and create and set the **Win32FavorRetainedPrinterSettings** registry key to **False**. This registry key is located on:

- `HKEY_LOCAL_MACHINE\SOFTWARE\Citrix\ICA Client\Engine\Lockdown Profiles\All Regions\Lockdown\Virtual Channels\Printing`
- `HKEY_CURRENT_USER\Software\Citrix\ICA Client\Engine\Lockdown Profiles\All Regions\Lockdown\Virtual Channels\Printing`

When we create this registry key, the plugin gives priority to settings from the printer, rather than retained settings

The client must have the same print driver installed on the client machine and server. If we don't have it, only the same settings are exchanged between the real printer and the virtual printer in the session.

Settings in the session stay synchronized with settings on the printing device. If the user makes a change in the printer inside the session, the plugin attempts to write the change back to the printer on the client machine when logging off. If a user makes a change outside a session, the plugin will update the printer configuration inside the session.

General locations of printing preferences

When we work in Windows, changes made to printing preferences can be stored on the client machine or in a document. However, in a XenApp environment, settings can be stored in three locations:

- On the client machine: Settings are stored on the client machine. Depending on the version of the operating systems, these settings are available in the **Control Panel | Device and Printers | Printing Preferences**.
- Inside a document: Mostly applications store settings inside documents and these settings are known as Document Settings. One example is Microsoft Office applications that typically store the printing preferences inside the document. These settings appear by default the next time we print that document.
- On the XenApp server: Some settings associated with a specific printer driver are stored on the XenApp server.

Because printing preferences can be stored in multiple places, XenApp processes them according to a specific priority.

XenApp searches for settings in this order:

- XenApp checks for retained printer settings. If XenApp detects retained settings, it applies these settings when the user prints.
- If there are no retained printer settings, XenApp searches for any changes to the printer settings for the default printer for the client machine. If XenApp detects any changes to printer settings on the client machine, it applies these settings when the user prints.
- If there are no retained or client printer settings, XenApp applies the default printer settings stored on the XenApp server when the user prints.

Generally, XenApp merges any retained settings and the settings inherited from the client machine with the settings for the default printer driver on the server.

By default, XenApp always applies any printer settings modified by the user during a session, that is, the retained settings, before considering any other settings.

Printing for mobile users

Sometimes we have users moving between different workstations, floors in the building, or even branch offices, and we need to present them to the closest printers.

XenApp provides two features designed for mobile users:

- SmoothRoaming
- Proximity Printing

SmoothRoaming

This feature, also known as Workspace control, lets a user disconnect from one session, move to a different client machine, and reconnect to continue that same session. The printers assigned on the first client machine are replaced on the reconnection with printers appropriate for the second client machine.

Proximity printing

The proximity printing feature is based on the use of two Citrix policies: Session printer and Default printer. We can use the location of the client machine to assign the closer network printer.

Proximity printing requires that we filter the policy using a location setting like:

- Network's IP addresses, if they are related to user locations
- The name of the client machine, if the name relates to the location.

Configuring printers for mobile users

We need to configure the proximity printing solution, if we want to make sure that our users always have access to the closest printer to their client machine. Proximity printing allows users within a specified IP address segment to automatically access network printers within that same IP address segment.

The HQ (headquarters) of Brick Unit Construction is a large building with ten floors. Each floor holds multiple departments. Several users move between offices to have meetings or work on the same projects, so they need access to a closer printer. William deployed two network printers on each floor, one at each side of the floor.

To configure proximity printing in the Brick Unit building, William needs to:

- Set up the DHCP server to assign IP addresses to each floor of the building.
- He needs to assign a unique designated IP address segment to each floor within the company. For example, he will assign segment 172.16.31.xxx to the first floor, 172.16.32.xxx to the second floor, and so on.

- He needs to provide IP addresses to each network printer within the range of IP addresses for the floor in which they are located. He will reserve the first ten IP addresses for network printers. So, for example, he will assign IP addresses 172.16.31.2 and 172.16.31.3 to network printers on the first floor.
- Then he needs to create a separate Citrix policy for each floor and add the printers in that to the session printers setting.
- Set the default printer setting to **Do not adjust the user's default printer**.
- Filter the policies by Client IP address.

Improving printing performance

By default, XenApp routes jobs to network printers from the XenApp server directly to the print server using the network printing pathway.

Print jobs sent over the network printing pathway are not compressed. When routing printing jobs across a network with limited bandwidth, we can disable the **Direct connection to print servers** policy, so we route jobs through the client machine, and the ICA protocol compresses the jobs.

Also, we can limit the bandwidth used by the client printing to avoid performance issues caused by using multiple virtual channels at the same time (like printing and multimedia applications).

When we limit the data transmission rate for printing, we can make more bandwidth available for video, keystrokes, and mouse data. More available bandwidth can help prevent degradation of the user experience during printing.

> The printer bandwidth limit is always enforced, even when no other channels are in use.

There are two ways we can limit printing bandwidth in client sessions using printer settings in the **Bandwidth** category:

- We can use the Citrix policy bandwidth printer settings in the Delivery Services Console to enable and disable the printing bandwidth session limit for the farm.
- Use individual server settings to limit printing bandwidth in the farm. We can perform this task using `gpedit.msc` locally on each server to configure the Citrix policy Bandwidth printer settings.

Limit printing bandwidth

William can configure one of the following options in the Citrix policy **ICA | Bandwidth** setting. If he enters values for both settings, the most restrictive setting (with the lower value) is applied.

- **Printer redirection bandwidth limit:** Specifies the bandwidth available for printing in Kbps
- **Printer redirection bandwidth limit percent:** Sets the percentage of the overall bandwidth available for printing

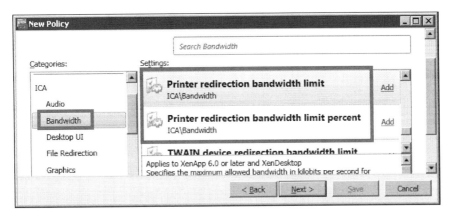

Third-party printing solutions

There are two Citrix partners that provide third-party solutions for printing. They provide a simple printer driver, great performance, fast printing, and more. He can find more info at:

- ThinPrint: www.thinprint.com
- UniPrint: www.uniprint.com

XenApp Printing Optimization Pack

By the end of October 2010, Citrix released the XenApp Printing Optimization Pack designed to improve printing speed, reduce printing bandwidth, and more.

After we download and decompress the file `XA6PrintPack.zip`, we will find three files inside it:

- `XA600W2K8R2X64010.msp`: This file installs the XenApp Printing Optimization Pack on the XenApp server
- `XenAppGPMX64.msi` and `XenAppGPMX86.msi`: This is an updated version of the Citrix XenApp Group Policy Management Experience for each platform (64bit and 32bit)

After we install the pack on our XenApp servers, we will note new policies available on our management console.

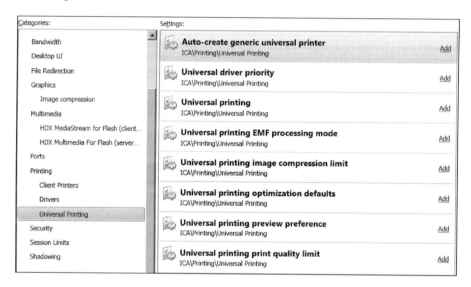

The following are the new policies available in the XenApp Printing Optimization Pack:

- Universal printing EMF processing mode
- Universal printing image compression limit
- Universal printing optimization defaults
- Universal printing print quality limit

Universal printing EMF processing mode

This policy allows us to send the EMF spool file directly into the spooler on the client machine (default option) or reprocess the EMF records on the client machine. By default, EMF records are spooled directly to the printer.

Reprocessing EMF records on the client machine allows some printer drivers to prompt users for additional information when generating printed output.

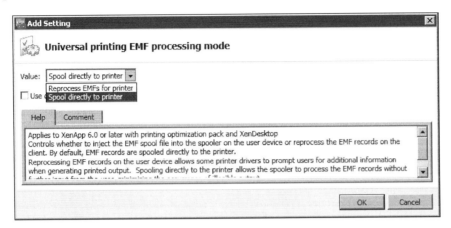

Universal printing image compression limit

This policy allows us to set the maximum quality and the minimum compression level available for images printed with the Universal Printer Driver. By default, the image compression limit is set to **Best quality (lossless compression)**.

If we select the **No compression** option, compression is disabled for EMF printing only; this option doesn't apply for XPS printing.

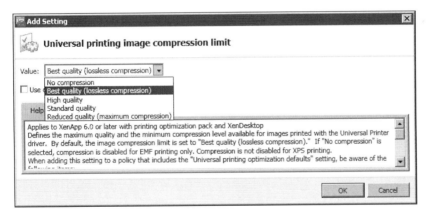

Universal printing optimization defaults

This rule specifies the default settings for the Universal Printer when it is created for a session, including the following options:

- **Desired image quality**: Sets the level of image compression. By default, the **Standard quality** option is selected.
- **Enable heavyweight compression:** This option enables or disables (default option) reducing bandwidth beyond the **Desired image quality** compression level without losing image quality.
- **Allow caching of embedded images:** This option allows (default option) or prevents embedded images to be cached.
- **Allow caching of embedded fonts:** This option allows (default option) or prevents embedded fonts to be cached.
- **Allow non-administrators to modify these settings:** This option allows or prevents (default option) standard users from modifying any of these options through the printer driver's advanced print settings.

Please note that all these options are supported for EMF printing; only the **Desired image quality** option is supported for XPS printing.

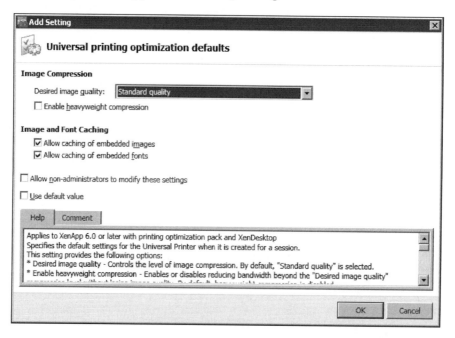

Universal printing print quality limit

This setting sets the maximum DPI (dots per inch) available for generating printed output in the session. By default, no limit is specified.

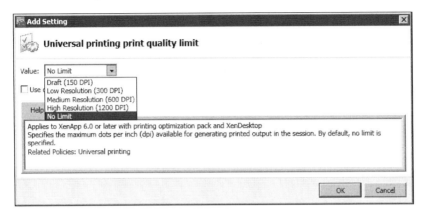

Summary

In this chapter, we learned about printing in XenApp environments, Windows and XenApp printing concepts, and how to use Citrix policies to manage printing. In the next chapter, we are going to talk about Multimedia Content on XenApp.

9
Multimedia Content on XenApp

In the last chapter, we learned about printing in XenApp environments, starting with Windows and XenApp printing concepts, and how to use Citrix policies to manage printing. In this chapter, we will discuss how to improve the multimedia experience of users using Citrix HDX technologies. HDX means High Definition eXperience. Citrix HDX is a big set of technologies that enables better multimedia and peripheral support and provides improvements in audio quality, enabling us to deliver multimedia and conference applications on XenApp 6.0 (and 5.0) farms.

In this chapter, we will talk about:

- Description of HDX technologies
- Using HDX 3D technologies to improve image display
- Using HDX Broadcast Display settings
- Using HDX MediaStream Multimedia Acceleration
- Using HDX MediaStream for Flash to optimize Flash content
- Configuring Audio using policies
- Configuring Audio for user sessions

Description of Citrix HDX technologies

XenApp includes various HDX technologies that allow us to improve user experience and session responsiveness. In this chapter, we are going to help William Empire from Brick Unit Construction to install and configure Citrix HDX technologies on his XenApp farm.

We have two major issues affecting the performance of playback Multimedia applications or content. These two issues are network latency and bandwidth availability. The following Citrix HDX technologies will help us to deal with these two issues:

- **HDX 3D Image Acceleration:** Helps us to manage quality of images and bandwidth used by images.
- **HDX 3D Progressive Display:** This feature increases session responsiveness, providing a low quality (compressed) image first, and if the image does not change, XenApp replaces the image with a high quality one.
- **HDX Broadcast Browser:** Enables our XenApp servers to respond to client machines broadcast. We can save bandwidth by disabling this option.
- **HDX Broadcast Display:** Helps us to manage and reduce bandwidth use, analyzing the queue of images, and omitting some of them to provide a better response to the user.
- HDX MediaStream Multimedia Acceleration: Helps us to manage and optimize audio and video content delivery.
- **HDX MediaStream for Flash:** Helps us to accelerate the delivery of Adobe Flash content.

Using HDX 3D technologies to improve image display

Citrix provides HDX 3D technologies to improve image display and reduce CPU load of graphics-intensive applications.

In environments with intensive use of graphics applications, like image editing or manipulation applications, large images are transferred between XenApp servers and client machines.

This is a common issue at Brick Unit Construction, where large images of building plans or presentations with a lot of graphics are used every day. William wants to enable HDX 3D technologies to reduce bandwidth and improve image display. XenApp includes Citrix policies to manage image compression and improve image display:

- Lossy compression
- Progressive compression

Both policies are located under **Graphics | Image Compression Policy Settings**.

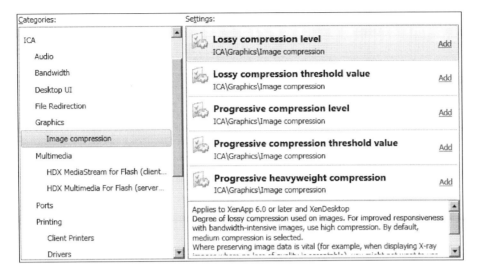

Using HDX 3D Image Acceleration to reduce bandwidth

The first HDX 3D technology William wants to implement is SpeedScreen Image Acceleration. This technology uses compression to reduce the size of image files that the XenApp server sends to the client machine.

This feature, enabled by default, uses compression to remove redundant data from the files before the transfer to a client machine.

He can configure the **Lossy Compression Level** Citrix User policy setting with one of the following options:

- **High**: Provides low image quality
- **Medium** (default option): Provides good image quality
- **Low**: Provides high image quality
- **None**: No compression is applied and quality is almost the same as the original file

Multimedia Content on XenApp

William can set up multiple policies depending on user membership or application and assign different levels of compression. He needs to choose **none** or **low compression** for users who need to view images at the original or near the original quality levels.

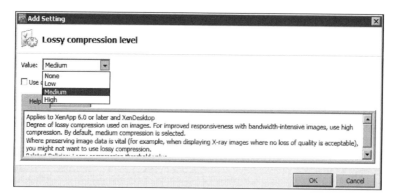

Another important setting in this policy is the **Lossy Compression Threshold Value**. This setting represents the maximum bandwidth in kilobits per second for a connection to which lossy compression is applied. By default, the threshold value is 2,000 kilobits per second.

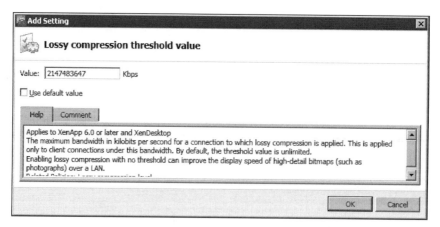

Using HDX 3D Progressive Display to improve the display of images

Citrix HDX 3D Progressive Display helps us to improve the performance of an application, showing an initial compressed version of an image file, and if the image doesn't change, the image is processed in the background and replaced by a high quality image.

If Lossy compression is enabled, the progressive compression must be higher than the Lossy compression level setting.

William can set the **Progressive Compression Level** setting to provide a less detailed, but faster, display of images. By default, progressive compression is not applied.

He needs to use the **Very High** or **Ultra-High** option to enable viewing of bandwidth-intensive graphics such as building pictures or detailed building plans.

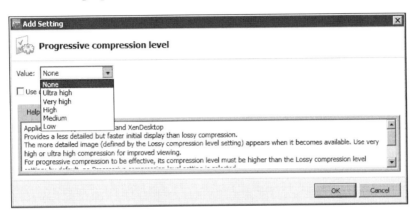

Another related setting is the **Progressive Compression Threshold Value**. This setting sets the maximum bandwidth in Kbps for client machine connections. This setting is applied to connections below this bandwidth. By default, the threshold value is 1440 Kbps.

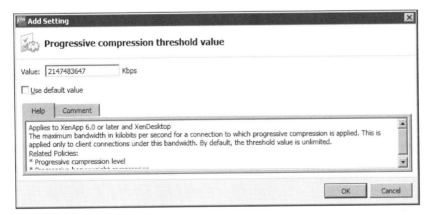

The **Progressive heavyweight compression** setting uses an advanced (and CPU-intensive) graphical algorithm to reduce bandwidth without losing image quality. By default, this setting is **Disabled**. Please note that this setting is supported on the Citrix Online Plug-in, but has no effect on other plugins.

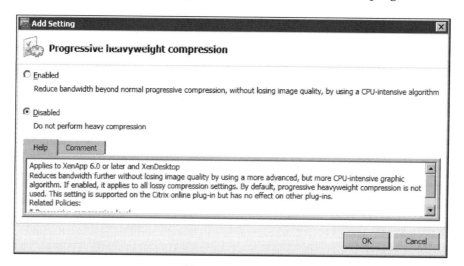

Reduce CPU use by moving processing to GPU

Using HDX 3D, we can move graphics-intensive processing from CPU to GPU (Graphics Processing Unit). Moving processing to the GPU will upload compressing and rendering operations from CPU, reducing the CPU use. This feature is only available on physical servers with a GPU (HDX 3D can't run on Virtual Machines) that supports DDI (Display Driver Interface) versions 9 or later.

William can enable published applications to render using the physical server's GPU, adding the **Enable WPFHook** key (type **REG_DWORD**) and set its value to **1** in the following registry key on the XenApp server:

```
HKLM\SOFTWARE\Wow6432Node\Citrix\CtxHook\AppInit_Dlls\Multiple
Monitor Hook
```

Using HDX Broadcast Display settings

HDX Broadcast Display settings are used to improve the response when graphics are sent to the client machine. William can configure HDX Broadcast Display settings using the ICA Graphics policy. This policy manages how images are handled in user sessions.

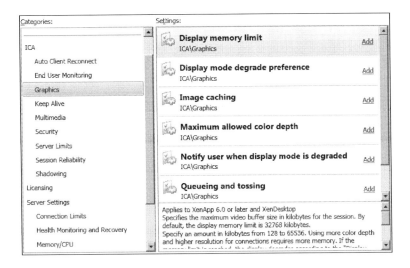

William can use the **Display Memory Limit** setting to change the maximum video buffer size for the session. By default, the display memory limit is **32768 kB**. He can specify an amount between 128 and 65536 KB. If the memory limit is reached, the display degrades according to the **Display Mode Degrade Preference** setting, described below.

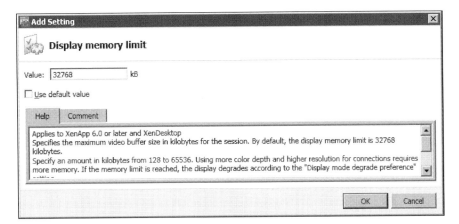

The **Display Mode Degrade Preference** setting specifies color depth or resolution degrades first when the session display memory limits are reached. By default, color depth is degraded first. William also can notify users when either color depth or resolution is degraded, using the **Notify User When Display Mode is Degraded** setting, described below.

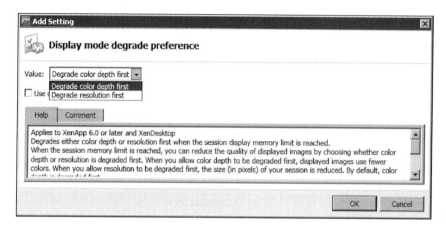

William can use the **Image caching** setting to enable (default option) or disable caching of images in sessions. This setting, when enabled, makes scrolling smoother.

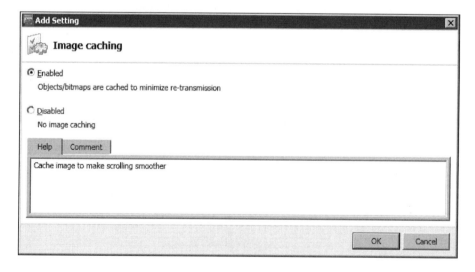

The **Maximum allowed color depth** setting specifies the maximum color depth allowed for a session. By default, the maximum allowed color depth is **32 Bits Per Pixel**. William can reduce high color depth to save memory.

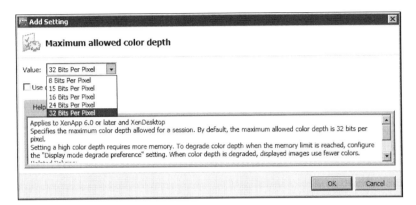

The **Notify user when display mode is degraded** setting shows a message to the user when the color depth or resolution is degraded. By default, this option is **Disabled**.

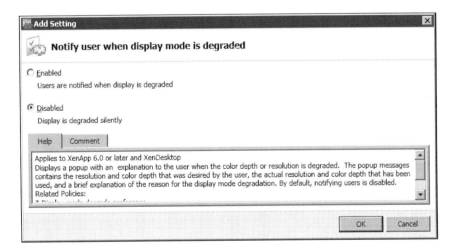

The **Queueing and tossing** setting is enabled by default. This setting discards queued images that are replaced by another image. This improves the response when graphics are sent to the client machine.

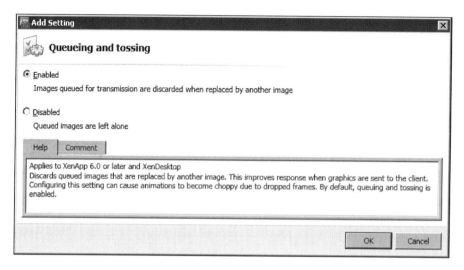

Using HDX MediaStream Multimedia Acceleration

William can improve the multimedia experience of the users by enabling the HDX MediaStream Multimedia Acceleration feature. This feature optimizes multimedia playback running in Internet Explorer, Windows Media Player, and RealOne Player, and offers significant performance improvements in these areas:

- CPU use: William can reduce the CPU use of XenApp servers by moving the multimedia content process to the client machine. Without HDX, when users play multimedia content in a session, XenApp decompresses and renders the multimedia file, increasing the server's CPU use.

- Network bandwidth: The multimedia content is compressed and delivered to client machines, reducing bandwidth consumption. Without HDX MediaStream Multimedia Acceleration, XenApp delivers the file uncompressed over the network, using more bandwidth.

HDX MediaStream Multimedia Acceleration optimizes playback of multimedia files that are encoded with codecs (programs used to encode or compress files) compatible with Microsoft's DirectShow and DirectX. A codec, compatible with the encoding format of the multimedia file, must be present on the client machine.

The following are the client machine's requirements to use HDX MediaStream Multimedia Acceleration:

- The codec required to decompress and play the multimedia file must be installed on the client machine. Audio and video are not synchronized, or only video or audio played are signs of missing or wrong codec.
- Citrix Online Plug-in must be installed on the client machine.
- The client must have enough memory and CPU available to process multimedia playback. A desktop computer is recommended because almost thin clients can't support multimedia playback.

> Playback of multimedia files protected with Digital Rights Management (DRM) is not supported by HDX MediaStream Multimedia Acceleration.

By default, Windows Server 2008 R2 doesn't install Windows Media Player. If William wants to play multimedia content on the XenApp farm, he needs to install the feature **Desktop Experience**.

To install **Desktop Experience**, he needs to open **Server Manager** (located in **Administrative Tools**), select **Features**, and choose **Desktop Experience**.

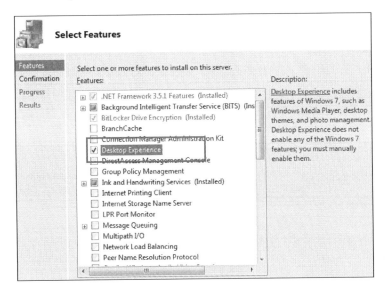

Using Citrix policies to configure HDX MediaStream

William can manage HDX MediaStream settings using the ICA Multimedia policy. This section contains policy settings for managing streaming audio and video in user sessions.

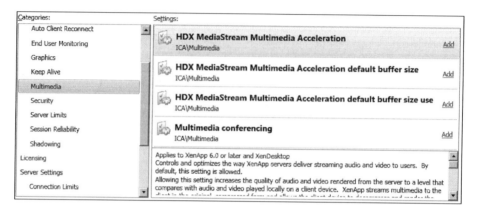

William can use the **HDX MediaStream Multimedia Acceleration** setting to enable (default option) or disable HDX MediaStream Multimedia Acceleration. This setting controls and optimizes the way XenApp servers deliver streaming audio and video to clients.

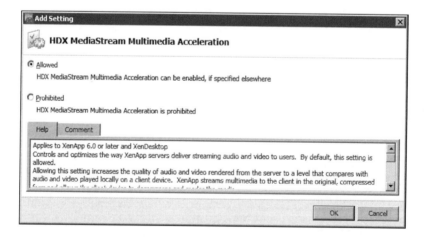

The **HDX MediaStream Multimedia Acceleration default buffer size** setting specifies a buffer size (from 1 to 10 seconds) used for multimedia acceleration. By default, the buffer size is **5 seconds**. William can increase this setting in high latency networks.

Chapter 9

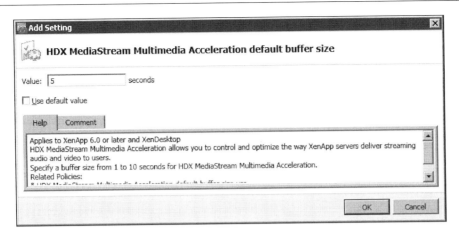

The **HDX MediaStream Multimedia Acceleration default buffer size use** setting enables (default option) or disables using the buffer size specified in the HDX MediaStreamMultimedia Acceleration default buffer size setting.

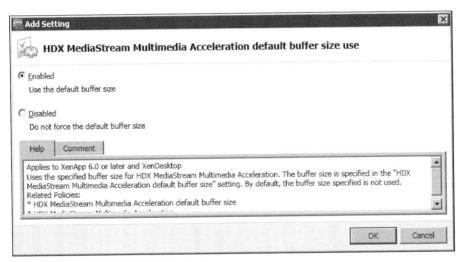

The **Multimedia conferencing** setting allows or prevents support for video conferencing applications. By default, video conferencing support is **Enabled**. William needs to set the HDX MediaStream Multimedia Acceleration setting to **Allowed** to enable multimedia conferencing.

Before using multimedia conferencing, William needs to check the following conditions:

- Drivers for the webcam used for multimedia conferencing are installed on the client machines. Drivers are not required on XenApp.
- The webcam is connected to the client machine before starting a video conferencing session.
- Office Communicator client software must be published on the XenApp server.
- The Office Communicator server must be present in the XenApp farm environment (but not installed on any XenApp server).

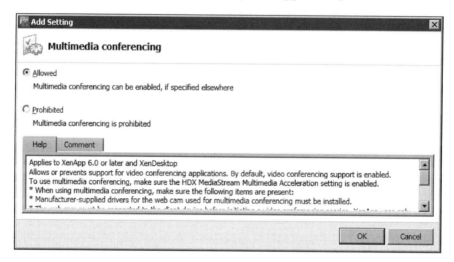

When users take part in audio or video conferences, they may hear an echo in their audio. Echoes usually occur when speakers and microphones are too close to each other. For that reason, Citrix recommends the use of headsets for audio and video conferences.

The success of echo cancellation is related to the distance between the microphone and the speakers. These devices must not be too close to each other or too far from each other.

Echo cancellation is available with only Citrix Online Plug-in 12.0 or later for Windows and Web Interface 5.3 or later.

Configuring echo cancellation

William needs to open the registry editor on the client machine and navigate to the following key:

- 32-bit machines: `HKEY_LOCAL_MACHINE\SOFTWARE\Citrix\ICA Client\Engine\Configuration\Advanced\Modules\ClientAudio\EchoCancellation`
- 64-bit machines: `HKEY_LOCAL_MACHINE\SOFTWARE\Wow6432Node\Citrix\ICA Client\Engine\Configuration\Advanced\Modules\ClientAudio\EchoCancellation`

William needs to set the **Value** data field to **TRUE** to enable or **FALSE** to disable echo cancellation.

Using HDX MediaStream for Flash to optimize Flash content

William can enable HDX MediaStream for Flash to move or redirect the processing of Adobe Flash content to the client machine rather than using network resources, reducing the XenApp server and network load, and improving the amount of sessions per server. HDX produces a high-definition experience when users are using Microsoft Internet Explorer to access Flash content, including animations, videos, and applications.

Playing Flash content on a XenApp server usually is slow because the Adobe Flash Player renders the content on the server, by default, in high-quality mode. This causes high bandwidth use.

Enabling HDX MediaStream at server side

HDX MediaStream server-side Flash functionality is enabled by default at the farm level, but if we enable HDX MediaStream client-side Flash, server-side rendering is overridden.

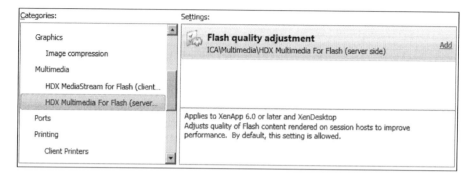

William can configure the **Flash quality adjustment** setting to adjust the quality of Flash content rendered on session hosts to improve performance. By default, Flash content is optimized for low bandwidth connections only.

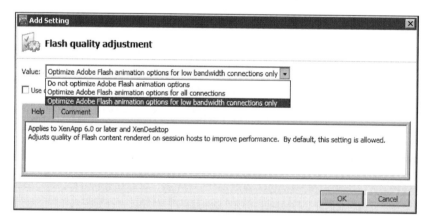

He can configure the **Flash quality adjustment** setting, located on ICA, HDX MediaStream for Flash (server side) policy with one of the following options:

- **Do not optimize Adobe Flash animation options:** This option plays all Flash content in high-quality mode.

- **Optimize Adobe Flash animation options for all connections**: This option reduces the CPU use and the amount of Flash data sent to users.

- **Optimize Adobe Flash animation options for low bandwidth connections only**: This option improves client responsiveness when Flash content is sent to users on connections with low bandwidth (below 150Kbps). When our users are located on a LAN where bandwidth is not limited, Flash content is played in high-quality mode.

System requirements for HDX MediaStream for Flash

The following is a list of the requirements:

- Windows-based client machine with Citrix Online Plug-in v11.2 or later installed.
- Low latency LAN-type network connection.
- Adobe Flash Player 10.x or later installed on the client machine and XenApp servers. If an earlier version of the Flash Player is installed, or the Flash Player is not installed on the client machine, the Flash content is rendered on the XenApp server.
- Microsoft Internet Explorer 7.0 or later with ActiveX capabilities should be available to the client machine.

Install/uninstall HDX MediaStream for Flash

Installing Citrix HDX MediaStream for Flash is a very straightforward process. We just need to run the file `CitrixHDXMediaStreamForFlash-ServerInstall-x64.msi`, located in the folder `HDX MediaStream for Flash\X64` on the root of the DVD.

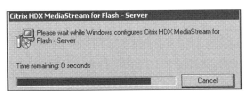

To remove HDX MediaStream for Flash from the XenApp server, we need to use the **Uninstall a program** option accessed in the Control Panel, under Programs and then select **Citrix HDX MediaStream for Flash - Server**.

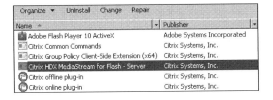

Configuring HDX MediaStream for Flash settings

After installation on the XenApp server, HDX MediaStream for Flash is enabled for client-side acceleration by default, and no further configuration is needed.

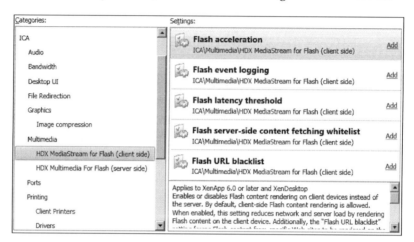

William can configure HDX MediaStream for Flash settings for handling Flash content in user sessions on the XenApp server using the **Policies** node of the Citrix Delivery Services Console. He can control the settings for the HDX MediaStream for Flash features through the following Citrix User policy settings, located on ICA, HDX MediaStream for Flash (client side) policy:

- **Flash acceleration**
- **Flash event logging**
- **Flash latency threshold**
- **Flash server-side content fetching whitelist**
- **Flash URL blacklist**

Setting up Flash Acceleration

William can use the **Flash acceleration** setting, located on ICA, HDX MediaStream for Flash policy, to enable (default option) or disable Flash content rendering on client machines instead of the XenApp server.

- When this setting is **Enabled**, it reduces network and server load by rendering Flash content on the client machine. Also, William can use Flash URL blacklist setting (described below) to force Flash content from specific websites to be rendered on the XenApp server.

- When this setting is **Disabled**, Flash content from all websites, regardless of the URL, is rendered on the XenApp server. William can configure the Flash server-side content fetching whitelist setting to allow only certain websites to render Flash content on the client machine.

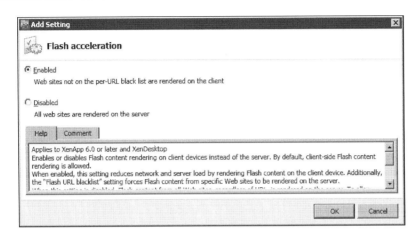

Enable server-side event logging

HDX MediaStream for Flash uses Windows event logging on the XenApp server to log events. William can review the Windows Event Log to check the usage or troubleshoot issues with HDX MediaStream for Flash.

The following are common to all events logged by HDX MediaStream for Flash:

- HDX MediaStream for Flash reports events to the Application log
- The Source value is Flash
- The Category value is None

An HDX MediaStream for a Flash-specific log appears in the **Applications and Services Logs** node on the servers running Windows Server 2008 R2.

The **Flash event logging** setting, located on ICA, HDX MediaStream for Flash policy allows (default setting), or prevents, Flash events to be recorded in the Windows application event log.

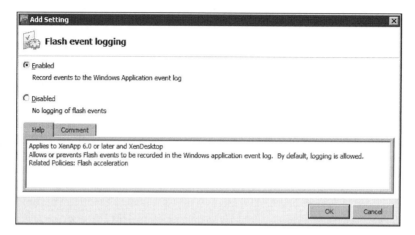

The **Flash latency threshold** setting, located on ICA, HDX MediaStream for Flash policy specifies a threshold between 0 and 5,000 milliseconds to determine where Adobe Flash content is rendered. By default, the threshold is **30 milliseconds**. During startup, HDX MediaStream for Flash analyzes the current latency between the server and client machine, and if the latency is under this value, HDX MediaStream for Flash is used to render Flash content on the client machine.

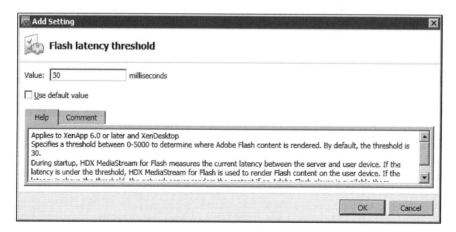

Chapter 9

The **Flash server-side content fetching whitelist** setting specifies websites whose Flash content is allowed to be rendered on the client machine and unlisted websites are rendered on the XenApp server.

William needs to set the **Flash acceleration** setting to **Enabled**, otherwise websites listed on the whitelist are ignored.

Note that listed URL strings do not need the `https://` prefix. These prefixes are ignored, if found. Wildcards (*) are valid at the beginning and end of a URL.

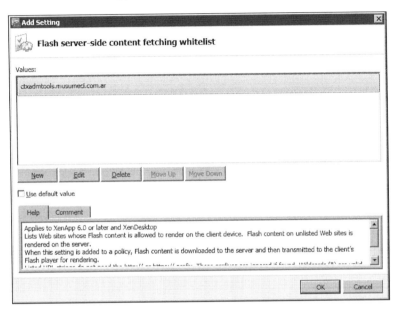

The **Flash URL Blacklist** setting is used by websites whose Flash content is rendered on the XenApp server. Flash content on unlisted websites is rendered on the client machine.

William needs to set the **Flash acceleration** setting to **Enabled**, otherwise websites listed in the URL blacklist are ignored.

Listed URL strings do not need the `https://` prefix. These prefixes are ignored, if found. Wildcards (*) are valid at the beginning and end of a URL.

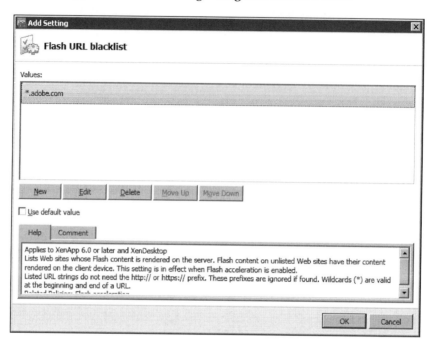

Configuring HDX MediaStream for Flash on the client machine

William can configure HDX MediaStream for Flash on client machines locally using the Group Policy Management Editor and apply it to a group of machines using the following procedure:

- Open the **Group Policy Management Editor** console
- Open **Computer Configuration | Policies | Administrative Templates**
- Right-click on **Administrative Templates** and select **Add/Remove Templates**
- Import and add the **HDX MediaStream for Flash - Client administrative template** (`HdxFlash-Client.adm`), available, depending on CPU platform:
    - 32-bit: `%Program Files%\Citrix\ICA Client\Configuration\language`
    - 64-bit: `%ProgramFiles(x86)%\Citrix\ICA Client\Configuration\language`

Chapter 9

Where language represents the two letter folder, for example: EN for English template, ES for Spanish template, and so on.

After installation of HDX MediaStream for Flash, William can see three policies:

- Enable HDX MediaStream for Flash on the user device
- Enable synchronization of the client-side HTTP cookies with the server side
- Enable server-side content fetching

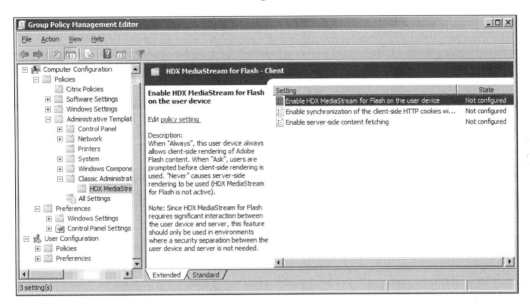

William can configure the HDX MediaStream for Flash on the client machine, by editing the **Enable HDX MediaStream for Flash on the user device** policy and selecting **Not Configured**, **Enabled**, or **Disabled**.

If he selected **Enabled**, from the Use HDX MediaStream for Flash list, he can select **Always**, **Ask**, or **Never**.

- **Always**: This option uses HDX MediaStream for Flash to play Flash content on the client machine
- **Ask:** Users will receive a dialog box the first time they access Flash content in each XenApp session

- **Never:** Uses HDX MediaStream for Flash and has Flash content play on the XenApp server

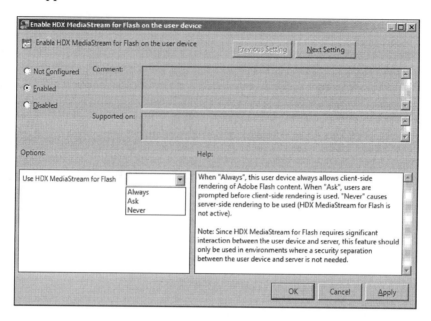

By default, HDX MediaStream for Flash downloads Adobe Flash content and plays the content on the client machine. Enabling server-side content fetching causes it to download the Flash content to the XenApp server and then sends it to the client machine. William can configure this setting using the **Enable server-side content fetching** policy.

 The Flash server-side content fetching whitelist setting on the XenApp server must be enabled and populated with target URLs for server-side content fetching to work.

Configuring audio using policies

William can configure audio through the **Policies** node of the Citrix Delivery Services Console. He can control the audio settings using two policies located under the ICA policy: **Audio** and **Bandwidth**.

Audio policy settings

William can use the **Audio** policy to enable client machines to send and receive audio in sessions.

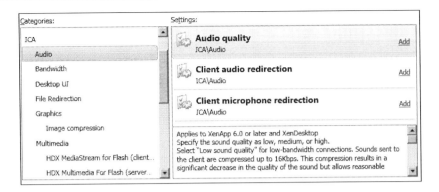

The **Audio quality** setting controls sound quality; available options are **Low**, **Medium**, and **High** (default option).

- **Low (low speed connections for low-bandwidth connections)**: Sounds delivered to the client machine are compressed up to 16 Kbps, causing a significant decrease in the quality of the sound, but provides a good performance for a low-bandwidth connection. With both audio playback and recording, the total bandwidth consumption is 22 Kbps at maximum.

- **Medium (optimized for speech for most LAN-based connections)**: Sounds delivered to the client machine are compressed up to 64 Kbps. With both audio playback and recording, the total bandwidth consumption is 33.6 Kbps at maximum.

- **High (high definition audio for LAN connections where sound quality is important)**: This setting can cause high CPU and bandwidth utilization because client machines play sound at its native rate. Sounds can use up to 1.3 MBps of bandwidth.

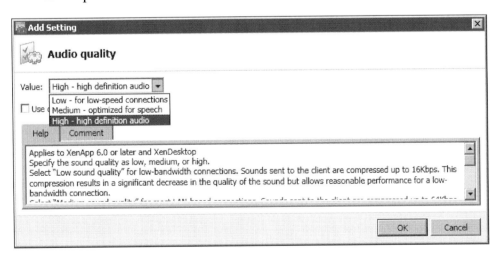

Multimedia Content on XenApp

The **Client audio redirection** setting allows (default option) or prevents applications hosted on the XenApp server to play sounds through a sound device installed on the client machine. Also, allows or prevents users from recording audio input. After enabling this setting, we can limit the bandwidth consumed by playing or recording audio, using the **Audio redirection bandwidth limit** or the **Audio redirection bandwidth limit percent** settings (explained later, under *Bandwidth policy settings*). When William limits the amount of bandwidth consumed by audio, using previously-mentioned policies, audio quality decreases but application performance increases.

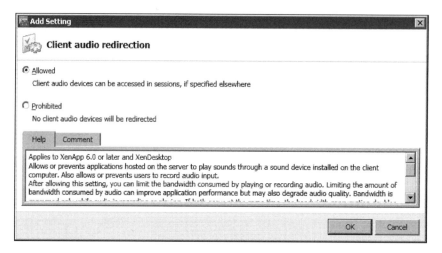

The **Client microphone redirection** policy allows (default option) or prohibits users from recording audio using input devices like a microphone on the client machine. The client machine needs either a built-in microphone or a device that can be plugged into the microphone jack.

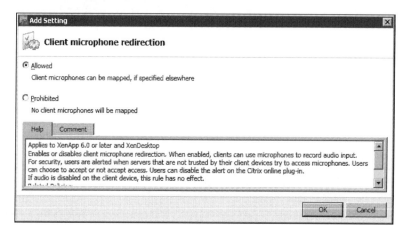

Bandwidth policy settings

The **Bandwidth** section contains policy settings that William can configure to reduce performance problems related to client session bandwidth use.

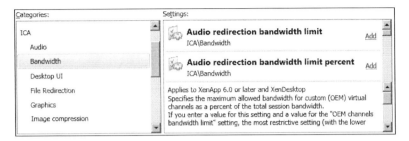

William can configure the **Audio redirection bandwidth limit** setting to set the maximum allowed bandwidth in Kbps for playing or recording audio in a user session. If William enters a value for both these settings and the **Audio redirection bandwidth limit percent** setting, the most restrictive setting (with the lower value) is applied.

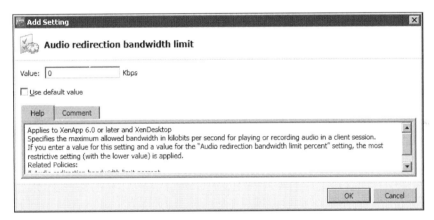

This **Audio redirection bandwidth limit percent** setting specifies the maximum allowed bandwidth limit for playing or recording audio as a percent of the total session bandwidth.

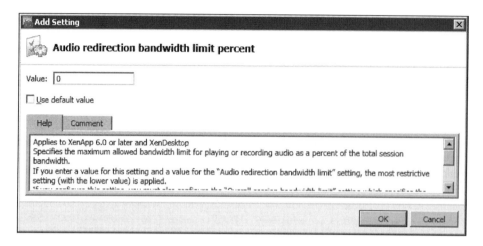

Configuring audio for user sessions

If we disable audio for a published application, then audio will not be available within the application under any condition. If we enable audio for an application, then we can use policy settings to set the conditions where audio is available within the application.

In the Citrix Delivery Services Console, William needs to select the published application for which he wants to enable or disable audio and select **Action | Application Properties**.

In the **Application Properties** dialog box, he clicks on **Advanced | Client options**. Then he selects or clears the **Enable legacy audio** checkbox.

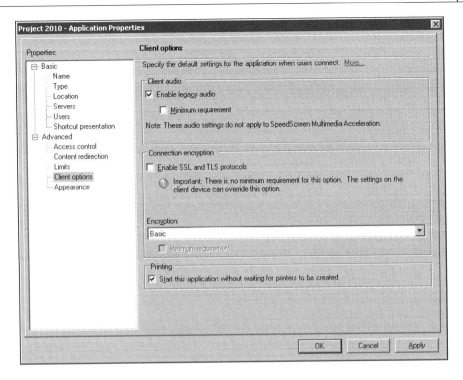

HDX Experience Monitor for XenApp

This tool released in August 2010 provides detailed information about the various HDX technologies, including performance and diagnostics information, for the following items:

- Graphics
- HDX MediaStream for Flash
- USB
- Smart card
- Printer redirection

The HDX Monitor is available at `http://support.citrix.com/article/CTX126491`.

After we completed the simple setup, we can run HDX Monitor. This tool runs only in an ICA session. If we try to run in the XenApp server console or in an RDP session, it exits after showing a warning message.

Multimedia Content on XenApp

The home page of HDX Monitor shows a summary of technologies installed and their statuses.

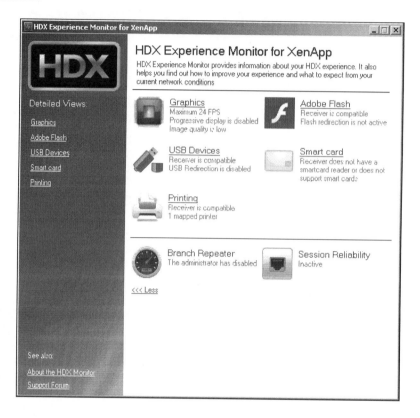

The **Graphics** page shows us setting and network performance, including:

- Maximum output bandwidth used (from Windows Performance Monitor)
- Using heavyweight JPEG (from Citrix policies)
- Using progressive display (from Citrix policies)
- Maximum FPS (frames per second) (from Windows registry)
- Image compression quality (from Citrix policies)

Also, a Graphics Network Performance is provided with information from Windows Performance Monitor.

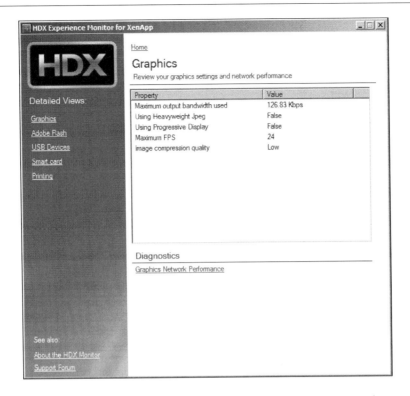

The **HDX MediaStream for Flash** page provides information about Flash settings, including:

- **HDX MediaStream for Flash** feature is enabled on the XenApp server
- Flash service is running or not
- Internet Explorer and Adobe Flash Player version installed
- Estimated Network latency and Network latency threshold
- Server-side content fetching configured
- Number of instances of Internet Explorer using HDX Flash redirection

Multimedia Content on XenApp

Also, extra options are available such as **Shake Active Flash Windows** which will shake all windows with Flash content, **Flash Network Graphics** shows a network chart based on Windows Performance Monitor and the **Flash System Verifier** option which provides us with a lot of information about IE, Flash, and Citrix configuration. If the server-side content fetching is enabled, there is an extra option called **Server Side content fetching URLs** to show the list of URLs allowed to run on the client machine.

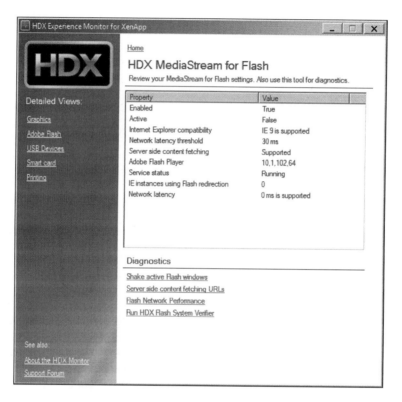

The **USB** page shows a list of USB-redirected devices and network information.

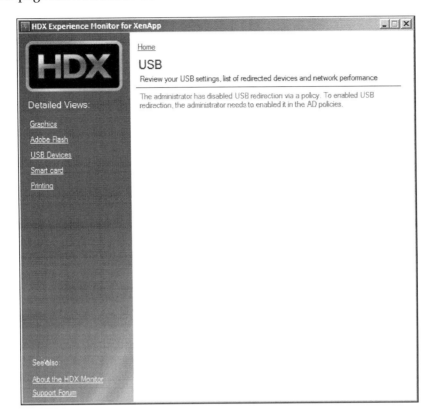

Starting with Windows Server 2008 R2 with SP1, the enable USB Redirection in the default domain group policy setting is disabled. To enable USB Redirection in the **Default Domain Group Policy** setting, we need to use the following steps:

- Open the Group Policy Management Console, right-click **Default Domain Policy**, and then click **Edit**
- Click on **Computer Configuration | Policies | Administrative Templates | Windows Components | Remote Desktop Services | Remote Desktop Connection Client | RemoteFX USB Device Redirection**
- Double-click the **Allow RDP redirection of other supported RemoteFX USB devices from this computer** policy
- Select the **Enabled** option, and then choose **Administrators and Users** in the **RemoteFX USB Redirection Access Rights** box

The **Smart Card** page shows smartcard information:

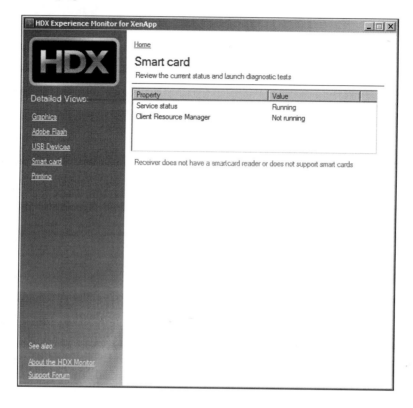

The **Printer Redirection** page provides a lot of information about the printing setting in our session, including:

- Printer redirection is enabled and active
- Maximum input and output bandwidth used
- Printer mapping is enabled at logon
- Universal print driver is installed

Also, a **Printing Network Performance** option is available at the end of the page. This option shows a network performance chart based on the information from Windows Performance Monitor.

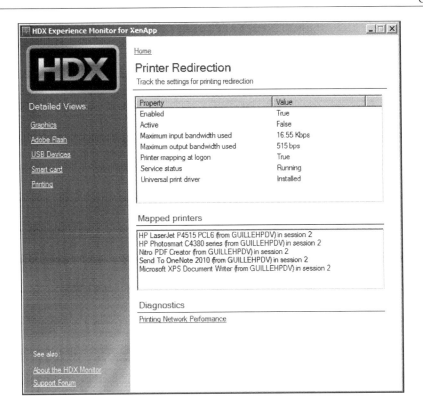

Summary

In this chapter, we learned about multimedia on XenApp farms. In particular, we talked about optimizing user sessions for XenApp using different Citrix HDX features like HDX MediaStream Multimedia Acceleration, HDX 3D Image Acceleration, HDX 3D Progressive Display, HDX MediaStream for Flash, and more. We learned in detail how to set up Configuring HDX MediaStream for Flash on the Server and configure different multimedia, audio, and video settings using Citrix policies.

In the next chapter, we will learn how to manage sessions.

10
Managing Sessions

In the last chapter, we learned how to improve the multimedia experience of users using Citrix HDX technologies. Citrix HDX enables better multimedia and peripheral support, provides improvements in audio quality, and enables us to deliver multimedia and conference applications on XenApp farms. In this chapter, we will discuss Citrix sessions and how to manage session environment, and in particular, we will talk about:

- Understanding sessions
- Managing and monitoring sessions using Citrix Delivery Services Console
- Viewing and shadowing sessions
- Maintaining session activity using Session Reliability, Auto Client Reconnect, and ICA Keep-Alive
- Customizing user environments in XenApp
- Limiting concurrent connections
- Optimizing user sessions for XenApp
- Redirection of local special folders in sessions

Understanding sessions

Each time we establish a session to a XenApp server, we use a protocol called Citrix ICA (Independent Computing Architecture), created by Citrix. ICA uses virtual channels to transmit keyboard strokes and mouse movements, printing, video and audio traffic, and more from the client machine to the XenApp server and the response back from the XenApp server to the client machine.

ICA uses port 1494 by default, but when we enable the **XenApp Session Reliability** feature in our XenApp farm, port 2598 is used instead of port 1494.

Managing Sessions

When a client machine initiates communication to the XenApp server with an ICA client and the user is successfully authenticated against the XenApp farm, a session is created on the server. The session is the core of the XenApp experience.

We can find a session in three main states: active, idle, and disconnected:

Let's use an example to understand these states. Our friend William Empire at Brick Unit Construction starts a session in XenApp. He opens Microsoft Word and starts working on a letter, now the session is considered to be in an active state.

The active state is maintained as long as there is a communication between the client machine and the XenApp server. If William left his machine for a few minutes to get a coffee, the session state changes to idle.

While a session is in an idle state, communication channels are kept open, but the communication between the client machine and the XenApp server is stopped.

When William returns and continues using the Word document, the session moves back to the active state.

When a session is open and idle on the server, the applications (and the environment) still use resources (and a license!) on the XenApp servers. To avoid wastage of the server's resources, it is best practice to establish an idle timeout value. If a session has remained idle longer than the allowed threshold, the session will change states.

Here we can decide to change idle sessions to a disconnected or terminated state. When the XenApp server retains an open session but the user is no longer actively connected this is a disconnected session. Also, disconnected sessions can happen for other reasons like network issues or loss of network connectivity.

Some applications that rely on virtual channels, such as media players, may act differently. For example, if we disconnect a user from a session running multimedia applications while playing audio, the audio stops playing because the audio virtual channel is no longer available. If the user then connects to the same XenApp server running the disconnected session, the disconnected session is reconnected.

Similar to an idle session, a disconnected session remains running on the XenApp server consuming resources, until the disconnected session is terminated, using the disconnected timeout value.

We can customize users' environments, including whether or not users can access mapped drives, printers available, bandwidth used for audio and redirect, or limited access to special folders. We can use policies or script to detect the location of users and apply different settings on the session.

If we keep multiple versions of Citrix farm running, we need to avoid our users logging in to different versions at the same time. This can cause a lot of unexpected results. Also, if we are using roaming profiles, we need to keep multiple versions of profiles and policies for Windows 2003 and Windows 2008. Profiles are different and can cause profile corruption (Number one administrator's nightmare!)

Citrix provides the ability of monitoring or troubleshooting users' sessions, using shadowing and keeping sessions running on high latency network connections.

Keeping the Citrix Plug-in (formerly known as Citrix Client) updated is very important. This ensures our users are able to use the latest features in their sessions and makes session troubleshooting a lot easier (one of the first questions from Citrix Technical Support is which version of Citrix Plug-in our users are running). The next chapter provides a lot of information about the Citrix Plug-in.

Monitoring XenApp sessions

In this chapter, we are going to help William Empire and his team to manage sessions on the Brick Unit Construction farm, using the **Citrix Delivery Services Console** and the following procedure:

He opens the console, and selects the XenApp server on which he wants to monitor sessions.

In the results pane, he clicks on the **Sessions** tab. This tab shows sessions running on the XenApp server.

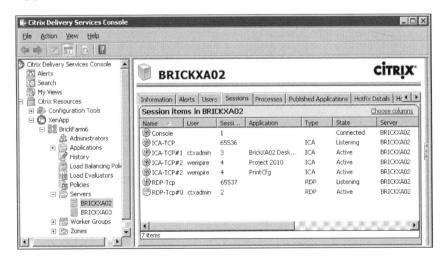

Managing Sessions

By default, the results pane shows the following information for all sessions (William can click the **Choose columns** link to specify which columns to display and the display order):

- **User**: Username that initiated the session. The username of anonymous connections begins with "Anon" followed by a session number.
- **Session ID**: This is a unique number that begins with 0 for the first connection to the console. Listener sessions are numbered from 65,537 and numbered backward sequentially.
- **Application Name**: Name of the published application running in the session.
- **Type**: Session type, ICA or RDP.
- **State**: Active, listen, idle, disconnected, or down.
- **Client Name**: Name of the client machine running the session.
- **Logon Time**: When the user started the session.
- **Idle Time**: Shows how long the session has been idle.
- **Server**: XenAppserver on which the application is running.

William can select a session and depending on the session, some tasks become available in the **Actions** pane; these can include **Reset**, **Log off**, **Disconnect**, and **Send Message**.

The lower portion of the results pane displays tabs containing additional information like **Information**, **Client Cache**, **Session Information**, **Client Modules**, and **Processes** tabs.

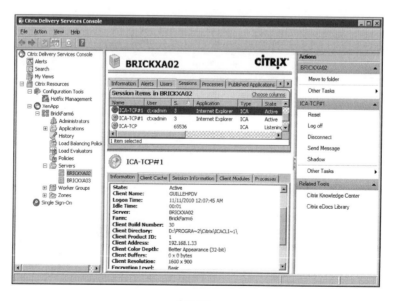

Managing XenApp sessions

Administrators and help desk specialists interact with sessions by resetting, disconnecting, logging off sessions, shadowing, or sending messages to users.

Detailed information to provide permissions to manage sessions on **Citrix Delivery Services Console** is provided in the section *Managing Citrix Administrators* in *Chapter 4, Using Management Tools*.

Disconnecting, resetting, and logging off sessions

William can log off users or reset a user's active or disconnected session.

Resetting a session terminates all processes that are running in that session. He can reset a session to remove the remaining processes in the case of a session error or sometimes because users left the sessions open. However, resetting a session can cause applications to close without saving data.

When he resets a disconnected session, the session state shows Down. When he refreshes the console or when the next automatic refresh occurs, the session no longer appears in the list of sessions.

He can select one or multiple sessions, right-click over it (or them), and select one of the options, like **Reset**, **Log off**, or **Disconnect** from the drop-down menu. He can also use the same menu to send messages or shadow user's sessions. Another option is using the **Action** panel, located at the right of the screen.

Note that we cannot send messages to disconnected sessions, so if there are such sessions selected, the option is not available.

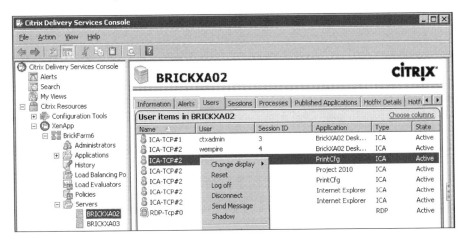

Managing Sessions

The process to reset, disconnect, or logoff a session is pretty similar.

- William selects the XenApp server to which the user is connected and in the results pane, he clicks the **Sessions** tab
- Then he selects the session he wants to reset/disconnect/logoff (he can select one or more sessions)
- In the **Actions** pane, he selects reset/disconnect/logoff

Resetting or ending user sessions using **Log off** can result in a loss of data, if users do not close their applications first.

When William clicks on the **Sessions** tab, he will find two special sessions (**ICA-TCP** and **RDP-TCP**) displaying Listening in the session state. If he resets a listener session, the server resets all sessions that use the protocol associated with the listener.

For example, if he resets the ICA listener session, he resets the ICA sessions of all users connected to the XenAppserver.

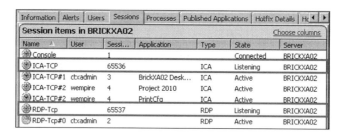

Terminating processes in a user session

Sometimes, a process inside a session is hung. This happens when the application calls another application, and the second one is not responding. William can kill the process for the second application without affecting the first one or reset the session, using the following process:

- William selects the XenApp server to which the user is connected and in the results pane, he selects the session from the **Users** tab
- In the lower portion of the results pane, he clicks the **Processes** tab and selects the process he wants to terminate
- Then in the **Actions** pane, he selects **Terminate**

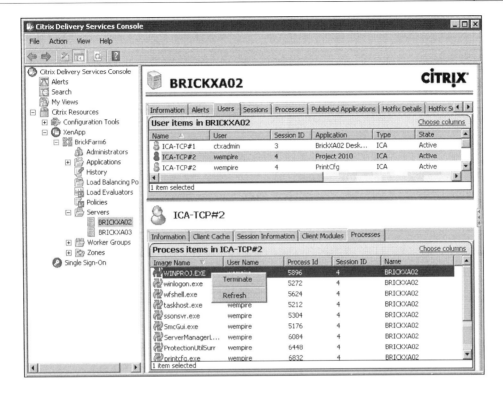

 Terminating a process may abruptly end a critical process and leave the XenApp server in an unusable state.

Sending messages to users

Sending a message to user sessions is a common practice to notify users of XenApp server reboots, to alert users about issues with published applications, or requesting a shadowing session to a user. The following is the procedure used by William:

- From the **Citrix Delivery Services Console**, he selects the XenAppserver to which the users are connected. Also, he can send a message to all user sessions in the farm, selecting a farm node instead of a XenApp server.
- In the results pane, he clicks the Users tab and then he selects one or more sessions.
- In the Actions pane, he chooses **Send Message**. The **Send Message** dialog box appears.

- He can edit the title of the message, if required, and enter the message text.

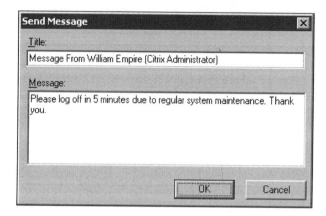

Viewing XenApp sessions

William can view another user's session running on a remote machine by using shadowing. When shadowing is enabled, he can monitor the session activity, and if configured, he can also use our keyboard and mouse to control the user's keyboard and mouse remotely in the shadowed session. Shadowing a session provides a powerful tool to assist and monitor users.

Shadowing is a very useful option for the Brick Unit Construction help desk staff who can use it to help users. They can view a user's screen or actions to troubleshoot problems and can demonstrate correct procedures. Also, it is possible to use shadowing for remote diagnosis and as a training tool.

They can shadow using both the Citrix Delivery Services Console and the Shadow Taskbar.

We enable shadowing on a XenApp server when we configure XenApp and select the default option, which allows shadowing on all connections on the server. If we do not leave the shadowing option enabled during configuration, we need to reinstall XenApp to get the shadowing functionality.

The following screenshot explains the installation and configuration process (more details about the setup process are available in *Chapter 3, Installing XenApp 6*).

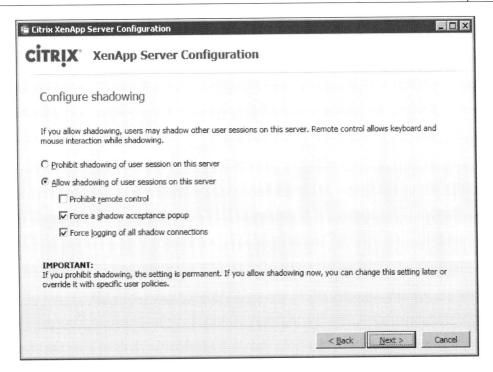

By default, the user is notified of the pending shadowing and asked to allow or deny shadowing.

> Our client machine and shadowing ICA session must support the video resolution of the user's ICA session (the shadowed session), if not, the operation fails. Also, we cannot shadow a system console from another session.

Viewing sessions using the Shadow Taskbar

William and his team can use the Shadow Taskbar to shadow multiple ICA sessions from a single location, including the XenAppserver console.

He can use the **Shadow** button to start shadowing one or more users. The Shadow Taskbar uses the client to launch an ICA session to monitor a user. A separate ICA session is started for each shadowed user.

William needs to enter his username and password to start an ICA session on the XenApp server running the Shadow Taskbar.

Managing Sessions

Please note:

- The administrator or help desk engineer uses a license to log on to the XenApp server and start shadowing a user.
- The Shadow Taskbar shows sessions on the server or domain we are logged in to. If we are using multiple domains, we need to logon with an account of the same domain users are connected to.
- Each shadow session consumes memory on the XenAppserver, so we need to avoid wastage of resources on XenApp servers and limit the number of simultaneous shadow sessions.
- Each shadowed session is represented by a task button on the Shadow Taskbar. We can use this button to switch quickly between the shadowing sessions we have opened.

Starting the Shadow Taskbar

From the Start menu, William needs to choose **All Programs | Citrix | Administration Tools | Shadow Taskbar**.

To configure shadowing options, he needs to right-click on an empty area of the Shadow Taskbar or press *Shift + F10*. He can switch between shadow sessions, using buttons in the Shadow Taskbar.

To close the Shadow Taskbar, he needs to right-click on an empty area of the Shadow Taskbar and select **Exit**.

Initiating shadowing

On the Shadow Taskbar, William clicks on the **Shadow** button. The **Shadow Session** dialog box appears.

The **Available users** list shows user sessions that can be selected for shadowing in the current domain. User sessions are organized by XenApp servers, published applications, and users.

The **Shadowed users** list shows user sessions selected for shadowing and existing shadow sessions; it also displays the username of currently shadowed users next to the shadow icon.

In the **Available users** list, he needs to select one or more users to shadow and then click on the **Add** button. At that moment, the selected users move to the **Shadowed users** list. Clicking on the **OK** button will cause shadowing initiated for all users in the **Shadowed users** list.

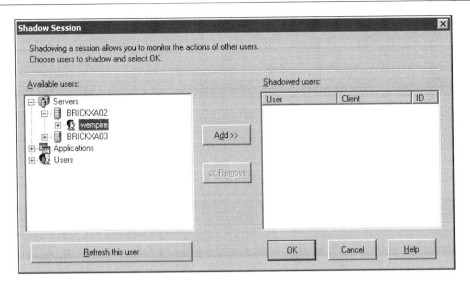

Ending a shadowing session

On the Shadow Taskbar, William needs to click on the **Shadow** button. The **Shadow Session** dialog box appears.

In the **Shadowed users** list he needs to select the users to stop shadowing and click **Remove**.

> We can end a shadow session by right-clicking the session's task button on the Shadow Taskbar and clicking **Stop Shadow**. We can end all shadow sessions by right-clicking the Shadow Taskbar and clicking **Stop All Shadowed Sessions**.

Enabling logging for shadowing

After configuring XenApp, William can enable shadow logging and configure shadow logging output to one of two locations on the XenApp server:

- **In a Central File:** This option records a limited number of logging events, like date and user being shadowed. When he configures shadow logging through the Shadow Taskbar, logged events are not recorded in the Windows Event log and they go to the file specified.

- **Windows Event Log:** This option logs events in the Application log of the Windows Event log. These include user shadowing requests, such as when users stop shadowing, failure to launch shadowing, and access to shadowing denied.

Managing Sessions

Logging events in a central file makes the management of a log easy. Because just shadowing events go in to this file, they are easy to review.

William can use the following process to configure shadow logging in a central file:

- He clicks on an empty area of the Shadow Taskbar and presses *Shift + F10*
- Then he clicks **Logging Options**
- He enables the **Enable Logging** checkbox and specifies a log file path
- Finally, he clicks on the **Clear Log** button to empty the current log file

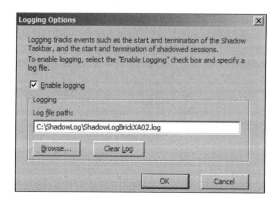

Also, William can enable shadow logging in the Windows Event log by configuring the Citrix User policy **Log shadow attempts** setting to **Enabled**:

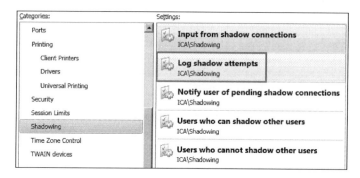

Enabling user-to-user shadowing

William can create a user policy to enable user-to-user shadowing, which allows users to shadow other users without requiring them to be members of the Citrix administrator group. With user-to-user shadowing, multiple users from different locations can view present and training sessions, allowing one-to-many, many-to-one, and many-to-many online collaborations.

Also, William can enable Help Desk personnel to shadow users' sessions or allow Brick Unit Project Managers and Architects to hold online meetings to review the current project status.

William enables user-to-user shadowing by creating policies that define users who can and cannot shadow, then he assigns these policies to the users to be shadowed.

Creating a shadowing policy

Creating a policy requires us to go through the following steps:

- Create a user policy that lists the users who can shadow other users' sessions
- Assign the policy to the users to be shadowed
- Publish the Citrix Shadow Taskbar and assign it to the users who will shadow

 The Shadow Taskbar cannot function in seamless mode.

Now we are going to help William to enable Brick Unit Help Desk staff shadow the Project Manager group, using the following procedure:

1. William creates a new policy named **Project Manager Shadowing**.

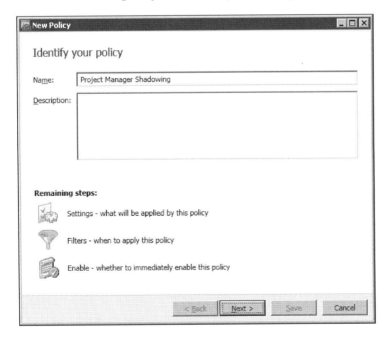

Managing Sessions

2. He adds the **Shadowing** Citrix computer policy setting and sets it to **Allowed**.

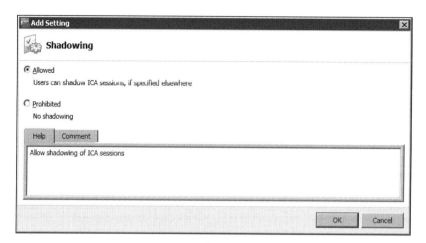

3. Because the Project Managers may work with sensitive data, William wants to add the **Notify user of pending shadow connections** Citrix User policy setting and sets it to **Enabled**. Also, because the Project Managers group does not want other users to take control of their mouse and keyboard, he adds the **Input from shadow connections** Citrix User policy setting and sets it to **Prohibited**.

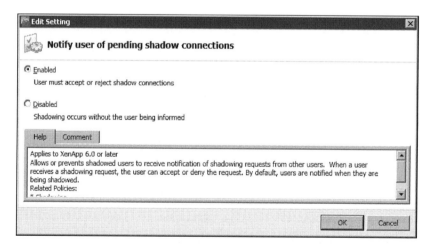

4. Now he needs to add users to the **Users who can shadow other users** setting and select the users who can shadow the Project Managers group: Help Desk staff and Domain Admins in Brick Unit.

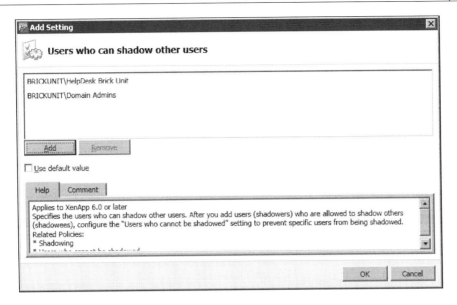

5. He adds the user filter and selects the users who can receive shadowing requests. Here William adds the Project Managers group.

6. Finally, he finishes the wizard, enabling and saving the policy.

Maintaining session activity

Users can lose network connectivity for various reasons, including unreliable networks, and change of wireless network for mobile users. We can increase the reliability of sessions and reduce the amount of inconvenience, downtime, and loss of productivity using the following features:

- Session Reliability
- Auto Client Reconnect
- ICA Keep-Alive

Configuring Session Reliability

When we enable Session Reliability, any minor disconnection from the network keeps the session active, allowing users to remain connected but with the screen frozen and the cursor changed to the hourglass; it will continue to queue keyboard input until network connectivity resumes or the timeout is reached.

This feature was originally designed to help users connected to their application sessions on low bandwidth conditions, like remote locations, but now this feature is especially useful for mobile users with wireless connections.

For example, one Brick Unit project manager with a wireless connection is taking notes in a construction site and momentarily loses connectivity. Usually, the session is disconnected and disappears from the user's screen, and the user has to reconnect to the disconnected session.

Session Reliability reconnects users without re-authentication prompts.

 We can use Session Reliability with Secure Sockets Layer (SSL).

By default, Session Reliability is enabled through policy settings. William can set the port on which XenApp listens for session reliability traffic and the amount of time Session Reliability keeps an interrupted session connected using Citrix policies.

The Citrix Computer policy **Session reliability connections** setting allows or prevents session reliability.

The **Session reliability connections** policy setting lets us allow or prohibit the Session Reliability feature.

Incoming session reliability connections use the default port 2598, unless we change the port number using the **Session Reliability Port Number** policy setting.

The **Session reliability timeout** setting has a default of 180 seconds, or 3 minutes. This is the time allowed before the session is disconnected. If we do not want users to be able to reconnect to the interrupted sessions without having to re-authenticate, we can use the **Auto client reconnect** feature.

If we use both Session Reliability and Auto Client Reconnect, the two features work in sequence.

Session Reliability closes, or disconnects, the user session after the amount of time we specify in the Citrix Computer policy **Session reliability timeout** setting. After that, the **Auto client reconnect** policy setting takes effect, attempting to reconnect the user to the disconnected session.

Configuring automatic client reconnection

The **Auto client reconnect** feature allows Citrix Plug-ins for Windows and Java to detect broken connections and automatically reconnects users to disconnected sessions. When the plugin client machine detects an unintentional disconnection of a session, it tries to reconnect the user to the session until a successful reconnection, or the user cancels the reconnection attempts.

William can configure **Auto client reconnect** with the following Citrix computer policy settings:

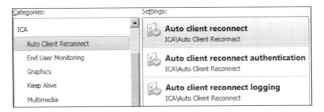

- **Auto client reconnect:** Enables or disables automatic reconnection by the same client after a connection has been interrupted
- **Auto client reconnect authentication:** Enables or disables the requirement for user authentication upon automatic reconnection
- **Auto client reconnect logging:** Enables or disables (default setting) logging of reconnection events in the Windows event log.

The **Auto client reconnect** incorporates an authentication mechanism based on encrypted user credentials. When a user initially logs on to a server farm, XenApp encrypts and stores the user credentials in memory, and creates and sends a cookie containing the encryption key to the plugin. The plugin submits the key to the XenApp server for reconnection. The server decrypts the credentials and submits them to Windows logon for authentication. When cookies expire, users must re-authenticate to reconnect to sessions.

Cookies are not used if we enable the **Auto client reconnection authentication** setting. Instead, XenApp displays a dialog box to the users requesting credentials when the plugin attempts to reconnect automatically.

We can disable **Auto client reconnect** on the Citrix Plug-in for Windows by using the `icaclient.adm` file. Detailed instructions to import the `icaclient.adm` file are available at http://xenapp6.musumeci.com.ar.

After we import the `icaclient.adm` file, we can modify the following setting:

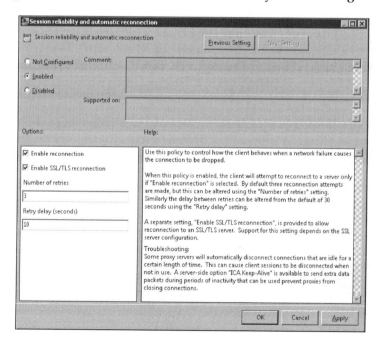

By default, **Auto client reconnect** is enabled through policy settings on the farm level.

By default, the ICA TCP connection on a XenApp server is set to disconnect sessions with broken or timed out connections. Disconnected sessions remain intact in system memory and are available for reconnection by the plugin. We need to keep in mind all disconnected sessions still running and use resources.

But, if a XenApp server's ICA TCP connection is configured to reset sessions with a broken communication link, automatic reconnection does not occur. **Auto client reconnect** works only if the XenApp server disconnects sessions when there is a broken or timed out connection.

The connection can be configured to reset, or log off, sessions with broken or timed out connections. When a session is reset, attempting to reconnect initiates a new session; thus, rather than restoring a user to the same place in the application in use, the application is restarted.

If XenAppserver is configured to reset sessions, **Auto client reconnect** creates a new session.

Configuring ICA keep-alive

Enabling the **ICA keep alive** feature prevents broken connections from being disconnected. When we enable it, if XenApp notices no activity (for example, no clock change, no mouse movement, no screen updates), this feature prevents Remote Desktop Services from disconnecting that session. XenApp sends keep-alive packets every few seconds to detect if the session is active. If the session is no longer active, XenApp marks the session as disconnected.

The **ICA keep alive** feature does not work if we are using Session Reliability. Session Reliability has its own mechanisms to handle this issue. We need to configure only ICA keep-alive for connections that do not use Session Reliability.

ICA keep alive settings override keep-alive settings that are configured in Microsoft Windows Group Policy.

Configure the following Citrix Computer policy settings:

- **ICA keep alive timeout:** Specifies the interval (1 to 3,600 seconds) used to send ICA keep-alive messages. In environments where broken connections are infrequent, enabling keep-alive is not required. The 60-second default interval causes ICA keep-alive packets to be sent to client machines every 60 seconds. If a client device does not respond in 60 seconds, the status of the ICA sessions changes to disconnected.
- **ICA keep alives:** Enables or disables sending ICA keep-alive messages periodically.

 Servers running the Citrix Access Gateway intercept packets being sent from XenApp servers to client machines. We need to set keep-alive values on the Access Gateway servers to match ICA keep-alive values on XenApp servers. This allows ICA sessions to be changed from active to disconnected.

Customizing user environments in XenApp

XenApp provides different ways to control what users experience in their session environments. We can customize user environments including suppressing or hiding login progress bars, allowing or restricting users from accessing their local devices, port, multimedia content (audio, video), or applications, and more.

We can also customize the user's experience by choosing whether we want published applications and desktops to appear in a window within a Remote Desktop window or "seamlessly". In seamless window mode, published applications and desktops appear in separate resizable windows, which make the application seem to be installed locally.

Controlling the appearance of user logons

When users connect to a XenApp server, they can see all connection and logon status information in a sequence of screens, from the time they double-click a published application icon on the client machine, through the authentication process, to the moment the published application launches in the session.

XenApp achieves this logon look-and-feel by suppressing the status screens generated by a server's Windows operating system when a user connects. To do this, XenApp setup enables the following Windows local group policies on the XenApp server on which we install the product:

- **Administrative Templates | System | Remove Boot | Shutdown | Logon | Logoff status messages**
- **Administrative Templates | System | Verbose versus normal status messages**

Active Directory group policies take precedence over equivalent local group policies on servers. So, if we enable these specific policies in our domain, this will override the Citrix local policies. We can disable these local GPO for troubleshooting but it is recommended to keep them enabled on production environments.

Controlling access to devices and ports

The Citrix Plug-in provides mapping disks or devices on the client machine so users can access their own devices within sessions. Client device mapping provides:

- Access to local drives and ports
- Cut-and-paste data between the client machine and the session
- Multimedia playback inside the session

During logon, the Citrix Plug-in lists available client drives and COM ports and sends the list to the XenApp server. By default, client drives appear as network resources, so the drives appear to be directly connected to the server. The client's drives are displayed with descriptive names so they are easy to locate among other network resources.

In general, XenApp displays client drive letters as they appear on the client machine; for example, the user device's hard disk drive appears as `C:` on `ClientName`, where `ClientName` is the name of the client machine. This allows the user to access client drive letters in the same way locally and within sessions.

Managing Sessions

These drives are used by Windows Explorer and other published applications like a network drive.

The following example shows the administrator using Windows Explorer running on a XenApp session. The hard drive C: is the drive in the XenApp server and CD/DVD and other disks are local disks on the client machine (note the label Local Disk). We can use GPO to hide the server's hard drive from users and avoid confusion.

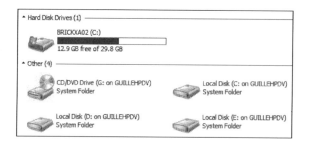

Mapping drives

We can use Citrix policies to allow or prevent device mapping. We can use the **File Redirection** user policy to enable or disable mapping to client floppy disk drives, hard drives, CD/DVD drives, or remote drives.

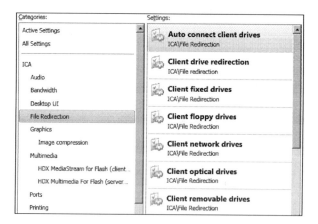

Redirecting COM ports and audio

Client COM port redirection allows a remote application running on the XenApp server to access devices attached to COM ports on the client machine. Both COM port and audio redirection are configured with the **Ports** user policy settings.

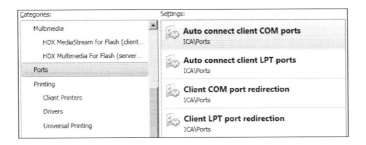

Limiting concurrent connections

William Empire can limit the number of connections to reduce the use of XenApp server resources, like CPU and memory, and increase the amount of concurrent users per server.

William can set a limit of two concurrent connections for users. If a user tries to establish more than two connections, a message tells the user that a new connection is not allowed. This is a common practice to reduce resource and licenses use.

We can also enable session sharing to limit the number of connections on a Citrix farm. Session sharing is a mode in which more than one published application runs on a single connection.

Session sharing occurs when a user has an open session and launches another application that is published on the same XenApp server; the result is that the two applications run in the same session. For session sharing to occur, both applications must be hosted on the same XenApp server. Session sharing is configured by default when we specify that applications appear in seamless window mode. If a user runs multiple applications with session sharing, the session counts as one connection.

Limit the number of sessions per server

When this setting is used, users can start sessions until the limit has been reached.

William can configure the **Server Settings | Connection Limits** computer policy using following settings:

- **Limit user sessions:** Sets the maximum number of concurrent connections, in the range 0 to 8192 per user. A value of 0 indicates no connections allowed.

- **Limits on administrator sessions**: Enables or disables connection limit enforcement for Citrix administrators. This setting affects their ability to shadow other users. Local administrators are exempted from the limit so they can establish as many connections as necessary.

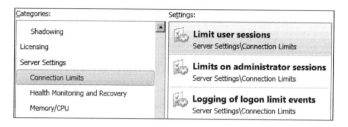

Limiting application instances

By default, XenApp does not limit the number of instances of a published application that can run at one time in a farm. By default, a user can launch more than one instance of a published application at the same time.

William can specify the maximum number of instances that a published application can run at one time or concurrently in the Citrix farm.

Brick Unit Construction bought 25 licenses of Adobe Acrobat Professional; they can publish the Acrobat application and set a limit of 25 concurrent instances in the farm. Once 25 concurrent users are running the application, no more users can launch it.

Another connection control option lets us prevent any user from running multiple instances of a particular published application. With some applications, running more than one instance in a single user context can cause errors.

Brick Unit Construction notices some issues with Outlook. Some are related with Outlook profiles being corrupted. They don't want to rebuild profiles every time users open Outlook to improve login times. Sometimes, users using a .PST file receive error messages. Help Desk staff found that the same issues occur when users run multiple copies of Outlook in different sessions and XenApp servers. Brick Unit Construction decided to limit users to run only one session of Outlook at the same time. This setting will reduce Help Desk calls (and wastage of resources in the Citrix farm).

 Connection control options apply to published applications and published desktops only and do not affect published content, such as documents and media files that execute on the client machine.

To set a limit for a published application or desktop, William needs to use the following procedure:

1. William needs to open the Citrix Delivery Services Console, select the farm, and then select **Applications**.
2. He needs to select the application or desktop he wants to modify. In the **Action** menu, he chooses **Application properties**.
3. In the **Properties** tree, he selects **Limits**, then he chooses one or both of the following options:
   - **Limit instances allowed to run in server farm**: He needs to enter the maximum number of instances that can run at one time in the server farm
   - **Allow only one instance of application for each user**: Prevents any user from running more than one instance of this application at the same time

Here, William limits concurrent sessions of Microsoft Project 2010 to 35 users. When a user tries to launch the application when 35 instances are running, XenApp denies the connection request and records the time and the name of the published application in the System log (if logging is enabled). See below to enable logging.

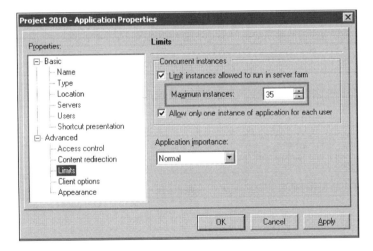

Logging connection denial events

William can enable event logging in the Windows Event Viewer System log each time a XenApp server denies a user connection because of a connection control limit. Each XenApp server records the data in its own System log. By default, this type of event logging is disabled.

William can configure XenApp to log when limits are reached (and connections are denied) for the following:

- Maximum connections per user
- Application instance limits
- Application instances per user

He needs to configure the **Logging of logon limit events** on the **Server Settings | Connection Limits** computer policy setting to enable or disable logging of connection denial events.

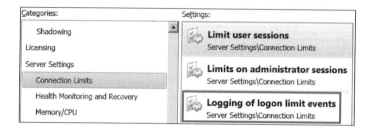

Sharing sessions and connections

Depending on the Citrix Plug-in, when a user opens an application, it can either appear in a seamless or non-seamless window. These window modes are available for most plugins, including the Web Interface and Citrix Online Plug-in.

- **Non-seamless window Mode:** Published applications and desktops are contained within an ICA session window. Desktops are typically published in non-seamless window mode. Publishing Desktop is the preferred option for thin clients or kiosks.

- **Seamless window Mode:** Published applications and desktops are not contained within an ICA session window. Each published application and desktop appears in its own resizable window, and looks like the application is installed on the client machine. Users can switch between published applications and the local desktop. This is the preferred mode to publish individual applications. Publishing individual applications is a preferred option for desktop computers or laptops.

When a user launches a published application, the Citrix Plug-in establishes a connection to a XenApp server and initiates a session. If session sharing is not configured, a new session is opened on the XenApp server each time a user opens an application.

If we want to share sessions, we need to ensure all applications are published with the same configuration, like encryption; unexpected results may occur when applications are configured for different requirements.

Session sharing always takes precedence over load balancing. Enabling session sharing can cause overload of XenApp servers, if our users have one application running on a server, and they launch a second application that is published on the same XenApp server and the server is at capacity, XenApp still opens the second application on that server.

William needs to use a policy to configure the client handling of remote applications. When this policy is enabled, it uses the list in the Application box to determine which published applications can be directly launched by the client.

This setting is not available by default. William needs to import the `icaclient.adm` and then access the policy located on **Citrix Components | Citrix Online Plugin | User experience | Remote applications**.

The session sharing feature can be enabled or disabled using the **Session sharing** checkbox.

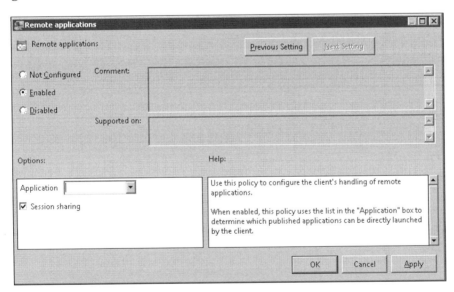

Preventing user connections during farm maintenance

William wants to prevent logons to a XenApp server when he performs maintenance or configuration tasks or installing applications.

By default, logons are enabled when we install XenApp and users can launch an unlimited number of sessions and instances of published applications. He can prevent users from connecting to a server in the farm by disabling logons, using the following procedure:

- He opens the **Citrix Delivery Services Console** and selects the XenApp server
- In the **Actions** pane, he selects **Other Tasks | Disable logon**

To re-enable disabled logons, he selects **Other Tasks | Enable logon**.

Optimizing user sessions for XenApp

XenApp includes various features to improve user experience by improving keyboard and mouse responsiveness.

SpeedScreen Latency Reduction is a collective term used to describe features such as Local Text Echo and Mouse Click Feedback that help enhance user experience on a slow network.

Mouse click feedback

On high latency connections, users often click the mouse multiple times because there is no visual feedback that a mouse click resulted in an action. Mouse click feedback, which is enabled by default, changes the appearance of the pointer from idle to busy after the user clicks a link, indicating that the system is processing the user's request.

William can enable and disable mouse click feedback at the server level.

He needs to use **SpeedScreen Latency Reduction Manager**, located at **Start | All Programs | Citrix | Administration Tools**.

Then from the **Application** menu, he selects **Server Properties** to enable or disable mouse click feedback.

Chapter 10

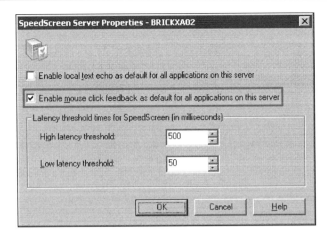

Local text echo

On high latency connections, our users frequently experience significant delays between typing text and when it is displayed (echoed) on the screen. When a user types text, the keystrokes are sent to the XenApp server, which renders the fonts and returns the updated screen to the client machine.

By default, local text echo is disabled. William can enable and disable this feature both at the XenApp server and application level. Also, he can configure local text echo settings for individual input fields within an application.

He needs to open **SpeedScreen Latency Reduction Manager**, located at
Start | All Programs | Citrix | Administration Tools.

Then from the **Application** menu, select **Server Properties** to enable or disable local text echo.

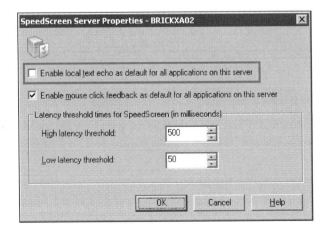

[317]

[Only Windows applications that use the standard Windows APIs for displaying text support local text echo.]

Configuring SpeedScreen Latency Reduction

William can use the SpeedScreen Latency Reduction Manager to configure SpeedScreen Latency Reduction settings for a XenApp server, for single or multiple instances of an application, as well as for individual input fields within an application. He can also use it as a troubleshooting tool to improve SpeedScreen Latency Reduction behavior for applications.

To launch the tool, William needs to select **SpeedScreen Latency Reduction Manager**, located at **Start | All Programs | Citrix | Administration Tools**.

William can configure common SpeedScreen Latency Reduction settings for all applications on a XenApp server or select custom settings for individual applications.

He can use the **Add New Application** wizard, included with the SpeedScreen Latency Reduction Manager, to adjust latency reduction functionality for a published application showing abnormal behavior after it is configured to use SpeedScreen Latency Reduction.

To optimize usability of the application, he needs to use the following procedure to adjust, turn on, or turn off SpeedScreen Latency Reduction for the application:

- William needs to open the application. The application must be running before he can use this wizard to modify existing settings.
- He launches **SpeedScreen Latency Reduction Manager** from **Start | All Programs | Citrix | Administration Tools**.
- From the **Applications** menu, he selects **New** to start the wizard.
- He uses the **Define the Application** screen to select an application instance on the XenApp server. To specify the application, he clicks the icon at the bottom of the page and drags the pointer onto the window of an application or uses the **Browse** button and navigates to the application.
- He can disable local text echo by selecting or clearing the **Enable local text echo for this application** checkbox.
- Finally, he chooses to apply settings to all instances of the application on the XenApp server or just the instance selected.

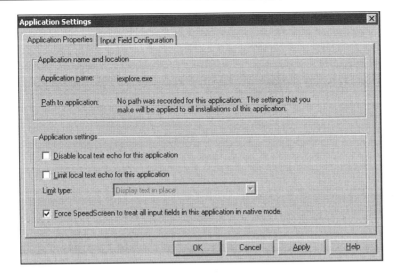

 When we configure the SpeedScreen Latency Reduction Manager on a particular XenApp server, settings are saved in the `ss3config` folder in the Citrix installation directory of that server. We can replicate settings to other servers by copying this folder and its contents to the same location on the other servers.

Redirection of Local Special Folders in sessions

William can enable Special Folder Redirection to simplify the way Brick Unit's users save files to their special folders locally. Special folders are Windows folders such as Documents, Computer, and the Desktop.

When Special Folder Redirection is disabled, the Documents and Desktop icons that appear in a session point to the user's Documents and Desktop folders on the XenApp server.

When Special Folder Redirection redirects is enabled, and users open or save a file from special folders, they are accessing the special folder on a file server (the preferred option) instead of their local computers.

There are two scenarios where enable Special Folders Redirection to client machine is not recommended: when users connected to the same session from multiples client machines simultaneously or when remote users accessing through Access Gateway or VPN.

For Special Folder Redirection to work, the user must log off from the session on the first client machine and start a new session on the second client machine, or we need to use roaming profiles or set a home folder for that user in the User Properties in the Active Directory. These are the preferred options for most of Citrix deployments.

Currently, for seamless and published desktops, Special Folder Redirection to the client machine works only for the `Documents` folder.

For seamless applications, Special Folder Redirection only works for the `Desktop` and `Documents` folders. Citrix does not recommend using Special Folder Redirection with published Windows Explorer.

If we need to provide Special Folder Redirection for all folders like `Favorites` or `Music`, for example, we need to use roaming profiles and network file share.

Using roaming profiles is a best practice because it allows users to have a consistent experience, they can see and save files and settings all the time, but also reduce the storage wastage on local XenApp hard drives.

Special Folder Redirection support is enabled by default, but we must configure this feature for users through the Citrix Online Plug-in and web interface. We can either enable Special Folder Redirection for all users or configure that users must enable the feature themselves in their client settings.

Also, we can allow or prevent specific users from having redirected special folders with the **Special folders Redirection** user policy setting located **ICA | File Redirection**.

We can create a policy to use the Special Folder Redirection policy setting. Then we can apply filters to provide or disable access to the users accessing local special folders.

Enable Special Folder Redirection in the web interface

The following is the procedure used by William to enable Special Folder Redirection. This requires a XenApp website. Detailed instructions to create and configure a XenApp website are available in *Chapter 3, Installing XenApp 6*.

1. He opens the **Citrix Delivery Services Console** and selects **Citrix Resources**, **Configuration Tools**, **Web Interface**, and the XenApp website name.
2. From the **Action** menu, he chooses **Manage Session Preferences**.
3. In the **Managing Session Preferences** page, he selects **Remote Connection**, **Local Resources**.

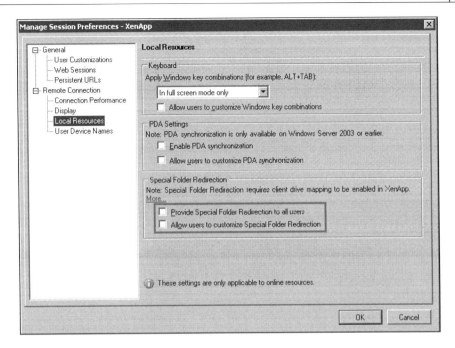

Now he can choose:

- **Provide Special Folder Redirection to all users**: Enables Special Folder Redirection to all users
- **Allow users to customize Special Folder Redirection**: Disables Special Folder Redirection, by default, but lets users turn it on in their session options

Enable Special Folder Redirection for the Citrix Online Plug-in

The following procedure is used by William to enable Special Folder Redirection for the Citrix Online Plug-in. This procedure requires a XenApp Services site. Detailed instructions to create and configure a XenApp website are available in *Chapter 3, Installing XenApp 6*.

1. He opens the **Citrix Delivery Services Console** and selects **Citrix Resources**, **Configuration Tools**, **Web Interface**, and the XenApp services site name.
2. From the **Action** menu, he chooses **Change session options**.

3. In the **Change Session Options** page, he selects **Remote Connection, Local Resources**.

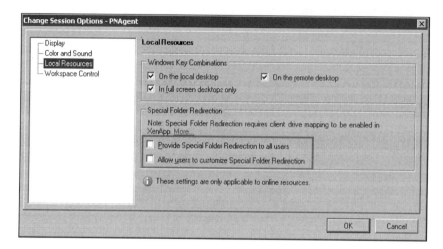

Now he can choose:

- **Provide Special Folder Redirection to all users**: Enables Special Folder Redirection by default
- **Allow users to customize Special Folder Redirection:** Disables Special Folder Redirection, by default, but lets users turn it on in their session options

Using Group Policy to redirect Special Folders

We can use GPO (Group Policies) and Windows Roaming Profiles to redirect Citrix or Terminal Server profiles to a network file server. This is a common scenario in almost all Citrix implementations. There are plenty of options to redirect profiles, including several profile tools, scripts, or GPOs.

Now let's take a look at how Brick Unit Construction will use GPO to redirect profiles.

William Empire decided to use Special Folder redirection to a file server. Implementing file redirection will provide a lot of benefits to the company, including centralization of all documents in one place, simplification of backup of data, and so on.

1. The first step is creating a GPO in the OU where the Citrix servers are located, using the Group Policy Management Console.

2. He opens the console and then he expands **User Configuration | Policies | Windows Settings | and Folder Redirection**.

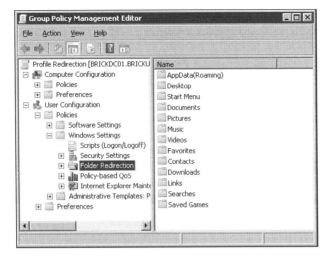

3. He right-clicks the special folder that he wants to redirect (for example, **My Documents** or **Desktop**) and then clicks **Properties**.

4. He clicks the **Target** tab, and then in the Settings box, selects **Basic - Redirect everyone's folder to the same location**.

5. Under **Target folder location**, he selects **Create a folder for each user under the root path**.

6. In the **Root Path** box, he enters the UNC (Universal Naming Convention) path of the file server, here it is **\\brickfs01\Users**, and then he clicks **OK**.

7. In the **Properties** dialog box for the special folder, he clicks **OK** to finish the process.

Summary

In this chapter, we learned about Managing Sessions on XenApp farms. In particular, we talked about:

- Understanding XenApp sessions
- Managing and monitoring sessions using Citrix Delivery Services Console, including disconnecting, resetting, and logoff sessions, and sending messages to users
- Viewing and shadowing sessions, using Shadow Taskbar
- Maintaining session activity using Session Reliability, auto client reconnect and ICA keep-alive features
- Customizing user environments in XenApp, including controlling the appearance of user logons and access to devices and ports, mapping drives, and redirecting COM Ports and Audio
- Limiting concurrent connections per server and limiting application instances and sharing sessions and connections
- Optimizing user sessions for XenApp, using local text echo, and mouse click feedback
- Redirection of Local Special Folders in Sessions, including setup of Special Folder Redirection on web interface and using GPO

In the next chapter, we will learn about Receiver and Plug-in Management, including installing Citrix Receiver for Windows and Macintosh and deploying and configuring Citrix Merchandising Server on VMware and XenServer Virtual Machines.

11
Receiver and Plugins Management

In the last chapter, we discussed about Managing Sessions on XenApp farms. In this chapter, we will talk about Citrix Receiver and Plugins Management.

Citrix Receiver turns any device, from a PC running Windows or Linux, Macintosh, thin client, tablet like iPad or Android devices, or Smartphone, like Android, Blackberry, and iPhones into a powerful business tool, providing the ability to work from anywhere, any time. In this chapter, we will talk about Citrix Receiver and plugins management, including:

- Introduction to Citrix Receiver, including features and compatibility
- Installing Citrix Receiver for Windows and Macintosh
- Deploying Citrix Merchandising Server on VMware and XenServer Virtual Machines
- Setting up Merchandising Server and Receiver plugins

Introduction to Citrix Receiver

Citrix Receiver is a light software client that makes accessing virtual applications and desktops possible on almost any client machine, including Windows and Macintosh computers and mobile devices like Android, Blackberry, Apple iPhone, and iPad devices.

Citrix describes the Citrix Receiver as similar to a satellite or cable TV receiver in a broadcast media service. Citrix Receiver allows IT organizations to deliver desktops and applications as an on-demand service to any device in any location with a rich "high-definition" experience.

The information in this chapter is based on Citrix Receiver 2.1 and Merchandising Server 2.1.

Citrix Receiver features

Citrix Receiver provides:

- Secure access to any Windows or web application or virtual desktop on any network or device
- Universal browser support
- Centralized administrative control of virtual and physical desktops; applications and IT services distribute automatic updates to users based on preferences and credentials
- A complete SDK that offers a simple, extensible, architectural framework; allows third-party software and technology vendors to integrate new customized services

Citrix Receiver plugin compatibility

The following table lists the plugins compatible with the Merchandising Server and required operating systems:

Plugins	Compatible operating systems
MS Application Virtualization Desktop Client 4.5 or later	Microsoft Windows XP (32-bit), Windows Vista (32 and 64-bit), Windows 7 (32 and 64-bit)
Acceleration plug-in 5.5 or later	Microsoft Windows XP(32-bit), Windows Vista (32 and 64-bit)
Receiver for Windows 2.x or later	Microsoft Windows XP, Windows Vista, Windows 7, Windows Server 2003 and 2008 (32 and 64-bit)
Dazzle plug-in 1.1.2 or later	Microsoft Windows XP, Windows Vista, and Windows 7 (32 and 64-bit)
EasyCall 3.x or later	Microsoft Windows XP, Windows Vista, Windows 7, Windows Server 2003 and 2008 (32 and 64-bit)
Offline plug-in 6.x or later	Microsoft Windows XP, Windows Vista, Windows 7, Windows Server 2003 and 2008 (32 and 64-bit)
Online plug-in 12.x or later	Microsoft Windows XP, Windows Vista, Windows 7, Windows Server 2003 and 2008 (32 and 64-bit)
Profile Management plug-in 2.0 or later	Microsoft Windows XP, Windows Vista, Windows Server 2003 and 2008 (32 and 64-bit)
Secure Access plug-in 4.6.2 or later	Microsoft Windows XP, Windows Vista, and Windows 7(32 and 64-bit)
Service Monitoring plug-in 5.3 or later	Microsoft Windows XP, Windows Vista, Windows 7 (64-bit)
Citrix Receiver for Mac 2.x or later	Apple Mac OSX 10.5-10.6 (32 and 64-bit)

Plugins	Compatible operating systems
Communication plug-in for Mac 3.0 or later	Apple Mac OSX 10.5-10.6 (32 and 64-bit)
Online plugin 11.2 or later	Apple Mac OSX 10.5, 10.6 (32 and 64-bit)
Secure Access plug-in 1.2 for Mac or later	Apple Mac OSX 10.5, 10.6 (32 and 64-bit)

Citrix Receiver system requirements and compatibility

The following are the system requirements for Windows and Macintosh users:

Citrix Receiver for Windows

To install Citrix Receiver on a Windows machine, we need:

- .NET framework version 2.0 or later.
- Administrator privileges on the user's computer. Users must have administrator privileges on their client machines to install Receiver for Windows manually. The recommended option is deploying Citrix Receiver for Windows using Active directory GPOs, SCCM (Microsoft System Center Configuration Manager), or similar tools to users' client machines.

The following browser versions are required to download Receiver for Windows:

- Microsoft Internet Explorer 7.x or later
- Mozilla Firefox version 2.x or later

The following operating systems are supported by Citrix Receiver for Windows:

- Microsoft Windows XP Professional SP3 (32 and 64-bit)
- Microsoft Windows Vista SP2 (32 and 64-bit)
- Microsoft Windows 7 (32 and 64-bit)
- Microsoft Windows Server 2003 SP2 (32 and 64-bit)
- Microsoft Windows Server 2008 SP2 (32 and 64-bit)

Citrix Receiver for Macintosh

Our users must run the following operating systems and versions to install Citrix Receiver for Mac:

- Apple Mac OSX 10.5 for Intel CPUs (32 and 64-bit)
- Apple Mac OSX 10.6 (32 and 64-bit)

Installing Citrix Receiver

Depending on our environment, we can use different methods for installing Receiver:

- **Internal Users with Administrative Rights**: Installs Receiver for Windows or Receiver for Macintosh through the **Download** page at the Merchandising Server
- **Internal Windows users without Administrative Rights**: Needs to push the Receiver for Windows installation to client machines
- **Remote Users**: Needs to publish the **Download** page of the Merchandising Server to an external site and users need to connect to this site to download and install the Receiver for Windows or Receiver for Macintosh

Now it's time to help William Empire, from Brick Unit Constructions, install Citrix Receiver and implement Citrix Merchandising Server on his network.

Deploying Citrix Receiver for internal users with administrative rights

A majority of internal users at Brick Unit Constructions are local administrators of their client machines as they generally need to connect devices like cameras or install applications that require administrative rights.

William will notify a few test users, with an e-mail, with the URL of the Merchandising server. The URL is similar to `https://[serverAddress]/appliance/download`, where `[serverAddress]` is the Merchandising server address or host name, for example, the URL at Brick Unit is `https://receiver.brickunit.local/appliance/download`.

Installing Citrix Receiver for Windows

Brick Unit's users must connect to the Merchandising Server URL, agree to the terms of use, and then they click the **Download Receiver** button to start the download:

Then Receiver for Windows prompts to log on, and users must enter their Active Directory credentials and click the **Log On** button.

The Receiver for Windows starts the initial delivery from the Merchandising Server and installs plugins. The user may be asked to reboot their client machine, depending on the plugins installed.

When the process is complete, the Receiver icon is present in the notification area.

If we install Citrix Receiver for Windows in a Windows server with Remote Desktop Services (formerly known as Terminal Services), users will notice that the status of the service under **Preferences**, **About** show in red: **Plug-in updates are disabled**:

This is caused because when the Receiver client detects Remote Desktop Services, it automatically disables the plugin to avoid disrupting the sessions of active users. We can re-enable updates when we want to update the server by adding the `allowadminTSupdates` switch to the Receiver command line.

Installing Citrix Receiver on XenApp servers

Sometimes, to publish XenApp desktops, we need to install Citrix Receiver and plugins to simplify management and keep all servers at the same version level. Citrix Receiver will disable automatic installation of plugins, so we need to manually trigger updates.

To install Citrix Receiver on a XenApp Server William must:

1. Log on to the XenApp server as administrator.
2. Download and install Citrix Receiver for Windows from the Merchandising Server. Receiver is installed on the server.
3. Close the Receiver, right-click the Citrix Receiver icon in the notification area and select **Exit**.
4. Open a command prompt window and run Citrix Receiver in the updating mode using the following command:

    ```
    C:\Program Files\Citrix\Receiver\Receiver.exe -autoupdate-allowadminTSupdates
    ```

Once the updates have been installed, a reboot may be required.

Installing Citrix Receiver for Macintosh

Similar to the installation on a Windows system, Mac users must connect to the Merchandising Server URL, agree to the terms of use, and then click the **Download Receiver** button to start the download.

- Once the installation succeeds, the Receiver will start the connection with the Merchandising Server to install plugins and requires the user to enter the Active Directory user authentication credentials
- After the user enters credentials, he needs to select **Standard** and click the **Continue** button
- The Receiver for Windows starts the initial delivery from the Merchandising Server and installs plugins
- The user may be asked the password, depending on the plugins installed
- When the process is complete, the Receiver icon is shown in the menu bar

Deploying Citrix Receiver for internal Windows users without administrative rights

The next step that William Empire will take is to push the Citrix Receiver client to some users' workstations without administrative rights, like training machines and a few information kiosks.

Options include deploying the .MSI file using Active Directory or Microsoft SCCM (System Center Configuration Manager, formerly known as SMS) or similar tools.

William needs to use the following installation options, if he wants to push the Receiver installation to his users:

- **SERVER_LOCATION**: This is the server address (with or without the HTTP prefix).
- **AUTOUPDATE**: Controls whether the Receiver checks the Merchandising Server for updates automatically or not. Options are **True** or **False**.
- **VERBOSE**: Controls the level of debug information produced by Citrix Receiver. Options are **True** or **False**.

- **TOKEN:** The value from the **Token Value** field in the Merchandising Server Administrator Console (Configurations, Authentication). This value is generated when we click on the **Generate Token** button:

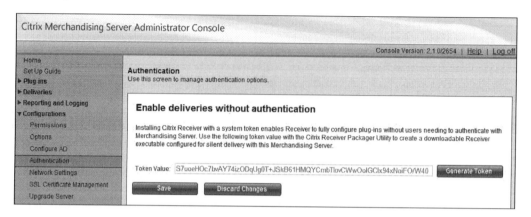

Based on the following information, William creates a script to install Receiver, plugins, and asks a user to reboot the machine (if required). As we mentioned before, this script can be used in unattended deployment:

```
msiexec /i "Receiver.msi" /qn ALLUSERS=1 REBOOT="ReallySuppress"SE
RVER_LOCATION=https://receiver.brickunit.local/appliance/services/
applianceService VERBOSE=true AUTOUPDATE=true TOKEN=S7uoeHOc7bvAY74izODqU
g0T+JSkB61HMQYCmbTIovCWwOoIGCIx94xNoiFO/W40
```

Deploying Citrix Receiver for remote users

Brick Unit's remote users can install Citrix Receiver remotely using the Citrix Secure Access (Standard or Enterprise Edition) Plug-in.

To allow Windows user's remote connection to the Merchandising Server, William must:

1. Download the package with Citrix Receiver Packager utility, sample download web, and support files from www.citrix.com. The package is called **Receiver for Windows 2.1 Packager** and is available under **Downloads | Receiver**.

2. Package the Citrix Secure Access (Standard or Enterprise Edition) plug-in and the Citrix Receiver for Windows application into a single file using the **Citrix Receiver Packager** utility and copy the generated file to an external web server.

3. Create a download web page using the sample included in the package, link it to the output file created by the Receiver Packager utility, and deploy the external web page on the web server (instructions to edit the sample website are given below).

Mac users must:

1. Download the package with the Citrix Receiver Packager utility, sample download web and support files from www.citrix.com. The Package is called **Receiver for Mac 2.1 Packager** and is available under **Downloads | Receiver**, and open the Citrix Receiver Packager.dmg file.

2. Under the Merchandising Server section, select **Use system token** (also he can choose **Prompt users for credentials**).

3. Enter the Token Value string from Merchandising Server Administrator Console, available under **Configurations | Authentication** and click **+** to select a dmg file.

4. Citrix Receiver Packager for Mac requires Receiver.dmg.

5. One can also include the Access Gateway Plug-in for Mac OS X (Citrix Access Gateway.dmg). This plugin is available for download at www.citrix.com under **Download | Access Gateway | Create button**:

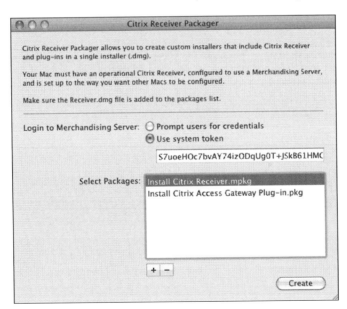

6. In the pop-up box, enter the filename and location for the new file, and click on the **Save** button, then click **OK**.
7. Copy the generated file and the modified sample web page to the web server (instructions to edit the sample website are below).

Instructions to edit the sample download page

The final step of the process for William includes editing the sample website and uploading it to the external website. To execute this final step, he must:

1. Extract the `.zip c` file using WinRAR, WinZIP, or similar compressing tool.
2. Go to the location where he extracts the file. Then he must copy the file created in the previous step to the same folder or another folder in the web server.
3. Edit the `resources.js` file and add the following data:
    - For Windows: Enter the relative path or URL of the generated Windows packaged file in the `downloadLocation` parameter
    - For Macintosh: Enter the relative path or URL of the generated Macintosh packaged file in the `macdownloadLocation` parameter

    Optional step: Modify the page styles or other information that is required.
4. Upload these files to a web server and e-mail the URL to all Brick Unit Construction users.

More information is available in **Enabling Remote Installation for Citrix Receiver** technical note at `http://support.citrix.com/article/CTX121355`.

Setting up Citrix Merchandising Server 2.1

Citrix Receiver for Windows, Receiver for Macintosh, and Merchandising Server are components of the Citrix Delivery Center solution. Citrix Merchandising Server and Citrix Receiver works together to update the installation and management of application delivery to the user desktops.

Merchandising Server is an administrative tool for configuring, delivering, and upgrading plugins for our users' devices and provides a great end-user experience on laptops and desktops.

Merchandising Server currently is supported on Citrix XenServer and VMware Servers.

Installing Merchandising Server software

The Merchandising Server software is delivered as a virtual appliance image that contains all of the software necessary for running the Merchandising Server.

William can download the virtual appliance image from www.citrix.com and then import the virtual machine into Citrix XenServer or VMware servers.

Two images are available under Receiver options:

- **XenServer**: the image name is similar to `citrix-merchandising-server-[releaseNumber].bz2`
- **VMware**: the image name is similar to `citrix-merchandising-server-VMware[releaseNumber].ova`

Merchandising Server System requirements

The following are the requirements to install and use the Merchandising Server:

Hypervisors (virtualization software) supported:

- Citrix XenServer 5.x or later. XenServer is available for free at www.citrix.com
- VMware ESX 3.5, VMware vSphere 4.x or later, and VMware Server 2.x. We can download VMware ESXi 4.x or VMware Server 2.x for free at www.vmware.com

Browsers required for the Citrix Merchandising Server Administrator Console:

- Microsoft Internet Explorer 7.x or later
- Mozilla Firefox version 3.x or later

Browsers supported for Citrix Receiver download pages:

- Microsoft Internet Explorer 7.x or later
- Mozilla Firefox version 3.x or later
- Apple Safari
- Google Chrome

Other requirements:

- Active Directory based on Windows 2003 or later is required

Based on the amount of users, the Merchandising Server virtual appliance will require more Memory or vCPU (virtual CPUs). Citrix recommends setting up at least 4 GB of RAM and 2 vCPUs to the virtual appliance, except in small deployments or testing environments.

Importing the virtual appliance into VMware vSphere 4.1

To deploy Merchandising Server on VMware, William must:

1. Use WinRAR or a similar tool to decompress the .ova file to a new folder.
2. Then he starts VMware vSphere Client and he needs to enter the IP address or host name of the VMware host or VMware vCenter server and then he enters the username, password, and clicks **Login**.
3. He chooses the **File and Deploy OVF Template** option. The **Deploy OVF Template** window appears and he needs to click on the **Browse** button, then selects the .ova file, and clicks the **Next** button:

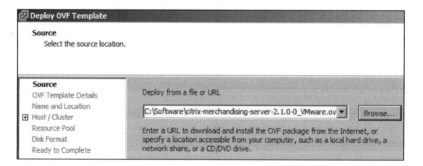

4. He verifies the OVF template details and then he clicks the **Next** button.
5. He clicks the **Accept** button to accept the EULA agreement and clicks the **Next** button.

Chapter 11

6. He needs to enter the name of the Merchandising Server virtual machine and clicks the **Next** button:

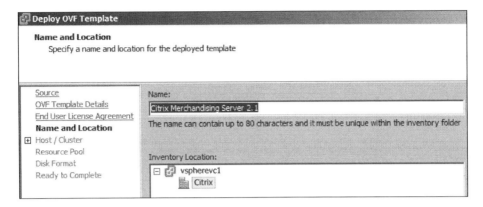

7. William chooses a datastore and then he clicks the **Next** button.
8. He reviews the deployment settings and then he clicks on the **Finish** button.
9. After the Virtual Machine build is complete, he chooses the Merchandising Server virtual machine name in the inventory and then in the **Getting Started** tab, he clicks **Edit virtual machine settings**. A properties pop-up window appears.
10. In the **Hardware** tab, William needs to select **Memory** and change the memory Size to 4 GB. Then he chooses **CPUs** and changes the **Number of virtual processors** to **2**. Citrix recommends allocating at least 4 GB of memory and configuring 2 vCPUs:

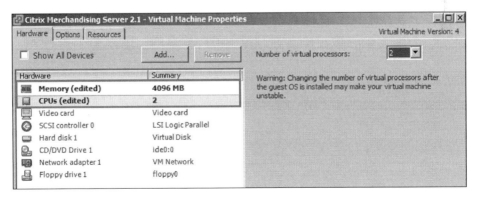

[337]

Importing the virtual appliance into Citrix XenServer 5.6

The following is the procedure to install the virtual appliance in Citrix XenServer, followed by William:

1. William starts the **Citrix XenCenter**, selects **File** and then the **Import VM** option. The **Import VM** pop-up window displays, he clicks on the **Browse** button, navigates to the .xva file, and clicks **Open**:

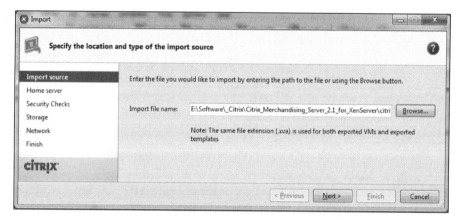

2. He selects Exported VM as the **Import Type** and then he clicks on the **Next** button.
3. In the **Home server** screen of the wizard, William selects the XenServer instance where this VM should be imported and then he clicks the **Next** button:

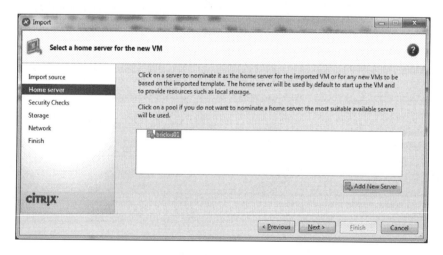

Chapter 11

4. In the **Storage** screen, William selects the storage repository to store the Virtual Machine and then he clicks on the **Import** button.

5. The import begins and the **Network** screen opens. In the **Network** screen, William needs to select the appropriate network and then he clicks on the **Next** button:

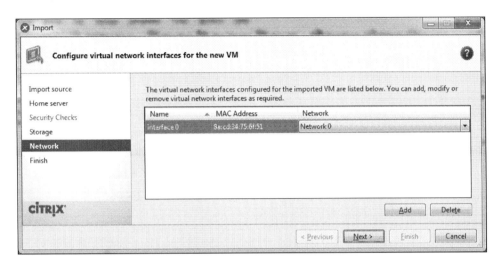

6. In the **Finish** screen, William clears the checkbox for **Start VM after Import** and he clicks the **Finish** button:

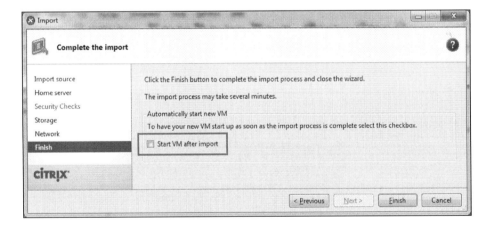

7. After the import process completes, William needs to right-click the **Virtual Machine** and choose **Properties**.

8. He needs to click the **CPU and Memory** tab and adjust the amount of memory and the number of vCPUs. Citrix recommends allocating at least 4 GB of memory and two vCPUs:

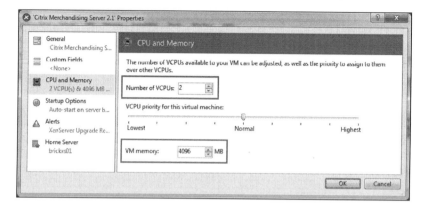

9. He clicks the **OK** button. He then selects the VM and clicks the **Network** tab.
10. Finally, he clicks the **Properties** button, selects **Auto-generate**, and clicks **OK**.

Setup Merchandising Server

As soon as William finishes adjusting memory and CPU settings, he is ready to start the virtual machine.

- In VMware, using the **Getting Started** tab, he clicks **Power on the virtual machine**. Then he needs to open the console by clicking the **Console** tab or open an independent console.
- In XenServer he needs to right-click the VM and choose Start, then he needs to select the **Console** tab.

Now he will configure network settings and enters **9** to save the configuration:

When prompted, he needs to enter a new password for the virtual appliance:

```
###########################################
#                                         #
#       New password for root user.       #
#                                         #
###########################################
New UNIX password: _
```

When this process is completed, he needs to reboot the virtual appliance to apply settings.

Configuring administrator users

The next step for William is configuring the virtual appliance to connect to Active Directory and provide access to his account and other administrators to the Administrator Console, using the following procedure:

1. He needs to open a browser window and enter the Administrator Console URL. The URL is similar to `https://[server_address]/appliance`, where `server_address` is the Merchandising Server host name or IP address. For example, he needs to enter `https://receiver.brickunit.local/appliance` and the login window will appear:

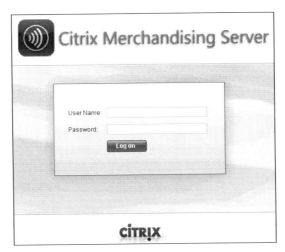

2. Now he needs to enter the default administrator console account, the default username is **root**, and the default password is **C1trix321**. Clicking on **Log on** will give him access to the console:

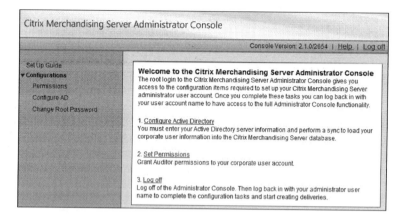

3. He needs to select the **Configurations** option, then the **Configure AD** option, and provide the Active Directory server information:

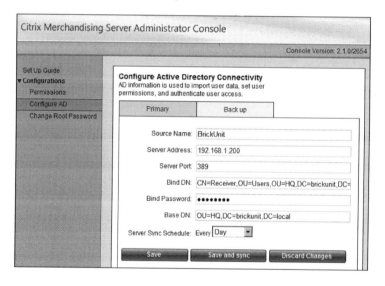

4. He clicks on the **Save Changes and Sync** button to load users into the Merchandising Server database.

5. The next step is choosing administrators; he needs to select the **Configurations** option and then the **Permissions** option.

6. He needs to enter the username, first or last name in the **Search** text box, and click **Search**. He chooses the name in the search results list and clicks the **Edit** button. He selects the **Administrator** role and clicks the **Save** button:

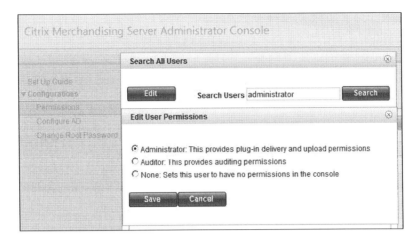

7. He needs to repeat the process for each of the users who will need **Administrator** or **Auditor** permissions.
8. Finally, he needs to log out of the **Administrator Console**.

Installing plugins

Now, William is ready to download plugins and create delivery rules.

The first step is to log in to the Merchandising Console using his Active Directory username and password, and then he has two different options to access plugins:

Because this is the first time William accesses the console, the home page will show the total number of new plugins available to download:

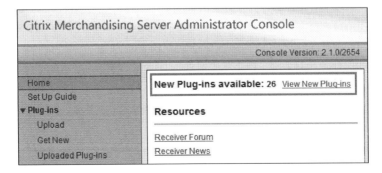

[343]

William can click on the **View New Plug-ins** link to access the list of plugins available to install. Also, he can click on the **Plug-ins | Get New** menu.

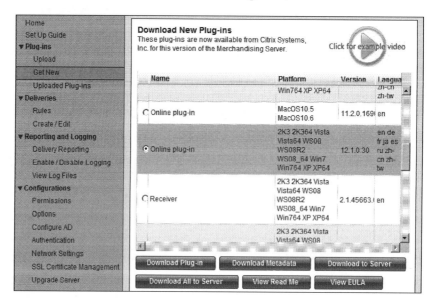

Now he can select the plugin from the list and click the **Download to Server** or the **Download All** button to download all available plugins. When the Success dialog box appears, he clicks the **Close** button.

He can repeat the process until he downloads all the plugins he wants to distribute to Brick Unit's users.

Create recipient rules

Delivery recipients are created based on the rules William will create. Rules can be defined by User Name, User Group, User Domain, Machine Name, IP Address, or Operating System. William can create as many rules as he needs and use them individually or in combination to define a set of delivery recipients, but only one delivery can be defined as the default delivery. The default delivery cannot contain rules.

This is the procedure used by William to create rules:

1. In the Administrator Console, William chooses the **Deliveries | Rules** option.
2. He clicks on the **Create** button (located at the bottom of the page). Also, he can use the **Edit** button to edit any existing rule.

Chapter 11

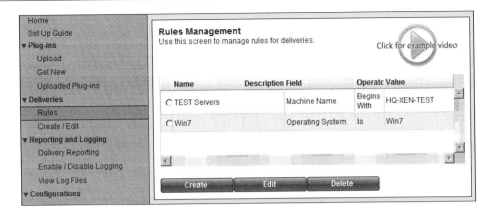

3. He types the rule **Name** and optionally the **Description**.
4. Then he chooses the rule type from the **Field** menu, from the list of available values: Machine Name, User Domain Membership, Computer Domain Membership, Operating System, LDAP User, and LDAP Group, Machine Name, and IP Address Range. Based on the **Field** he selects, different options are available:
   - The Search functionality is available when he selects LDAP User or LDAP Groups
   - If he chooses User Domain Membership, Machine Domain Membership, Operating System, or IP Address Range, he needs to select **Is** or **Is Not** for the **Operator** field and type the appropriate **Value** entry
   - If he selects Machine Name, he can choose **Begins With**, **Contains**, or **Is Exactly**, and types the appropriate **Value** entry

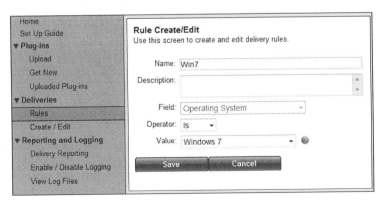

5. Finally, when the rule is ready, he needs to click the **Save** button to save the rule.

Creating deliveries

Deliveries are used to deploy and update the plugin to a client machine or device. To create deliveries, William has to:

1. Open the Administrator Console, and he chooses **Deliveries | Create / Edit**.
2. Click the **Create** button, located at the bottom of the page.
3. In the **General** tab, he enters the general information for the delivery.

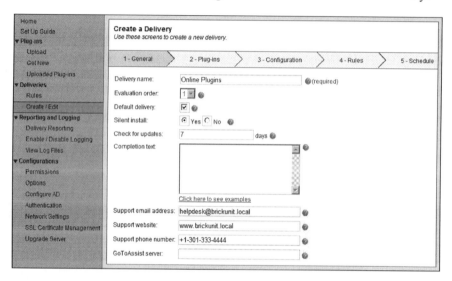

4. In the **Plug-ins** tab, he chooses plugins to deliver, using the **Add** and **Remove** buttons.

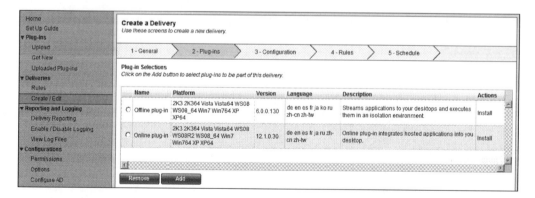

5. In the **Configuration** tab, he can modify plugin settings.

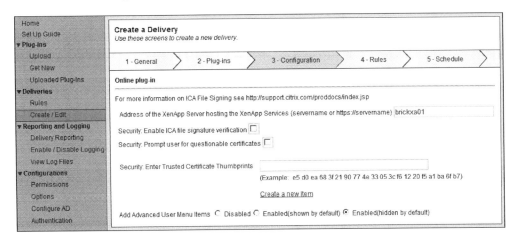

6. In the **Rules** tab, he can set up rules to apply in the delivery (note: in the default delivery, the option is not available).
7. In the **Schedule** tab, William can set the delivery schedule time and date or choose the **Deliver Now** option. Then he clicks the **Schedule** button to complete the process.

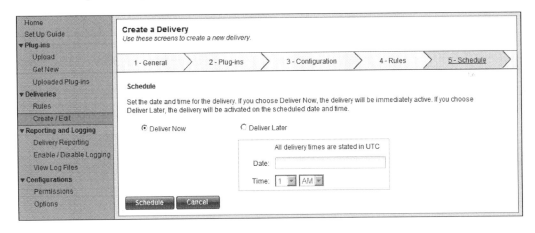

8. After the delivery is completed, he can review deliveries and modify, suspend, or resume any of them.

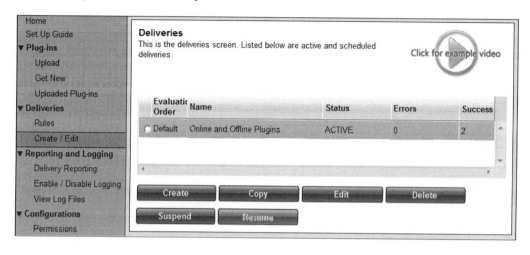

9. Merchandising Server setup now is complete. Brick Unit Construction users are ready to download and install Citrix Receiver. Once they have downloaded Receiver, Merchandising Server will install plugins based on the schedule created before.

Configure SSL certificates

By default, Merchandising Server uses SSL to encrypt communication with Receiver clients. This requires installing and configuring an SSL certificate for the Merchandising server.

The Merchandising Server includes a temporary 30-day certificate. William needs to replace or renew this certificate within 30 days to ensure continuous communication between the server and client machines.

[Merchandising Server supports only 1024-bit SSL certificates.]

William can use the following options to create the SSL certificate:

- Creating a Self-Signed SSL Certificate: He can renew every 30 days the installed certificate. This is the less preferred option.
- Use an Existing SSL Certificate: William can import an existing certificate, like a wildcard certificate generated in another server, using a private key file.
- SSL Certificate using a Certificate Signing Request from the Merchandising Server: William needs to send the certificate signing request to public certificate authority or use an internal one.
- Internal certificates: Generated using Microsoft Certificate Services.

Also, William can enable or disable the SSL communication with the HTTPS redirection option. By default, any attempt to access the Merchandising Server through HTTP protocol is automatically redirected to HTTPS.

William can change this setting using the **HTTPS Redirection** option, available at Administrator Console, under **Configurations | Options**.

Disabling SSL can be useful in some scenarios like multiple Merchandising Servers in different geographical areas or when the Merchandising Server is deployed behind NetScaler. William can use NetScaler in 'Transparent SSL' or 'SSL Offload' mode.

Receiver for Windows communicates with NetScaler using SSL and the NetScaler sends commands using HTTP protocol to the Merchandising Server.

Creating a self-signed SSL certificate

A self-signed certificate valid for 30 days is already installed on the Merchandising Server. If William chooses this option, he must renew it every 30 days by generating it again. The following is the procedure to generate the certificate:

1. He logs on to the Administrator Console and he select **Configurations | SSL Certificate Management**.
2. He chooses **Generate a self-signed certificate** from the **Select an action** drop-down box.
3. In the **Common Name** field, William needs to enter the host name or IP address of the Merchandising Server and then he needs to complete the rest of the fields.

4. He clicks on the **Submit** button to generate a self-signed certificate for the Merchandising Server.

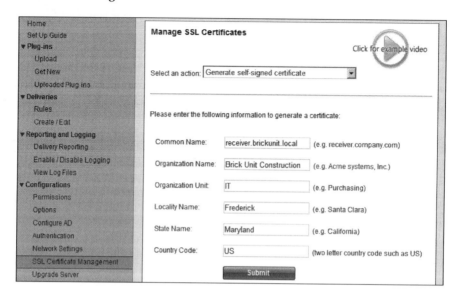

 This certificate requires that users accept a security exception for a certificate that was not issued by a trusted certificate authority.

Creating a Certificate Signing Request

William needs a CSR (Certificate Signing Request) to obtain an SSL certificate from a certificate authority. He can use the Administrator Console to generate the CSR required by the CA (Certificate Authority).

Then he can obtain a certificate from the CA by providing the completed CSR. Also, the Merchandising Server supports certificates whose CSR was generated by other servers.

1. He logs on to the Administrator Console and chooses **Configurations | SSLCertificate Management**.
2. He chooses **Export certificate signing request** from the **Select an action** drop-down box to create the CSR.
3. In the **Common Name** field, William needs to enter the host name or IP address for the Merchandising Server and then he needs to complete the rest of the fields.

4. He clicks the **Export** button to generate and download the `server.csr` file that he needs to provide to the CA to obtain a certificate.

5. He contacts the CA and follows the required procedure to acquire a certificate. He needs to provide the `.CSR` file generated in the previous step to the CA and sometimes the platform information (Note: The server platform is Apache and the certificate usage is WebServer).

6. Finally, the CA sends an SSL server certificate and the root certificate.

Importing SSL certificates

The following procedure is used by William to import certificates and private key files:

1. He logs on to the Administrator Console and chooses **Configurations | SSLCertificate Management**.

2. He chooses **Import certificate from a certificate authority** from the **Select an action** drop-down box.

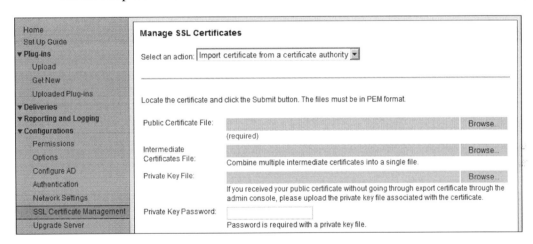

3. Now he needs to specify the files to be imported, based on the type of certificates he is using:
    ○ **Certificates Generated from the Merchandising Server**: He needs to use the **Browse** button next to the **Public Certificate File** field. The Merchandising Server already has the private key file needed for the certificate requests, so he does not need to upload a private key file.
    ○ **Intermediate Certificate File**: He needs to use the **Browse** button next to the **Intermediate Certificates File** field.

- **Certificates Generated from the Merchandising Server or Certificates Generated from Other Servers:** William uses the **Browse** button next to the **Public Certificate File** field. Then he uses the **Browse** button next to the **Private Key File** field to locate the private key file for the certificate. After that, he types the Private Key password (also known as the pass phrase) for the private key file.

    4. He clicks on the **Submit** button to finish the procedure.

The **Certificate Status** textbox displays information about the certificate after the successful completion of this process and Merchandising Server restarts.

Creating a signing request for Microsoft certificate services

The following is the procedure for requesting and downloading a signed certificate from an internal signing authority:

1. William opens the Internet browser and enters the company's certificate services URL.
2. He chooses the link to request a certificate.
3. He chooses the link to submit a request using a `base 64 encoded CMC` or `PKS #10` file or a renewal request by using a `base-64 encoded PKSCS #7` file.
4. He pastes the contents of the signed certificate request into the **Saved Request** field.
5. He selects the web server in the certificate template field.
6. He clicks on the **Submit** button to finish the procedure.

When the certificate is issued, he selects the **Base 64 encoding method** and downloads the signed certificate.

Installing SSL certificates on client machines

Merchandising Server uses SSL to encrypt communications with Receiver. William needs a root certificate on the client machine that can verify the signature of the Certificate Authority on the Merchandising Server certificate.

Using an external Certificate Authority, like VeriSign or similar, will automatically be trusted by most client machines.

But if William chooses to use SSL certificates from an internal Certificate Authority, he needs to distribute root certificates so that they are available for all users in the centralized local computer certificate store. If the root certificates are not available in the centralized local computer certificate store, Receiver for Windows cannot receive updates from the Merchandising Server.

William can use Active Directory Group Policies to distribute Certificates to client machines. The document that provides detailed instructions to install certificates using GPOs can be found at `http://technet.microsoft.com/en-us/library/cc731253(WS.10).aspx`.

Summary

In this chapter, we learned about Citrix Receiver for Windows and Macintosh, and how to install and use Merchandising Server to configure, deliver, and upgrade plugins for our users' devices.

In the next chapter, we are going to learn about managing XenApp with Windows PowerShell.

12
Scripting Programming

In the previous chapter, we learned about Citrix Receiver for Windows and Macintosh and how to use Citrix Merchandising Server for plugins management.

In this chapter, we will learn how to automatize common tasks using PowerShell scripts. This powerful scripting language combined with the Citrix XenApp Commands package will help us to create scripts to manage our XenApp farm. We can automatize common and simple tasks, like publishing or enabling/disabling applications, assign/remove users or disable logon on servers, however we can use PowerShell for more complex tasks like generating CPU usage reports, creating backup of policies, or migrating applications between XenApp farms.

In this chapter, we will cover:

- Installing and configuring PowerShell to manage Citrix farms
- Use of cmdlets to manage XenApp servers
- Using PowerShell commands from inside .NET code
- Converting our MFCOM scripts to PowerShell to manage XenApp 6
- Accessing MFCOM objects and managing previous versions of XenApp from PowerShell

MFCOM and PowerShell

Before XenApp 6 was released, MFCOM was used by developers and administrators to create utilities and scripts to automate administration tasks on Citrix XenApp farms.

MFCOM is very powerful and can be used from inside .VBS files (Visual Basic scripts), .WSH files (Windows Scripting Host), Visual Studio, Visual Studio.NET, and more.

Starting on XenApp 6, Citrix dropped support for MFCOM and moved scripting capabilities to Microsoft PowerShell. MFCOM-based scripts need to be completely re-written using XenApp cmdlets. A **cmdlet** is a command that is used in the Windows PowerShell.

On previous versions of XenApp, we can use multiple scripting or development languages to manage XenApp, but now on version 6.0, we have only one option: PowerShell, later we can learn how to run PowerShell commands from inside .NET code.

Microsoft is using PowerShell for management of different infrastructure products (Windows Server, Exchange Server, SQL Server, and so on), so the transition to PowerShell provides standardization across different Windows-based products.

We can use PowerShell with Citrix XenApp Commands to configure and administer servers and farms using the console, for example, we can use PowerShell to publish an application or add users to published applications.

Installing XenApp Commands on XenApp Servers

Windows Server 2008 R2 includes Microsoft PowerShell 2.0 preinstalled, so we just need to install XenApp Command to start using it. If we are using previous version of Windows, we need to download (for free) and install Microsoft PowerShell 2.0 from the Microsoft website.

We have two options to install XenApp Commands:

- Download the **Citrix XenApp 6 PowerShell SDK** (which includes the XenApp Command cmdlets), the SDK helps us to manage XenApp 6 farms using PowerShell, and also provides PowerShell cmdlets to manage common Citrix components and group policies
- Download **Citrix XenApp Commands**. This pack allows PowerShell to manage XenApp 4.5, 5.0, and 6.0 farms

Both tools are available for download at
http://community.citrix.com/display/xa/Download+SDKS.

Installing Citrix XenApp 6 PowerShell SDK

We need to decompress the downloaded .ZIP file using WinZip, WinRAR, or a similar utility, and then run the .EXE file.

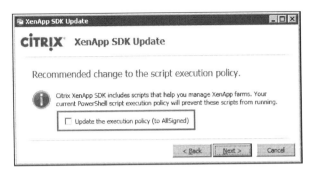

Enabling the option **Update the execution policy (to AllSigned)** requires that all scripts and configuration files are signed by a trusted publisher, including scripts that we write on the local computer.

The XenApp 6 PowerShell SDK includes multiple components: Citrix Common Commands, Citrix XenApp Commands, Citrix XenApp Server SDK, and Citrix Group Policy Management.

Installing PowerShell XenApp Commands

We need to decompress the downloaded .ZIP file using WinZip, WinRAR, or similar utility, and then run the appropriate .MSI file:

- `Citrix.XenApp.Commands.Install_x64.msi` for 64-bit systems
- `Citrix.XenApp.Commands.Install_x86.msi` for 32-bit systems

We can only install the XenApp Commands on systems with XenApp 4.5 or later installed.

> The PowerShell sample code in this chapter is based on Citrix XenApp Command CTP3, this version of Citrix XenApp Command is not the final release, so some code or commands can change when the final version will be released.

Using PowerShell for basic administrative tasks

This chapter requires that we are familiar with Microsoft PowerShell. If you are not familiar with it, I recommend downloading **Windows PowerShell Graphical Help File** and **Windows PowerShell Quick Reference**. Both the files are located in the **Download** section of this page at `http://technet.microsoft.com/en-us/scriptcenter`.

Also, you can review the **XenApp Commands Help**, available in **Start | All Programs | Citrix and XenApp Commands**.

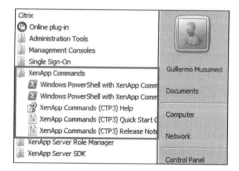

Installing Citrix XenApp Commands snap-in

The Citrix XenApp Command snap-in is an add-on developed by Citrix to manage XenApp from PowerShell.

To open the PowerShell Citrix Commands console, we need to use the **Windows PowerShell with XenApp Command** shortcut available at **Start | All Programs | Citrix | XenApp Commands**.

Another option is to open the PowerShell shortcut and load the Citrix XenApp snap-in. This option is required when we want to use a PowerShell to manage multiple products or we are using the PowerShell console version 1.0.

```
Add-PSSnapin Citrix.XenApp.Commands
```

To verify the XenApp Commands are working properly, we need to type:

```
Get-command -psSnapin Citrix.XenApp.Commands
```

```
PS C:\> get-command -module Citrix.XenApp.Commands

CommandType   Name                           Definition
-----------   ----                           ----------
Cmdlet        Add-XAAdministratorPrivilege   Add-XAAdministratorPrivilege [-AdministratorName...
Cmdlet        Add-XAApplicationAccount       Add-XAApplicationAccount [-BrowserName] <String[...
Cmdlet        Add-XAApplicationFileType      Add-XAApplicationFileType [-BrowserName] <String...
Cmdlet        Add-XAApplicationServer        Add-XAApplicationServer [-BrowserName] <String[]...
Cmdlet        Add-XASessionPrinter           Add-XASessionPrinter [-PolicyName] <String> [-Se...
Cmdlet        Clear-XAConfigurationLog       Clear-XAConfigurationLog [-Credential <PSCredent...
Cmdlet        Connect-XASession              Connect-XASession [[-ServerName] <String>] [[-So...
Cmdlet        Copy-XAApplication             Copy-XAApplication [-BrowserName] <String[]> [-F...
Cmdlet        Copy-XAFolder                  Copy-XAFolder [-FolderPath] <String[]> [-ToFolde...
Cmdlet        Disable-XAAdministrator        Disable-XAAdministrator [-AdministratorName] <St...
Cmdlet        Disable-XAApplication          Disable-XAApplication [-BrowserName] <String[]> ...
Cmdlet        Disable-XAPolicy               Disable-XAPolicy [-PolicyName] <String[]> [-Pass...
Cmdlet        Disable-XAServerLogOn          Disable-XAServerLogOn [-ServerName] <String[]> [...
Cmdlet        Disconnect-XASession           Disconnect-XASession [[-ServerName] <String>] [-...
Cmdlet        Enable-XAAdministrator         Enable-XAAdministrator [-AdministratorName] <Str...
Cmdlet        Enable-XAApplication           Enable-XAApplication [-BrowserName] <String[]> [...
Cmdlet        Enable-XAPolicy                Enable-XAPolicy [-PolicyName] <String[]> [-PassT...
Cmdlet        Enable-XAServerLogOn           Enable-XAServerLogOn [-ServerName] <String[]> [-...
Cmdlet        Get-XAAccount                  Get-XAAccount [[-SearchPath] <String>] -AccountA...
Cmdlet        Get-XAAccountAuthority         Get-XAAccountAuthority [[-Name] <String[]>] [-Ve...
Cmdlet        Get-XAAdministrator            Get-XAAdministrator [[-AdministratorName] <Strin...
```

The `Get-Command` cmdlet gets commands in the session, such as aliases, functions, filters, scripts, and applications.

Also, we use the following command to check if the snap-in is installed:

`Get-command -psSnapin Citrix*`

We can use the `Get-Help` command to show information about a command:

`Get-help Get-XAServer`

This command will generate this output:

```
PS C:\> get-help Get-XAServer

NAME
    Get-XAServer

SYNOPSIS
    Retrieves XenApp servers.

SYNTAX
    Get-XAServer [[-ServerName] <String[]>] [-Full] [<CommonParameters>]

    Get-XAServer [-BrowserName <String[]>] [-Full] [<CommonParameters>]

    Get-XAServer [-FolderPath <String[]>] [-Full] [<CommonParameters>]

    Get-XAServer [-ZoneName <String[]>] [-OnlineOnly] [-Full] [<CommonParameters>]

    Get-XAServer [-AccountAuthorityName <String[]>] [-Full] [<CommonParameters>]

    Get-XAServer [-LoadEvaluatorName <String[]>] [-Full] [<CommonParameters>]

    Get-XAServer [-DriverName <String[]>] [-Full] [<CommonParameters>]

    Get-XAServer [-InputObject <XAServer[]>] [-Full] [<CommonParameters>]

    Get-XAServer [-Full] [-VirtualIPLoopbackEnabled] [<CommonParameters>]
```

Using PowerShell for farm management

Use the following command to show farm information:

`Get-XAFarm`

```
PS C:\> Get-XAFarm
FarmName                          : BrickFarm6
ServerVersion                     : 6.0.6410
AdministratorType                 : Full
SessionCount                      : 10
DefaultOfflineLicenseLeasePeriod  : 21
MinimumOfflineLicenseLeasePeriod  : 2
MaximumOfflineLicenseLeasePeriod  : 365
```

We can also use the `Get-XAFarmConfiguration` cmdlet for more detailed information about the farm.

To show the list of XenApp servers in our farm, we can use the following cmdlet:

`Get-XAServer`

```
PS C:\> Get-XAServer
ServerName           : BRICKXA02
FolderPath           : Servers
ZoneName             : Frederick
ElectionPreference   : MostPreferred
IPAddresses          : {192.168.1.203}
OSVersion            : 6.1.7600
OSServicePack        :
Is64Bit              : True
CitrixProductName    : Citrix Presentation Server
CitrixVersion        : 6.0.6410
CitrixEdition        : Platinum
CitrixEditionString  : PLT
CitrixServicePack    : 0
CitrixInstallDate    : 7/3/2010 8:58:11 AM
CitrixInstallPath    : C:\Program Files (x86)\Citrix\
LogOnsEnabled        : True
IcaPortNumber        : 1494
RdpPortNumber        :
VirtualIPInUse       :
SessionCount         :
```

Now we can use a pipeline character (|) to pass the output generated by one command to another command. We can filter specific information about our XenApp servers, for example, we want to see a list with the server name, and if the logon is enabled, we use `Select` to filter commands.

`Get-XAServer | select ServerName, LogOnsEnabled`

Also, we can order the results using `Sort` and extra pipe. The following example orders the results based on the `LogOnsEnabled`:

`Get-XAServer | select ServerName, LogOnsEnabled | Sort LogOnsEnabled`

```
PS W:\> get-XAServer | select ServerName, LogOnsEnabled | sort LogOnsEnabled

ServerName                                                    LogOnsEnabled
----------                                                    -------------
HQ-XEN-005                                                            False
HQ-XEN-TEST3                                                          False
HQ-XEN-014                                                             True
HQ-XEN-011                                                             True
HQ-XEN-007                                                             True
HQ-XEN-008                                                             True
HQ-XEN-009                                                             True
HQ-XEN-TEST2                                                           True
HQ-XEN-DC1                                                             True
HQ-XEN-TEST1                                                           True
HQ-XEN-015                                                             True
HQ-XEN-016                                                             True
HQ-XEN-013                                                             True
HQ-XEN-002                                                             True
HQ-XEN-003                                                             True
```

We can disable logons on a specific XenApp server using the following command:

`Disable-XAServerLogOn-ServerName "HQ-XEN-001"`

If we need to enable logons on a specific XenApp server, we can use the following command:

`Enable-XAServerLogOn -ServerName "HQ-XEN-001"`

To show application information, we can use:

`Get-XAApplication`

```
PS C:\>  Get-XAApplication
ApplicationType                       : ServerInstalled
DisplayName                           : Project 2010
Description                           : Project 2010 64-bit
FolderPath                            : Applications
BrowserName                           : Project 2010
Enabled                               : True
HideWhenDisabled                      : False
ContentAddress                        :
CommandLineExecutable                 : "C:\Program Files\Microsoft Office\Office14\WINPROJ.EXE" "%*"
WorkingDirectory                      : C:\Program Files\Microsoft Office\Office14
ProfileLocation                       :
ProfileProgramName                    :
ProfileProgramArguments               :
AnonymousConnectionsAllowed           : False
ClientFolder                          :
AddToClientStartMenu                  : False
PlaceUnderProgramsFolder              : True
StartMenuFolder                       :
AddToClientDesktop                    : False
ConnectionsThroughAccessGatewayAllowed: True
OtherConnectionsAllowed               : True
AccessSessionConditionsEnabled        : False
AccessSessionConditions               : {}
InstanceLimit                         : 35
MultipleInstancesPerUserAllowed       : False
CpuPriorityLevel                      : Normal
AudioType                             : Basic
AudioRequired                         : False
SslConnectionEnabled                  : False
EncryptionLevel                       : Basic
EncryptionRequired                    : False
WaitOnPrinterCreation                 : False
WindowType                            : 1024x768
ColorDepth                            : TrueColor
TitleBarHidden                        : False
MaximizedOnStartup                    : False
```

Scripting Programming

Now we can use pipes, `Select`, and `Sort` to filter some commands:

```
Get-XAApplication | Select DisplayName, ApplicationType, Enabled | Sort DisplayName
```

```
PS W:\> Get-XAApplication | Select DisplayName, ApplicationType, Enabled | Sort DisplayName

DisplayName                    ApplicationType    Enabled
-----------                    ---------------    -------
Adobe Acrobat Professional 9   ServerInstalled    True
Alert Monitor                  ServerInstalled    True
Answer Wizard                  ServerInstalled    True
Business Rule Editor           ServerInstalled    True
Call Logging                   ServerInstalled    True
Create New User                ServerInstalled    True
EdgeSight Console              ServerInstalled    True
Firefox                        ServerInstalled    True
HQ-XEN-001 Desktop             ServerDesktop      True
HQ-XEN-002 Desktop             ServerDesktop      True
Inventory System               ServerInstalled    True
KVM Console                    ServerInstalled    True
Managers Console               ServerInstalled    True
NetApp System Manager          ServerInstalled    True
QuickBook 2008                 ServerInstalled    True
VMware 3                       ServerInstalled    True
VMware 4                       ServerInstalled    True
VNC Viewer                     ServerInstalled    True
```

We can use the `Export-CSV` command to save the result to a CSV file (comma separated values text file). We can open the CSV file using Excel:

```
Get-XAApplication | Select DisplayName, ApplicationType, Enabled | Sort DisplayName | Export-CSV C:\farm-apps.csv
```

	A	B	C
1	DisplayName	ApplicationType	Enabled
2	Adobe Acrobat Professional 9	ServerInstalled	TRUE
3	Alert Monitor	ServerInstalled	TRUE
4	Answer Wizard	ServerInstalled	TRUE
5	Business Rule Editor	ServerInstalled	TRUE
6	Call Logging	ServerInstalled	TRUE
7	Create New User	ServerInstalled	TRUE
8	EdgeSight Console	ServerInstalled	TRUE
9	Firefox	ServerInstalled	TRUE

Also, we can use the `ConvertTo-HTML` command to generate an HTML file, then we need to redirect the output using the `Out-File` command. We can open the HTML file using Internet Explorer, Firefox, or another Internet browser:

```
Get-XAApplication | Select DisplayName, ApplicationType, Enabled | Sort DisplayName | ConvertTo-HTML | Out-File C:\farm-apps.html
```

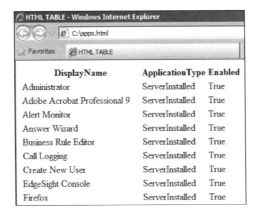

To list sessions on our Citrix farm, we can use:

`Get-XASession`

The following command will generate a lot of information in the farm. We are going to use pipeline to limit the information shown. In the following example, we are to going to use `select` to show the XenApp server (`ServerName`), username (`AccountName`), application (`BrowseName`), and session state.

`Get-XASession| Select ServerName, AccountName, BrowseName, State`

Now we can add an extra pipeline to filter the `Disconnected` sessions.

`Get-XASession | Select ServerName, AccountName, BrowseName, State | Where-Object {$_.State -eq "Disconnected"}`

Scripting Programming

To close all disconnected sessions, add an extra pipeline and the `Stop-XASession` command:

```
Get-XASession | Select ServerName, AccountName, BrowseName, State | Where-Object {$_.State -eq "Disconnected"} | Stop-XASession
```

Now we are going to learn how to publish an application using cmdlets. The following example will publish WordPad on the farm:

```
New-XAApplication -BrowserName "WordPad" -ApplicationType "ServerInstalled" -DisplayName "WordPad" -FolderPath "Applications" -Enabled $true -CommandLineExecutable "C:\Program Files\Windows NT\Accessories\wordpad.exe" -WorkingDirectory "C:\Program Files\Windows NT\Accessories" -AnonymousConnectionsAllowed $false -ServerNames HQ-XEN-001, HQ-XEN-002 -Accounts "XEN\Domain Admins"
```

Let's review this command in detail:

- `BrowserName`: Specifies the browser name of the published application. The browser name must be unique among all published applications.
- `ApplicationType`: Specifies the application type. Options are `ServerInstalled`, `ServerDesktop`, `Content`, `StreamedToServer`, `StreamedToClient`, `StreamedToClientOrInstalled`, and `StreamedToClientOrStreamedToServer`.
- `DisplayName`: Specifies the display name of the published application. The display name needs to be unique.
- `FolderPath`: Specifies the parent folder name of the published application.
- `Enabled`: Specifies whether to enable or disable the published application. Valid parameters are `$true` and `$false`.
- `CommandLineExecutable`: Specifies the application full path.
- `WorkingDirectory`: Specifies the default working directory for the application.
- `ServerNames`: Specifies a list of servers where the published application is installed.
- `Accounts`: Specifies the user accounts that can access the published application.

```
PS W:\> New-XAApplication -BrowserName "WordPad" -ApplicationType "ServerInstalled" -DisplayName "WordPad" -FolderPath "
Applications" -Enabled $true -CommandLineExecutable "C:\Program Files\Windows NT\Accessories\wordpad.exe" -WorkingDirect
ory "C:\Program Files\Windows NT\Accessories" -ServerNames HQ-XEN-001, HQ-XEN-002 -Accounts "AFT\domain admins"

ApplicationType                            : ServerInstalled
DisplayName                                : WordPad
Description                                :
FolderPath                                 : Applications
BrowserName                                : WordPad
Enabled                                    : True
HideWhenDisabled                           : False
ContentAddress                             :
CommandLineExecutable                      : "C:\Program Files\Windows NT\Accessories\wordpad.exe"
WorkingDirectory                           : C:\Program Files\Windows NT\Accessories
ProfileLocation                            :
ProfileProgramName                         :
ProfileProgramArguments                    :
AnonymousConnectionsAllowed                : False
ClientFolder                               :
AddToClientStartMenu                       : True
PlaceUnderProgramsFolder                   : True
StartMenuFolder                            :
AddToClientDesktop                         : False
ConnectionsThroughAccessGatewayAllowed     : True
OtherConnectionsAllowed                    : True
AccessSessionConditionsEnabled             : False
AccessSessionConditions                    : {}
InstanceLimit                              : -1
MultipleInstancesPerUserAllowed            : True
CpuPriorityLevel                           : Normal
AudioType                                  : Basic
AudioRequired                              : False
SslConnectionEnabled                       : False
EncryptionLevel                            : Basic
EncryptionRequired                         : False
WaitOnPrinterCreation                      : True
WindowType                                 : 1024x768
ColorDepth                                 : TrueColor
TitleBarHidden                             : False
MaximizedOnStartup                         : False
```

We can add extra users to an existing published application using the following command line:

`Add-XAApplicationAccount -BrowserName "WordPad" -Accounts "XEN\gmusumeci"`

We can add extra XenApp servers to an existing published application using the following command line:

`Add-XAApplicationServer -BrowserName "WordPad" -ServerNames "HQ-XEN-002"`

The following command will remove specific XenApp servers from the WordPad application:

`Remove-XAApplicationServer -BrowserName "WordPad" -ServerNames "HQ-XEN-003"`

We can disable the application WordPad using the following command:

`Set-XAApplication -BrowserName"WordPad" -Enabled $false -HideWhenDisabled $true`

The `HideWhenDisabled` parameter can hide or show the application.

Using PowerShell Commands from .NET applications

Now we are going to learn how to develop simple .NET applications to call Citrix PowerShell cmdlets on both Visual Basic.NET (VB.NET) and C#.NET.

Requirement to develop applications:

- Citrix XenApp 6 PowerShell SDK or Citrix XenApp Commands
- Microsoft provides the Express Edition of Visual Studio.NET, Visual C#.NET, and Visual Basic.NET for free at www.microsoft.com/visualstudio

Creating a sample VB.NET application

Now we are going to create a sample application to list all XenApp servers in our farm using Citrix XenApp Commands with managed code.

The first step is to start VB.NET. Samples contained in this book are developed in **Microsoft Visual Basic 2008 Express Edition**.

Go to **File | New Project | Windows Forms Applications**.

Enter the desired name for our project and click on the **OK** button.

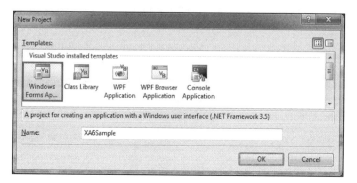

Adding references

The next step is to add a reference to the `System.Management.Automation.dll` assembly. Adding this assembly is tricky; first, we need to copy the assembly file to our application folder using the following command:

```
Copy %windir%\assembly\GAC_MSIL\System.Management.Automation\1.0.0.0_
31bf3856ad364e35\System.Management.Automation.dll C:\Code\XA6Sample
```

where `C:\Code\XA6Sample` is the folder of our application.

Then we need to add the reference to the assembly.

In the **Project** menu, select **Add Reference**, click on the **Browse** tab, search and select the file **System.Management.Automation.dll**.

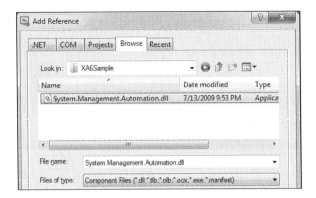

After referencing the assembly, we need to add the following directive statements to our code:

```
Imports System.Management.Automation
Imports System.Management.Automation.Host
Imports System.Management.Automation.Runspaces
```

Downloading the example code

You can download the example code files for all Packt books you have purchased from your account at http://www.PacktPub.com. If you purchased this book elsewhere, you can visit http://www.PacktPub.com/support and register to have the files e-mailed directly to you.

Also, adding the following directive statements will make it easier to work with the collections returned from the commands:

```
Imports System.Collections.Generic
Imports System.Collections.ObjectModel
```

Creating and opening a runspace

To use the Microsoft Windows PowerShell and Citrix XenApp Commands from managed code, we must first create and open a **runspace**. A runspace provides a way for the application to execute pipelines programmatically. Runspaces construct a logical model of execution using pipelines that contain cmdlets, native commands, and language elements.

Scripting Programming

So let's go and create a new `sub` called `ShowXAServers` for the new runspace.

```
Private Sub ShowXAServers()
```

Then the following code creates a new instance of a runspace and opens it.

```
Dim myRunspace As Runspace
myRunspace = RunspaceFactory.CreateRunspace()
myRunspace.Open()
```

The preceding piece of code only provides access to the cmdlets that come with the default Windows PowerShell installation. To use the cmdlets included with XenApp Commands, we must call it using an instance of the `RunspaceConfiguration` class. The following code creates a runspace that has access to the XenApp Commands:

```
Dim rsConfig As RunspaceConfiguration
rsConfig = RunspaceConfiguration.Create()
Dim info As PSSnapInInfo
Dim snapInException AsNew PSSnapInException
info = rsConfig.AddPSSnapIn("Citrix.XenApp.Commands", snapInException)
Dim myRunSpace As Runspace
myRunSpace = RunspaceFactory.CreateRunspace(rsConfig)
myRunSpace.Open()
```

This code specifies that we want to use Windows PowerShell in the XenApp Command context. This step gives us access to Windows PowerShell cmdlets and Citrix-specific cmdlets.

Running a cmdlet

Next, we need to create an instance of the Command class by using the name of the cmdlet that we want to run. The following code creates an instance of the Command class that will run the `Get-XAServer` cmdlet, add the command to the Commands collection of the pipeline, and finally run the command calling the `Pipeline.Invoke` method.

```
Dim myCommand As New Command("Get-XAServer")
pipeLine.Commands.Add(myCommand)
Dim commandResults As Collection(OfPSObject)
commandResults = pipeLine.Invoke()
```

Display results

Now we run the command `Get-XAServer` on the shell to get this output:

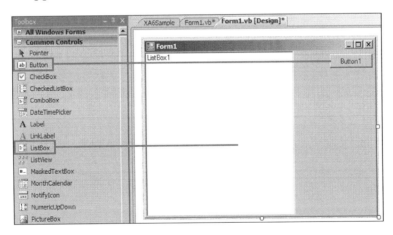

The left column displays the properties of the cmdlet, and in this case, we are looking for the first one, the `ServerName`, so we are going to redirect the output of the `ServerName` property to a listbox.

So the next step will be to add a **ListBox** and **Button** controls. The **ListBox** will show the list of XenApp servers when we click the button.

Then we need to add the following code at the end of `Sub ShowXAServers`:

```
For Each cmdlet As PSObject In commandResults
ListBox1.Items.Add(cmdlet.Properties("Servername").Value.ToString())
Next
```

Scripting Programming

The full code of the sample will look like this:

```vb
Imports System.Management.Automation
Imports System.Management.Automation.Host
Imports System.Management.Automation.Runspaces
Imports System.Collections.Generic
Imports System.Collections.ObjectModel

Public Class Form1

    Sub ShowXAServers()
        Dim rsConfig As RunspaceConfiguration
        rsConfig = RunspaceConfiguration.Create()
        Dim info As PSSnapInInfo
        Dim snapInException As New PSSnapInException
        info = rsConfig.AddPSSnapIn("Citrix.XenApp.Commands",
          snapInException)
        Dim myRunSpace As Runspace
        myRunSpace = RunspaceFactory.CreateRunspace(rsConfig)
        myRunSpace.Open()
        Dim pipeLine As Pipeline
        pipeLine = myRunSpace.CreatePipeline()
        Dim myCommand As New Command("Get-XAServer")
        pipeLine.Commands.Add(myCommand)
        Dim commandResults As Collection(Of PSObject)
        commandResults = pipeLine.Invoke()
        For Each cmdlet As PSObject In commandResults
            ListBox1.Items.Add(cmdlet.Properties("Servername").
              Value.ToString())
        Next
    End Sub

    Private Sub Button1_Click(ByVal sender As System.Object, ByVal e
   As System.EventArgs) Handles Button1.Click
        ShowXAServers()
    End Sub

End Class
```

And this is the final output of the application when we run it:

Passing parameters to cmdlets

We can pass parameters to cmdlets using the `Parameters.Add` option. We can add multiple parameters. Each parameter will require a line. For example, we can add the `ZoneName` parameter to filter server members of the US-Zone zone:

```
Dim myCommand As New Command("Get-XAServer")
myCommand.Parameters.Add("ZoneName", "US-ZONE")
pipeLine.Commands.Add(myCommand)
```

Creating a sample C#.NET application

Now we will create a sample application to list all XenApp servers in our farm using Citrix XenApp Commands with managed code. This sample is exactly the same as the VB.NET application. Open C#.NET. Samples contained in this book are developed in **Microsoft C# 2008 Express Edition**.

Then we need to go to **File | New Project | Windows Form Applications**. Type the desired name for our project and click the **OK** button.

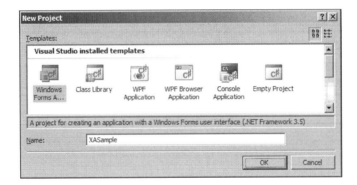

Adding references

We need to add a reference to the `System.Management.Automation.dll` assembly. Adding this assembly is tricky; first, we need to copy the assembly file to our application folder using the following command:

```
Copy %windir%\assembly\GAC_MSIL\System.Management.Automation\1.0.0.0__
31bf3856ad364e35\System.Management.Automation.dll C:\Code\XA6Sample
```

where `C:\Code\XA6Sample` is the folder of our application.

Scripting Programming

Then we need to add the reference to the assembly. In the **Project** menu, we need to select **Add Reference**, click on **Browse** tab, search and select the file **System.Management.Automation.dll**.

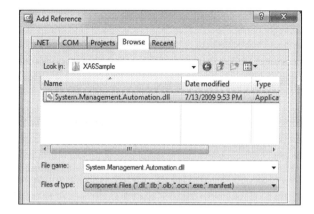

After referencing the assembly, we need to add the following directive statements to our code:

```
Using System.Management.Automation;
Using System.Management.Automation.Host;
Using System.Management.Automation.Runspaces;
```

Also, adding the following directive statements will make it easier to work with the collections returned from the commands:

```
Using System.Collections.Generic;
Using System.Collections.ObjectModel;
```

Creating and opening a runspace

To use the Microsoft Windows PowerShell and Citrix XenApp Commands from managed code, we must first create and open a runspace. A runspace provides a way for the application to execute pipelines programmatically. Runspaces construct a logical model of execution using pipelines that contains Cmdlets, native commands, and language elements.

So let's go and create a new function called `ShowXAServers` for the new runspace.

```
void ShowXAServers()
```

Then the following code creates a new instance of a runspace and opens it.

```
RunspacemyRunspace = RunspaceFactory.CreateRunspace();
myRunspace.Open();
```

The preceding piece of code provides access only to the cmdlets that come with the default Windows PowerShell installation. To use the cmdlets included with XenApp Commands, we must call it using an instance of the RunspaceConfiguration class. The following code creates a runspace that has access to the XenApp Commands:

```
RunspaceConfiguration rsConfig = RunspaceConfiguration.Create();
PSSnapInException snapInException = null;
PSSnapInInfo info = rsConfig.AddPSSnapIn("Citrix.XenApp.Commands",
out snapInException);
Runspace myRunSpace = RunspaceFactory.CreateRunspace(rsConfig);
myRunSpace.Open();
```

This code specifies that we want to use Windows PowerShell in the XenApp Command context. This step gives us access to Windows PowerShell cmdlets and Citrix-specific cmdlets.

Running a cmdlet

Next, we need to create an instance of the Command class by using the name of the cmdlet that we want to run. The following code creates an instance of the Command class that will run the Get-XAServer cmdlet, add the command to the Commands collection of the pipeline, and finally run the command calling the Pipeline.Invoke method.

```
Pipeline pipeLine = myRunSpace.CreatePipeline();
Command myCommand = newCommand("Get-XAServer");
pipeLine.Commands.Add(myCommand);
Collection<PSObject> commandResults = pipeLine.Invoke();
```

Display results

Now we run the command Get-XAServer on the shell and get this output:

```
PS C:\Users\ctxadmin> get-xaserver

ServerName            : BRICKXA02
FolderPath            : Servers
ZoneName              : Frederick
ElectionPreference    : MostPreferred
IPAddresses           : {192.168.1.203}
OSVersion             : 6.1.7600
OSServicePack         :
Is64Bit               : True
CitrixProductName     : Citrix Presentation Server
CitrixVersion         : 6.0.6410
CitrixEdition         : Platinum
CitrixEditionString   : PLT
CitrixServicePack     : 0
CitrixInstallDate     : 7/3/2010 8:58:11 AM
CitrixInstallPath     : C:\Program Files (x86)\Citrix\
LogOnsEnabled         : True
IcaPortNumber         : 1494
RdpPortNumber         :
VirtualIPInUse        :
SessionCount          :
```

Scripting Programming

In the left column, the properties of the cmdlet are located, and in this case, we are looking for the first one, the `ServerName`, so we are going to redirect the output of the `ServerName` property to a listbox.

So the next step will be to add a **ListBox** and **Button** controls. The **ListBox** will show the list of XenApp servers when we click the button.

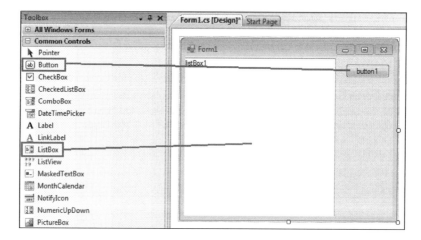

Then we need to add the following code at the end of `FunctionShowXAServers`:

```
foreach (PSObject cmdlet in commandResults)
{
   string cmdletName = cmdlet.Properties["ServerName"].Value.ToString();
   listBox1.Items.Add (cmdletName);
}
```

The full code of the sample will look like this:

```
using System;
using System.Collections.Generic;
using System.ComponentModel;
using System.Data;
using System.Drawing;
using System.Linq;
using System.Text;
using System.Windows.Forms;
using System.Management.Automation;
using System.Management.Automation.Host;
using System.Management.Automation.Runspaces;
using System.Collections.ObjectModel;
```

```csharp
namespace XASampleVC
{
    public partial class Form1 : Form
    {
        public Form1()
        {
            InitializeComponent();
        }

        private void Form1_Load(object sender, EventArgs e)
        {

        }

        void ShowXAServers()
        {
            RunspaceConfiguration rsConfig =
              RunspaceConfiguration.Create();
            PSSnapInException snapInException = null;
            PSSnapInInfo info = rsConfig.AddPSSnapIn(
              "Citrix.XenApp.Commands", out snapInException);
            Runspace myRunSpace = RunspaceFactory.CreateRunspace(
              rsConfig);
            myRunSpace.Open();
            Pipeline pipeLine = myRunSpace.CreatePipeline();
            Command myCommand = new Command("Get-XAServer");
            pipeLine.Commands.Add(myCommand);
            Collection<PSObject> commandResults = pipeLine.Invoke();
            foreach (PSObject cmdlet in commandResults)
            {
                string cmdletName = cmdlet.Properties["ServerName"].
                  Value.ToString();
                listBox1.Items.Add(cmdletName);
            }
        }

        private void button1_Click(object sender, EventArgs e)
        {
            ShowXAServers();
        }


    }
}
```

And this is the final output of the application when we run it:

Passing parameters to cmdlets

We can pass parameters to cmdlets, using the `Parameters.Add` option. We can add multiple parameters. Each parameter will require a line. For example, we can add the `ZoneName` parameter to filter server members of the US-Zone zone.

```
Command myCommand = newCommand("Get-XAServer");
myCommand.Parameters.Add("ZoneName", "US-ZONE")
pipeLine.Commands.Add(myCommand);
```

Using MFCOM on XenApp

We can use PowerShell to call MFCOM objects on XenApp 5.0 farms or older versions. This is useful when we want to use PowerShell to manage multiple versions of XenApp farms or migrate data from previous versions of XenApp.

The following is a simple example of how to call an MFCOM object, inside a PowerShell script. The script shows the XenApp farm name on a XenApp 5.0 or earlier version. This example will fail on XenApp 6.0:

```
$CtxXA = New-Object -ComObject "MetaFrameCOM.MetaFrameFarm"
$CtxXA.Initialize(1)
$CtxXA.FarmName
```

Convert MFCOM scripts to PowerShell

We can convert our MFCOM Scripts to PowerShell using the MFCOM Script Searcher tool, available for download at http://support.citrix.com/article/CTX125089.

This tool will help us to search existing MFCOM scripts and provide us with an alternate PowerShell cmdlet to perform a similar function. Also, the tool will show the syntax of the PowerShell and some examples.

To use the tool, download the file, decompress the .ZIP file, and run the .EXE file.

We need to set the location to search for the script file. Select the type of scripts we would like to search. Click the **Search Files** button. The application inspects the files located in the folder (and subfolders, if we enable the **Search Subfolders** checkbox) and returns PowerShell commands and examples.

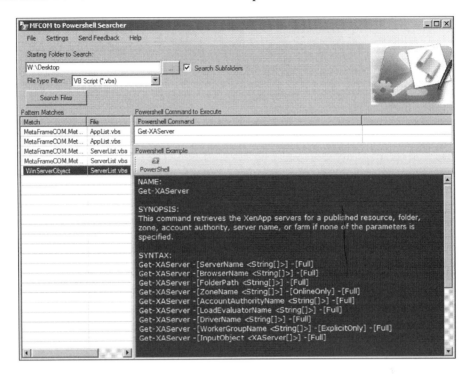

Summary

In this chapter, we have learned about managing XenApp with Windows PowerShell and developed sample .NET applications to call Citrix PowerShell cmdlets, on both Visual Basic.NET (VB.NET) and C#.NET.

- Difference between MFCOM and PowerShell scripts
- Installing XenApp Commands on XenApp servers
- Using PowerShell for basic administrative tasks
- Using PowerShell commands from .NET applications (VB.NET and C#.NET)
- Converting MFCOM scripts to PowerShell

In the next (and last) chapter, we will talk about advanced deployment of XenApp 6 farms, including deploying XenApp 6 in a virtualized environment (VMware vSphere, Citrix XenServer, and Microsoft Hyper-V).

13
Virtualizing XenApp Farms

In the last chapter, we learned about scripting programming, which included the installation of XenApp commands on XenApp servers and the use of PowerShell for basic administrative tasks. We also learned how to use PowerShell commands from inside .NET applications (VB.NET and C#.NET).

In this chapter, we will cover the basics of virtualization of Citrix XenApp farms. We have been hearing a lot about virtualization over the last few years and implementing XenApp in a virtualized environment is a very popular option today. Running XenApp on virtual machines helps reduce datacenter size and costs, cuts down on server deployment time, and saves money. In this chapter, we will learn more about implementing XenApp on virtual machines including:

- Deploying XenApp 6 in a virtualized environment
- Advantages and disadvantages of virtualization, virtual machine performance and host scalability, and more
- Deploying XenApp6 on Citrix XenServer, Microsoft Hyper-V, and VMware vSphere virtual machines
- Cloning XenApp6 virtual machines

Deploying XenApp 6 in a virtualized environment

Deploying virtualized XenApp farms today is a common scenario for any Citrix environment. In this chapter, we help William Empire from Brick Unit Construction to evaluate XenApp 6 on leading bare metal hypervisors in the market: Citrix XenServer, VMware ESX vSphere, and Microsoft Hyper-V.

Hypervisors allow multiple operating systems, called **guests**, to run concurrently on a host computer, a feature called **hardware virtualization**. The hypervisor presents to the guest operating systems a virtual operating platform and monitors the execution of the guest operating systems. Multiple instances of a variety of operating systems may share the virtualized hardware resources. Bare metal hypervisors run directly on the host's hardware to control the hardware and to monitor guest operating systems.

There are many good reasons to virtualize XenApp 6 farms, including:

- Faster server and application provisioning: In a (standard) non-virtualized environment, deploying new servers and increasing farm capability can take hours. In a virtualized environment, we can create templates and scripts to deploy VMs (virtual machines) in a few minutes.

- Server consolidation: Virtualization improves server utilization. The average server utilization in the datacenter is usually between 10 to 25 percent. The application silos utilization ratio is lower and can be around 5 percent to 10 percent. Consolidating multiple servers and application silos allows us to maximize the utilization of our hardware resources and reduce data-center expenses like energy and rack space. Also, we can consolidate multiple operating systems into the same host.

- Improved disaster recovery: By using snapshots, we can replicate production VMs to disaster recovery datacenters in a few minutes and keep our environment updated.

- Zero-downtime for hardware maintenance: In a virtualized environment, we can move VMs between hosts without service interruption, to update the hardware of our hosts' servers.

- Dynamic workload management: We can use VMs to support dynamic workload management, moving VMs to accommodate spikes in demand.

- Improved solution for test environment: We can build multiple copies of similar environments, and test new applications and hotfixes before we apply changes on production. Also, virtualized environments are great for training and development environments.

A few disadvantages of implementing virtualization:

- Server consolidation: Consolidation of servers and storage virtualization may create a larger, single point of failure, turning storage (SAN, NAS, and so on), and networking (switches, for example) in critical elements in our datacenter. A switch failure can affect our storage and may cause a virtual machine data-store failure. This issue can cause the downtime of virtual machines located in this data-store.

- Performance: Some applications can run slow on virtual machines. The performance of the applications sometimes is related with hardware. For example, using the SAS (Serial Attached SCSI) disk can provide better performance for critical applications than SATA (Serial ATA) disks.
- Licensing: Virtualization licensing is complex. We need to analyze the cost of hypervisor, hypervisor management tools, operating systems, and applications.

Virtual machine performance and host scalability

When we start a VM deployment, there are multiple questions that should be addressed to pin down the most appropriate host configuration:

- How many VMs should be deployed on a single host?
- Which CPU must be chosen and how many CPU cores must be used for the host?
- How much memory and NIC ports should be installed on the host?
- How many virtual CPUs and how much memory should be allocated to each VM?
- Do we have to use internal storage or use SAN storage to store the VM disks? For VM deployment in a production environment, it is always advisable to use SAN. Local storage is not recommended.

The key for a successful deployment is always testing. Our applications and users will determine the appropriate VM configuration. As a consultant, I have found clients with VMs that require a lot of memory and just a single vCPU and some who require a normal amount of memory (4 GB of RAM for 32-bit and 8 GB of RAM for 64-bit VMs), but many vCPUs.

One of the keys to improved performance is to avoid oversubscribed vCPUs; that means that Brick Unit Construction should allocate more vCPUs than the number of cores. For example, if we have a server with four CPUs and each of them have six cores, we have 24 cores, so in this example, it is recommended to avoid using more than 24 vCPUs. This will cause VMs to share CPUs, which will eventually lead to performance degradation.

Another key is to avoid oversubscribed memory, which in some hypervisors is not allowed. That means, William must assign more memory to VMs than existing physical memory and allocate enough memory on the host to run all VMs, plus 1 GB for the host and extra memory for the memory overhead caused for 64-bit.

Also, storage is crucial for the performance of VMs. As I mentioned before, using a SAS (Serial Attached SCSI) disk can provide better performance for critical applications than SATA (Serial ATA) disks. Using local storage is a cheaper solution and a valid option for PoC (Proof of Concepts), pilots, or small environments but medium to large environments must use storage technologies like SAN (Storage Area Network) or NAS (Network Attached Storage), for example. These technologies provide the ability to move VMs between hosts without any downtime.

Networking is important for the success and performance of our virtualization deployment, so we need to have enough network ports to avoid performance issues. Usually, XenApp requires a solid network infrastructure. Most of the environments store Windows roaming profiles on file servers, and every time a user logs into the Citrix farm, the profile is copied from the network to the XenApp server. Also, depending on our applications and type of storage, we will need less or more network ports. For example, if we are using iSCSI, we need at least one dedicated network port (two for redundancy) to connect with the storage. Also, it is very important to choose a server to have enough expansion slots, just in case we need to add more network ports.

Choosing the right CPU is also very important. AMD Opteron and Intel Xeon processors provide on-chip instructions to handle direct hardware calls from the hypervisor, minimizing the associated overhead. We need to choose a CPU that supports virtualization technologies like AMD-V or Intel-VT.

Also, Intel Hyper-Threading (HT) provides great benefit to virtualization; Hyper-Threading allows a single physical processor core to appear to behave like two logical processors. So for example, if we choose an Intel Xeon CPU with four cores and enabled Hyper-Threading, the operating system or hypervisor will see eight cores. Enabling Hyper-Threading allows us to use 8 vCPUs per physical CPU. The performance is not the same as having a CPU with eight "real" cores, but is pretty good.

Choosing the right virtualization platform

What is the best platform to deploy XenApp on virtual machines: Citrix, Microsoft, or VMware? The response: it depends. If we have the time and resources, building a test lab is a good option. Also, we can find some reviews on the Internet from independent professionals (for example, Virtual reality Check Project www.virtualrealitycheck.net) and some from hypervisor companies and hardware vendors. These tests show results based on simulated tests. A real environment can show the same or opposite results.

Every implementation is unique, and server loads are different, based on users and applications. So my recommendation. So my recommendation is to build a small PoC or Pilot with these three platforms and evaluate the best option for our needs, except our company chose a virtualization platform before.

A good practice recommended by Citrix is do not P2V (convert a physical server into a virtual machine) Citrix production servers into VMs. Build VMs from scratch, except when you don't have any options. The P2V process does not remove drivers and applications from hardware vendors. If you don't have any chances, remove all hardware tools like HP Proliant Support Pack or Dell OpenManage after the P2V process. If you are using HP Proliant servers, you can use the **HP Proliant Support Pack Cleaner** tool (available for free at http://ctxadmtools.musumeci.com.ar) to remove all HP Proliant Support Pack tools.

Deploying XenApp6 on Citrix XenServer

XenServer is an open and powerful server virtualization solution that cuts datacenter costs by transforming static and complex datacenter environments into more dynamic, easy-to-manage delivery centers.

XenServer, the Citrix server virtualization solution, is based on Xen, an open-source virtualization project that supports both Intel Virtualization Technology (INTEL VT) and AMD Virtualization (AMD-V) capabilities. Xen allows a single machine to host multiple isolated environments, each running on a different operating system.

In 2004, the Xen project released the first version of its hypervisor and in 2007 Citrix purchased XenSource, renaming Xen products as XenServer Standard Edition and XenServer Enterprise Edition.

Citrix XenServer free edition is available for free at www.citrix.com/xenserver. Also, we can buy the Advanced, Enterprise, or Platinum Editions. These versions provide different features such as high availability, workload balancing, storage links, provisioning services, lab and stage management, and site recovery.

The installation of XenServer 5.6 is relatively simple. Refer to the following XenServer documentation for details:

- XenServer 5.6 Installation Guide (http://support.citrix.com/article/CTX124889)
- XenServer Administrator's Guide (http://support.citrix.com/article/CTX124887)
- XenServer 5.6 Virtual Machine Installation Guide (http://support.citrix.com/article/CTX124888)

The information in this chapter is based on **Citrix XenServer 5.6 FP1**.

Install XenApp Evaluation Virtual Appliance on XenServer

The XenApp EVA (Evaluation Virtual Appliance) is a complete virtual machine system for evaluating Citrix XenApp 6. The Citrix XenApp EVA is the faster way to evaluate and test XenApp and enables customers and partners to evaluate application virtualization with XenApp 6 for Windows Server 2008 R2.

Now we are going to help William to evaluate the XenApp EVA. XenApp EVA is available for download from **citrix.com | Download | XenApp**. The image is available for XenServer and Hyper-V. This download requires a www.citrix.com account.

To install the EVA, William needs to do the following:

1. He needs to download and extract the file, running the .EXE file.
2. William imports the EVA.VHD disk into Citrix XenServer: he opens **XenCenter | Tools | Virtual Appliance Tools | Disk Image Import**.

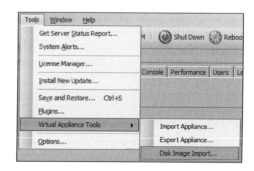

3. He uses the **Browse** button to search for the `.VXD` file and then clicks the **Next** button.
4. He types the VM name and disables the **Run Operating System Fixups** checkbox. Then he clicks the **Next** button.

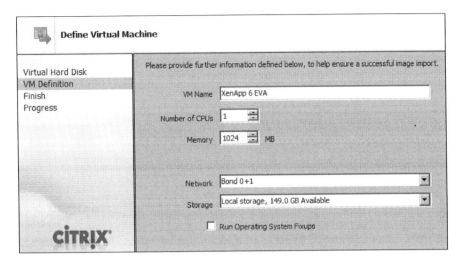

5. He logs on as **CTXS-XA1\Administrator** with the password **Evaluation1**.
6. He installs the **XenServer Tools** from the VM menu, and selects the **Install XenServer Tools** option. Then he reboots the server.
7. Finally, he downloads an Evaluation License from www.citrix.com and he installs the license in the server (instructions are discussed in *Chapter 3, Installing XenApp 6*).

That's it, William is ready to join the machine to the domain (if he wants) and start testing XenApp!

Creating a new XenApp 6 VM in XenServer

The process to create a new VM for XenApp 6 is very straightforward. The following is the process used by William to install a XenApp 6 VM in XenServer:

1. In the XenCenter console, William clicks on the VM menu and he selects **New VM**. Also, he can right-click on the XenServer host and click on the **New VM** option.

2. The creation of VM wizard starts. On the **Template** page, he needs to choose the **Citrix XenApp on Windows Server 2008 R2 (64-bit)** option. This will set up the VM with optimal settings for XenApp.

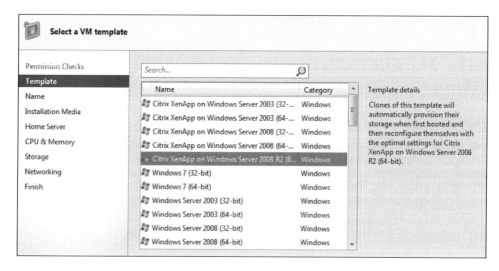

3. On the **Name** page, he needs to enter a VM name. He can change this name later, if he needs to. Also, he can enter a description for the VM.

4. On the **Installation Media** page, he can choose the location of operating system files. By default, he can boot from the host DVD or from the network. He can click on the **New ISO Library** link to create an ISO Library to store operating systems disks in ISO format. In the following screenshot, he selects a **Windows Server 2008 R2 ISO** image from their ISO library:

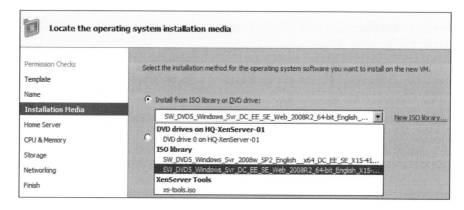

Chapter 13

5. On the **Home Server** page, he needs to select the XenServer where he is going to place the VM.
6. On the **CPU & Memory** page, he will set the number of vCPUs and the amount of memory for the VM. Also, he can adjust both values later.
7. On the **Storage** page, he can select the size and location of the VM's disk or disks. Also, he selects to create a diskless VM that can be booted from the network.
8. On the **Networking** page, William can set up the network card of the VM. He can add or remove network cards and choose the appropriate network host:

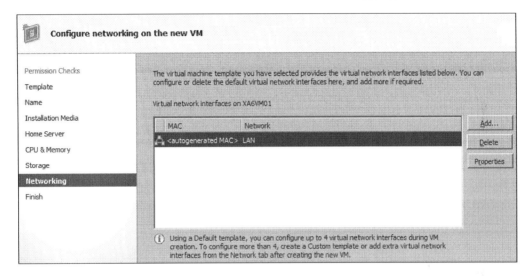

9. On the **Finish** page, he reviews all settings of the VM machine and he clicks the **Finish** button to start the VM build process.

[387]

10. Once the build process is complete and the virtual machine is started, the installation of Windows Server 2008 R2 starts.

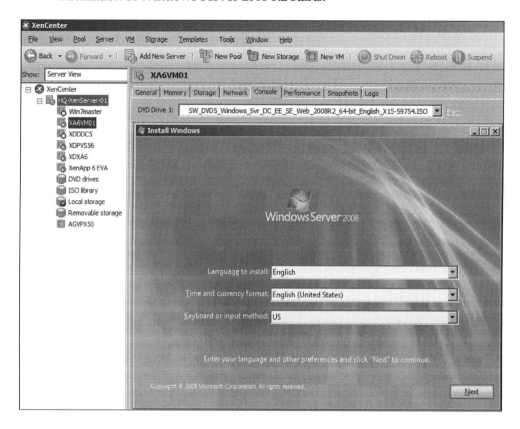

11. Once the setup of the operating system is complete, William can install XenServer tools in the VM, using the **VM** menu, **Install XenServer Tools** option. XenServer tools provide high performance Windows drivers and a management agent (this is a recommended step).

- After XenServer tools are installed and the server is rebooted, William is ready to configure the VM
- He needs to configure the IP Address, install Remote Desktop Services (optional step), and reboot the server

$\Big[$ Take a VM snapshot before any step of the install and setup process, until you are familiar with the procedure, just in case. $\Big]$

Now William is ready to set up XenApp on the VM! He needs to follow the instructions discussed in *Chapter 3, Installing XenApp 6* to set up the first server XenApp 6 on the farm. Also, you can read the section *Cloning XenApp 6 virtual machines* later in this chapter, to know how to prepare our VM for cloning.

Deploying XenApp6 on Microsoft Hyper-V

Microsoft Windows Server 2008 Hyper-V R2 (Hyper-V), the next-generation hypervisor-based server virtualization technology, is available as an integral feature of Windows Server 2008 R2 and enables you to implement server virtualization with ease.

Hyper-V allows us to make the best use of the server hardware investments by consolidating multiple server roles as separate virtual machines (VMs) running on a single physical machine.

Hyper-V requires 64-bit machines with AMD-V or Intel VT-enabled processors.

Virtualizing XenApp Farms

Hyper-V is not available for the Itanium edition or Windows Server 2008 R1 32-bit editions.

Hyper-V is available as two different versions:

- A standalone product called Microsoft Hyper-V Server 2008 R2: This version is free and available for download at www.microsoft.com. This version is a limited version of Windows Server 2008 R2 Core with the Hyper-V role enabled and other roles disabled. This version can be managed using command line, PowerShell, or using the managing console from a Windows Server 2008, Windows 7, or Windows Vista machine.
- As part of Microsoft Windows Server 2008 R2. We need to have a license of Windows Server 2008 Standard, Enterprise, or Datacenter editions (Windows Server 2008 Web Edition is not supported) and install the Hyper-V role.

For more information about **Microsoft Server 2008 Hyper-V R2**, check this link: www.microsoft.com/hyper-v-server/en/us/default.aspx.

The information in this chapter is based on Microsoft Windows Server 2008 R2 with the Hyper-V R2 role installed.

A management tool is required to manage the (free) standalone edition of Hyper-V or for specific features like Live Migration or cloning on the Windows Server 2008 edition.

Microsoft offers **System Center Virtual Machine Manager 2008 R2**, available for evaluation at http://www.microsoft.com/systemcenter/en/us/virtual-machine-manager.aspx.

Citrix also offers a management tool for Hyper-V called Citrix Essentials for Hyper-V. This product is available in three versions: one of them called **Express** is available for free. More information can be found at http://www.citrix.com/ehv.

Installing XenApp Evaluation Virtual Appliance on Hyper-V

The XenApp EVA (Evaluation Virtual Appliance) is a complete virtual machine system for evaluating Citrix XenApp 6. The Citrix XenApp EVA is the faster way to evaluate and test XenApp and enables customers and partners to evaluate application virtualization with XenApp 6 for Windows Server 2008 R2.

Chapter 13

Now we will help William to evaluate the XenApp EVA. XenApp EVA is available for download from **citrix.com | Download | XenApp**. The image is available for XenServer and Hyper-V. This download requires a `mycitrix.com` account.

To install the EVA, William needs to do the following:

1. He downloads and extracts the file, running the `.EXE` file.
2. He needs to create a new VM to import the `EVA.VHD` disk into Hyper-V by opening **Hyper-V Manager**, **Actions** menu, he chooses **New** and then **Virtual Machine**. Also, he can right-click on the hostname and select **New and Virtual Machine**.
3. On the **Specify Name and Location** page, he types the VM name and chooses the location of the folder to store the VM, and clicks the **Next** button.

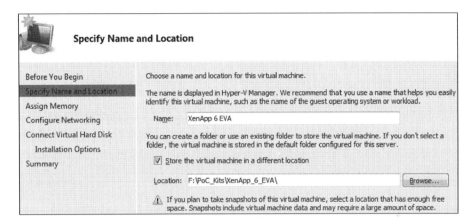

4. On the **Assign Memory** page, he enters the amount of memory for the VM and clicks on the **Next** button.
5. On the **Configure Networking** page, William selects the appropriate network connection and clicks on the **Next** button.

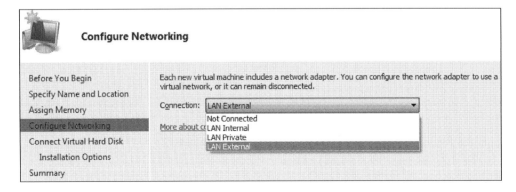

6. On the **Connect Virtual Hard Disk** page, William selects the **Use an existing virtual hard disk** option and uses the **Browse** button to search for the `CitrixXA6EVA.VXD` file and clicks on the **Next** button.

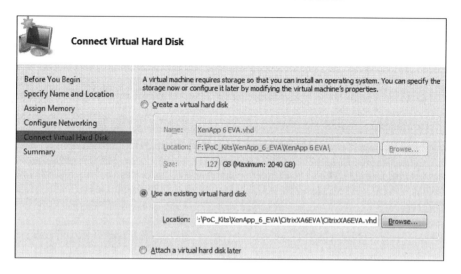

7. On the **Summary** page, he clicks on the **Finish** button to complete the process and creates the VM.
8. He logs in as **CTXS-XA1\Administrator** with the password **Evaluation1**.
9. He downloads an Evaluation License from `www.citrix.com` and installs the license on the server (Instructions are discussed in *Chapter 3, Installing XenApp 6*).

And now, he is ready to join the machine to the domain (if he wants) and start testing XenApp!

Creating a new XenApp 6 VM in Hyper-V

The process to create a new VM for XenApp 6 is pretty simple. The following is the process used by William to install a XenApp 6 VM in Hyper-V:

1. He opens **Hyper-V Manager**, clicks the **Actions** menu, and chooses **New** and then **Virtual Machine**. Also, he can right-click on the hostname, select **New**, and then **Virtual Machine**.

Chapter 13

2. On the **Specify Name and Location** page, William types the VM name, chooses the location to store the VM, and clicks the **Next** button.

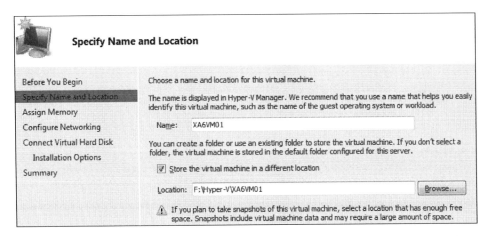

3. On the **Assign Memory** page, he enters the amount of memory for the VM and clicks on the **Next** button.

4. On the **Configure Networking** page, he selects the appropriate network connection and clicks the **Next** button.

5. On the **Connect Virtual Hard Disk** page, he selects the **Create a virtual hard disk** option, uses the **Browse** button to select the folder to store the .VXD file, sets the **Size** of the disk, and then clicks on the **Next** button.

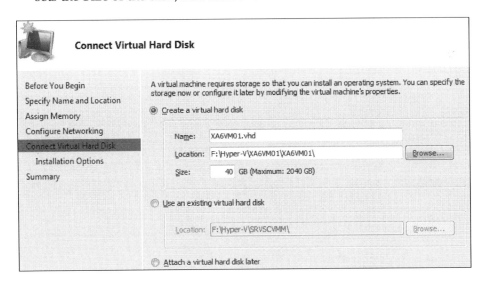

Virtualizing XenApp Farms

6. On the **Installation Options** page, William can select the **Install an operating system from a boot CD/DVD-ROM** option to boot from CD/DVD in the host or using an .ISO image. This is the most common scenario. Also, he can select the **Install an operating system from a boot floppy disk** option or the **Install an operating system from a network-based installation server** option.

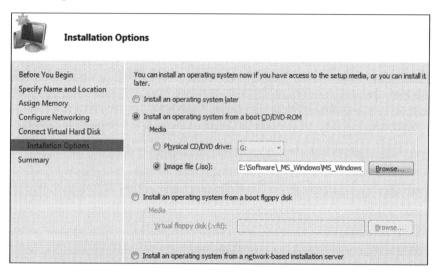

7. On the **Summary** page, he clicks on the **Finish** button to complete the process and creates the VM.

8. After the build process is complete and the virtual machine is ready, he right-clicks over the VM name and selects the properties to edit the settings of the VM. He can modify the amount of vCPUs (this is an optional step – he can keep the default 1 vCPU option).

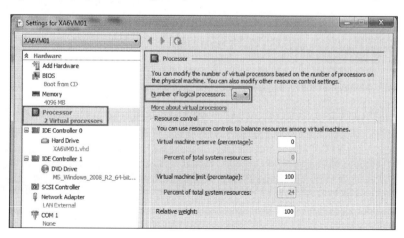

9. After that, William is ready to install Windows Server 2008 R2 operating system. When the setup of the operating system is complete, he is ready to configure the VM. He needs to configure the IP Address, install Remote Desktop Services (optional step), and reboot the server.

 Take a VM snapshot before any step of the install and setup process, until you are familiar with the procedure, just in case.

Now William is ready to setup XenApp on the VM! He needs to follow the instructions discussed in *Chapter 3, Installing XenApp 6* to set up the first server XenApp 6 on the farm. Also, you can read the section *Cloning XenApp 6 virtual machines* later in this chapter, to know how to prepare our VM for cloning.

Deploying XenApp 6 on VMware vSphere

VMware vSphere leverages the power of virtualization to transform datacenters into dramatically simplified cloud computing infrastructures, and enables IT organizations to deliver the next generation of flexible and reliable IT services, using internal and external resources, securely and with low risk.

VMware vSphere (formerly known as VMware ESX Server) is available in these versions:

- **VMware vSphere Hypervisor (ESXi):** This is the free version of vSphere. Perfect for testing, evaluating the platform, remote offices, and small environments.
- **VMware vSphere:** This is the full version of the hypervisor. Available in multiple versions, provides different features, depending on the cost of every product.

Some limitations of ESXi:

- Limited management capabilities: We need to buy a VMware vCenter Server license if we want to create templates or copy VMs from a GUI.
- Limited scripting capabilities: We can't create scripts to unattended installations. Also, VMware locks access to several APIs, so we can't manage some functionality using scripts.
- Host Active Directory Integration: ESXi doesn't support AD integration.

Choosing the right VMware vSphere product will depend on our environment, but I will give some advice based on my experience implementing XenApp on VMware.

Virtualizing XenApp Farms

First of all, build a dedicated cluster just for XenApp production VMs. We can use a different cluster for infrastructure servers, like Edgesight, Web interface servers, and so on.

The best version for most of the XenApp environments is vSphere Standard edition; this decision will depend on the hardware we choose to build our vSphere servers. Standard edition is limited to 4-way (four CPUs) servers with six cores. For example, choosing an AMD Opteron 6100 CPU with eight or twelve cores will require an Advanced or Enterprise license.

Standard edition provides the ability to build clusters with high availability, vMotion, thin provisioning, and more.

One of the features not supported by Standard Edition is VMware DRS (only available at Enterprise and Enterprise Plus). VMware DRS dynamically balances computing capacity across multiple VMware hosts. VMware DRS is a great feature when we have multiple VMs with different resource requirements, but because XenApp VMs are highly resource-intensive, there is no need for VMware DRS.

Also, I do not recommend using vMotion to move XenApp production VMs, except for a host emergency or maintenance tasks. Usually, because XenApp server load is similar between VMs and host, there is no reason to move VMs between hosts.

 The information in this chapter is based on VMware vSpherev4.1.

Create a new XenApp 6 VM in VMware vSphere

The process to create a new VM for XenApp 6 in vSphere is a little bit more complicated than in Citrix XenServer and Microsoft Hyper-V, because vSphere provides more options. Now we are going to help William to configure a VM to run XenApp:

1. On the **Configuration** page, he chooses **Custom** and clicks the **Next** button.

Chapter 13

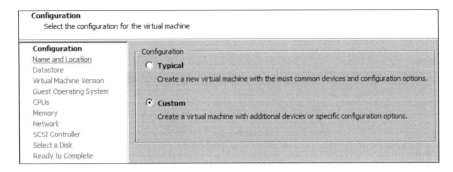

2. On the **Name and Location** page, he needs to type the name and the location of the VM and then click the **Next** button.

3. On the **Datastore** page, he needs to choose the datastore in which to store the VM and then click on the **Next** button.

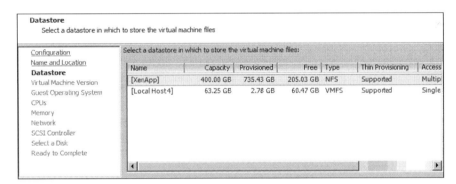

4. On the **Virtual Machine Version** page, he selects the **Virtual Machine Version 7** and clicks the **Next** button.

5. In the **Guest Operating System**, William needs to choose **Microsoft Windows Server 2008 R2 (64-bit)** and click the **Next** button.

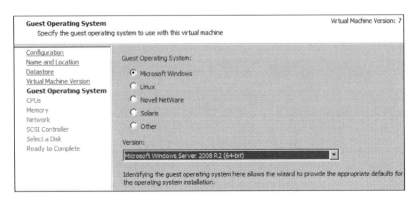

Virtualizing XenApp Farms

6. On the **CPUs** page, he needs to assign the number of vCPUs he wants and then clicks on the **Next** button.

7. On the **Memory** page, he needs to assign the amount of memory he wants and then clicks the **Next** button.

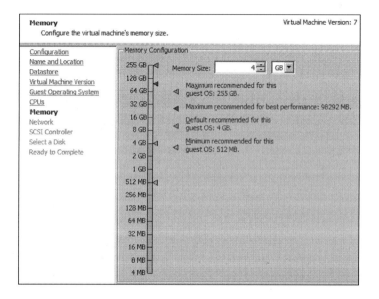

8. In the **Network** card, William can add one or more network card, choose the right network, and click on the **Next** button.

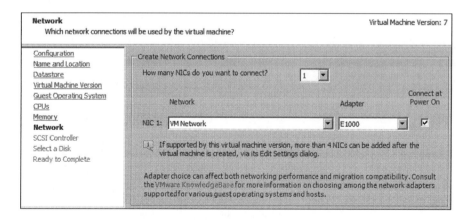

Chapter 13

9. On the **SCSI Controller** page, William needs to select the SCSI Controller, and depending on the VM configuration, he has multiple options. If he has a single disk for both operating systems and application, **LSI Logic SAS** is the recommended option. If he has two or multiple disks, it is recommended to set the operating system to the **LSI Logic SAS** controller and the **VMware Paravirtual** controller for all remaining data disks.

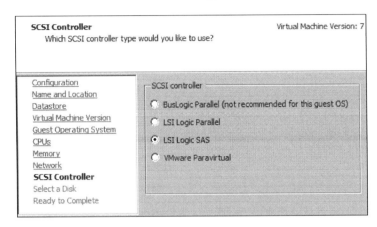

10. On the **Select a Disk** page, he chooses the **Create a new virtual disk** option and then clicks the **Next** button.

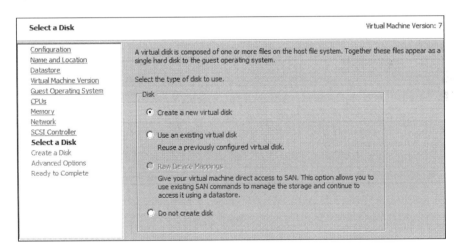

11. On the **Create a Disk** page, he sets the **Disk Size** and then clicks the **Next** button.

12. On the **Advanced Options**, he keeps the default settings, and clicks the **Next** button.

Virtualizing XenApp Farms

13. On the **Ready to Complete** page, William enables the **Edit the virtual machine settings before completion** checkbox and clicks the **Continue** button.

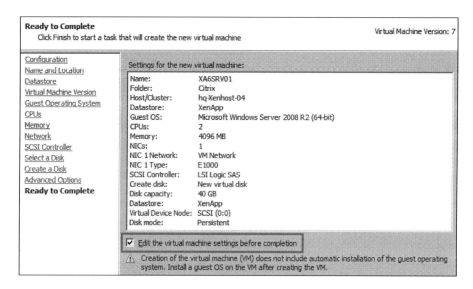

14. To remove the floppy disk, he selects it and clicks the **Remove** button.

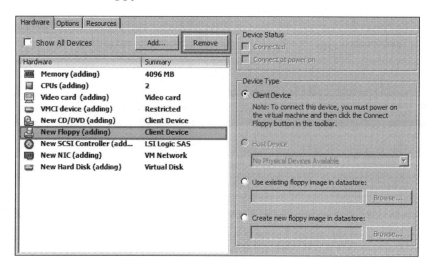

Chapter 13

15. Optional: To add an extra disk, William needs to click on the **Add** button and choose **Hard Disk**. He chooses **SCSI (1:0)** in the **Virtual Device Node**. This step will add a **New SCSI Controller** too. Change the **New SCSI controller** to **Paravirtual**.

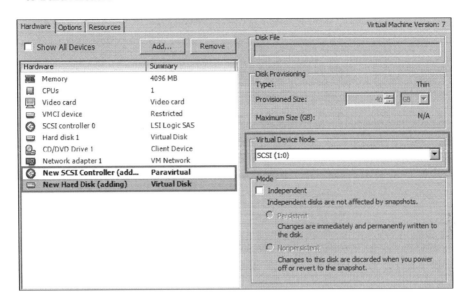

16. In the **Options** tab, he selects **Memory/CPU Hotplug**. This option allows him to increase the amount of memory and CPU without powering off the VM. This option only works on Windows Server 2008 Enterprise and Datacenter editions.

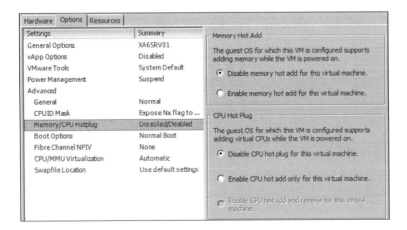

17. In the **Options** tab, he selects **CPU/MMU Virtualization**. Enabling this option will provide a significant increase in the performance of VM. Hardware-assisted MMU (Memory Management Unit) virtualization requires specific CPUs like Intel Xeon 5500 Series or later or AMD Opteron 4000 or 6000 Series or subsequent processors.

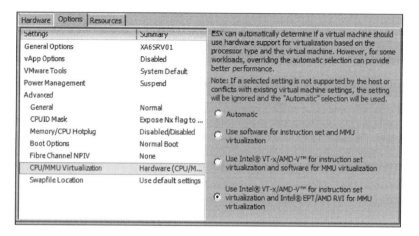

18. Now, he is ready to install the Windows Server 2008 R2 operating system.
19. Once the setup of the operating system is complete, William needs to install VMware Tools. To install VMware Tools, in the VM console, he clicks on the **VM** menu, selects **Guest** and then **Install/Upgrade VMware Tools**, follows the instructions, and restarts the server.

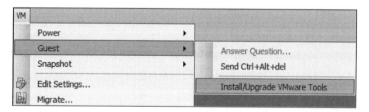

20. After VMware Tools is installed, he needs to configure the IP Address, install Remote Desktop Services (optional step), and reboot the server.

Take a VM snapshot before any step of the install and setup process, until you are familiar with the procedure, just in case.

Now William is ready to set up XenApp on the VM! He needs to follow the instructions discussed in *Chapter 3*, *Installing XenApp 6* to set up the first server XenApp 6 on the farm. Also, you can read the next section *Cloning XenApp 6 virtual machines* to know how to prepare our VM for cloning.

Cloning XenApp 6 virtual machines

After William creates the first XenApp 6 virtual machine and creates a Citrix farm (or joins an existing XenApp 6 farm), he is ready to start the cloning process.

[Cloning is not supported for the first server in the farm (the server where we created the XenApp farm).]

1. William downloads (and installs) the updated XenApp Server Configuration Tool for Citrix XenApp 6 for Microsoft Windows Server 2008 R2 from `http://support.citrix.com/article/CTX124981`.

2. After the update is installed and XenApp server is rebooted, William needs to open **XenApp Server Role Manager** (**Start | All Programs | Citrix | XenApp Server Role Manager**).

3. The wizard starts and he needs to click on the **Edit Configuration** link.

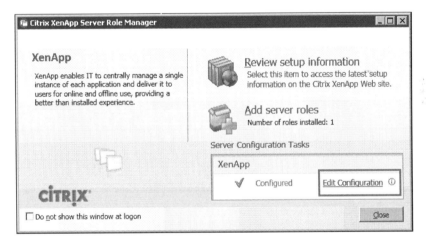

4. Then he needs to select the **Prepare this server for imaging and provisioning** option.

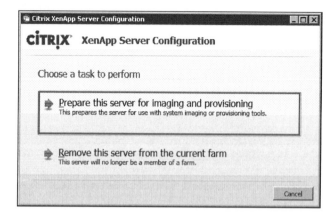

5. He selects the **Remove this current server instance from the farm** checkbox and selects the **Next** button.
6. William clicks on the **Apply** button to start the process.
7. This page shows the result of the process. William clicks on the **Finish** button to close the wizard.

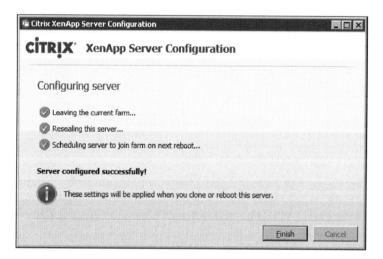

8. When the wizard is closed, he returns to the **XenApp Server Role Manager**, where he can choose to close the window or reboot the virtual machine. He needs to close the window, so he can run **SYSPREP** before cloning the virtual machine.

> The System Preparation Tool (SYSPREP) is a tool used to remove system-specific data from Windows, such as the Computer SID. Also, SYSPREP resets other machine-specific information that, if duplicated, can cause problems for certain applications like Windows Server Update Services (WSUS).
>
> Microsoft recommends to SYSPREP the image before cloning, but we can skip this step and replace a process like reset WSUS settings by scripts, if we want.
>
> To understand the SYSPREP tool, I recommend reading Mark Russinovich's article **The Machine SID Duplication Myth** at http://blogs.technet.com/b/markrussinovich/archive/2009/11/03/3291024.aspx.

9. William is going to run SYSPREP before the cloning process. He needs to choose the **Enter System Out-of-Box Experience (OOBE)** option, enable the **Generalize** checkbox, select **Shutdown** in the **Shutdown Options**, and click on the **OK** button.

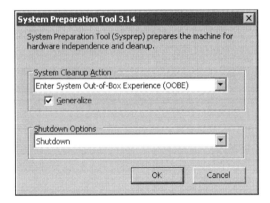

10. When the SYSPREP process is complete, the virtual machine is turned off. Now William is ready to copy the virtual machine.

11. When he turns on the VM, the setup process starts and after he chooses the language and keyboard, he is ready to configure the VM. He needs to rename the server, assign an IP address (optional), and join it to the domain. Once the setup is complete, the new VM is joined to the XenApp farm and the server is ready.

Unattended Install of XenApp 6

An unattended installation (also called silent installation) is one which does not require user interaction. Sometimes an unattended installation is silent installation when it does not display any indication of status or progress. Most of the people use one or the other name to refer to automatic deployments.

On XenApp 6, we can use two different commands to set up the server in unattended mode:

- `XenAppSetupConsole.exe`: Used to install XenApp components.
- `XenAppConfigConsole.exe`: Used to configure XenApp, join server to a farm, configure authentication, and so on.

We can use the following unattended install instructions to automatize the deployment of both physical and virtual XenApp servers.

Unattended Install of XenApp Components

We learned how to install XenApp 6 in *Chapter 3, Installing XenApp 6*. We found detailed information there. Let's take a quick look at the list of tasks used by William to prepare the server to install XenApp in unattended mode:

1. Install and configur Windows Server 2008 R2.
2. Join the server to domain (if required) and disable Windows Firewall and IE ESC (Enhanced Security Configuration).
3. Disable UAC (User Account Control) to avoid issues with unattended scripts. He can re-enable later, if he needs. He disables UAC clicking on **Start | Control Panel | User Accounts | Change User Account Control Settings** and set UAC to **Never notify**.

After the setup of the operating system is complete, he needs to add required Windows roles and install and configure XenApp 6 on the server. Following is the process used by William to install and configure XenApp:

1. Add required Windows roles using PowerShell. He opens a Windows PowerShell command and types the following command:

   `Import-Module Servermanager`

   This cmdlet will load the Server Manager module into the Windows PowerShell session (also he can create a PowerShell script with this and following cmdlets).

2. Then he adds required roles (.NET Framework 3.51 and Remote Desktop) using the following PowerShell cmdlets:

   `Add-WindowsFeatureAS-NET-Framework`

   `Add-WindowsFeatureRDS-RD-Server -restart`

   The last cmdlet will force a restart of the server.

> If we want to add an extra role, the GPMC console for example, and we do not know the command name of the role or feature, we can use the PowerShell cmdlet `Get-WindowsFeature` to show a list of all roles and features available. We need to use the command in the `Name` column.

Also, William can install roles from the command line, using the command `ServerManagerCmd.exe`. This command is deprecated and replaced by the previously explained PowerShell cmdlet `Add-WindowsFeature`, and is not guaranteed to work in future versions of Windows Server.

To install roles or features using `ServerManagerCmd.exe`, he can use the following command:

`ServerManagerCmd -install AS-NET-Framework`

`ServerManagerCmd-install RDS-RD-Server -restart`

If William wants to add an extra role, and he does not know the command name of the role or feature, he can use the following command:

`ServerManagerCmd-query`

This command will show a list of all roles and features available (and their names) and which of them are installed.

3. Prerequisite installations are complete. William needs to extract the XenApp 6 ISO file downloaded from the Citrix site to a folder in the server or mount the XenApp 6 DVD in the server.

4. The next step for William is to install XenApp running `XenAppSetupConsole.exe` file from the folder `\Xenapp Server Setup\Bin` in the local server folder or the XenApp 6 DVD, using the following command:

   `XenAppSetupConsole.exe /install:XenApp /Platinum`

   The `/install` parameter is used to select features to install. He can install multiple features using commas. Valid options are:

   ◦ EdgeSightServer: Installs EdgeSight Server role

   ◦ Licensing: Installs Citrix Licensing Server role

Virtualizing XenApp Farms

- ○ MerchandisingServer: Installs Merchandising Server role
- ○ PCMAdmin: Installs Power and Capacity Management administration components
- ○ Provisioning: Installs Provisioning Services
- ○ SecureGateway: Installs Secure Gateway
- ○ SmartAuditorServer: Installs SmartAuditor server
- ○ SsonService: Installs Single sign-on service
- ○ WebInterface: Installs Web Interface role
- ○ XenApp: Install XenApp server role

If he choosesthe **XenApp** feature, the Citrix Delivery Services Console, Citrix Online Plug-in, and Citrix Offline Plug-in are installed by default.

Also, he can use the `/exclude` parameter to omit the installation of same XenApp Role components. Options are:

- ○ XA_Console: Omits the installation of the Citrix Delivery Services Console
- ○ XA_IISIntegration: Omits the installation feature if the server has IIS role services installed

He used the `/Platinum` parameter to set the edition of XenApp to Platinum. If we doesn't specify an edition option, the Platinum edition is set by default. Other options available are:

- ○ /Enterprise: Sets the edition of XenApp to Enterprise
- ○ /Advanced: Sets the edition of XenApp to Advanced

> More information about `XenAppSetupConsole.exe` is available at `http://support.citrix.com/proddocs/index.jsp?topic=/xenapp6-w2k8-install/ps-install-command-line.html`.

5. After the XenApp role is installed, William reboots the server. He can automatize this step, using the following command:

`Shutdown/r /t 0`

Chapter 13

6. Once the server back up is complete, he is ready to join the XenApp server to existing farm and configure XenApp 6, using the `XenAppConfigConsole.exe` tool, located in the `\XenApp Server Configuration Tool` folder. The following command will join the server to the existing XenApp farm and uses the information stored in the SQL Server using a DSN file (instructions to create the file are below):

```
XenAppConfigConsole.exe /ExecutionMode:Join /FarmName:
BrickFarm6/DSNFile:c:\XA6\BrickFarm6.dsn/OdbcUsername:brickunit\
administrator/odbcPassword:Passw0rd/ZoneName:Frederick/
LicenseServerName:BrickXA01.brickunit.local/Log:C:\XA6\XA6Config.
log
```

> Use the `/Confirm` parameter to show a confirmation message before configuring the XenServer server. This option is very useful for testing an unattended script.

The `/ExecutionMode` parameter sets the task we want to execute. William can use this option to create a XenApp farm, join, or remove the XenApp from an existing farm, using following options:

- **Create**: Creates a new XenApp farm
- **Join**: Joins a XenApp server to an existing farm
- **Leave**: Removes the XenApp server from the farm. This option is valid only if we previously joined the XenApp server to an existing farm.

The `/FarmName` parameter specifies the XenApp farm name.

The `/DSNFile` parameter is used to set the path to the DSN file used to connect to the XenApp data store hosted on a SQL Server (or an Oracle database).

To create the DSN for the unattended install, William needs to open the `mf20.dsn` file located at `C:\Program Files (x86)\Citrix\Independent Management Architecture` folder of an existing XenApp server. Then he copies the content to a new DSN file located on local hard drive of the new XenApp server or in a network file server.

The DSN file should be look like this:

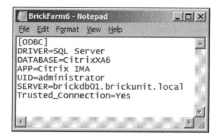

The `/OdbcUserName` parameter is used to set the data store username in format `DOMAIN\USER`.

The `/OdbcPassword` parameter specifies the data store password.

The `/ZoneName` parameter is used to set the Zone Name.

The `/LicenseServerName` parameter is used to specify the name of the Citrix license server.

The `/Log` parameter saves the progress of the configuration to the log file specified.

> More information about `XenAppConfigConsole.exe` is available at http://support.citrix.com/proddocs/index.jsp?topic=/xenapp6-w2k8-install/ps-config-command-syntax.html.

After the configuration process is completed successfully, William needs to reboot the server to complete the process.

Summary

In this chapter, we learned about Virtualization of XenApp farms. In particular, we talked about:

- Deploying XenApp 6 in a virtualized environment, including advantages and disadvantages, Virtual machine performance and host scalability and more
- Deploying XenApp6 on Citrix XenServer, Microsoft Hyper-V, and VMware vSphere virtual machines
- Cloning XenApp 6 virtual machines
- Unattended installation of XenApp 6

Virtualization will provide a lot of benefits and savings. However, one of my preferred reasons to implement VM over physical servers is not related with performance or management, it is related with reliability. Let's use an example to clarify the idea:

We have two identical servers. One is the physical server running XenApp. This server can support 120-140 users. Now we have the second server, running a hypervisor with four virtual machines. Each virtual machine can support 25 to 35 users, depending on the load. So the hypervisor can support around 100-140 users. If the physical server hangs or crashes, all users are affected. However, if only one virtual machine crashes or hangs, only one-fourth of the users are affected.

Index

Symbols

/DSNFile parameter 409
/exclude parameter 408
/ExecutionMode parameter 409
/FarmName parameter 409
/install parameter 407
/LicenseServerNameparameter 410
/Log parameter 410
/OdbcPassword parameter 410
/OdbcUserName parameter 410
/Platinum parameter 408
/ZoneName parameter 410
.NET applications
   C#.NET application, creating 371
   developing 366, 371
   developing, requirements 366
   VB.NET application, creating 366

A

Access Gateway, access infrastructure 22
access methods, Web Interface Console
   Alternate 89
   Direct 89
   Gateway alternate 89
   Gateway direct 89
   Gateway translated 89
   Translated 89
Accounts command 364
Add New Application wizard 318
administration tools
   Citrix SSL Relay Configuration tool 93
   Shadow taskbar 94
   SpeedScreen Latency Reduction Manager 94

Allowed option 201
Allow option 227
application
   content publishing, Publish Application wizard used 130-138
   delivery method, selecting 105
   hosted application publishing, Publish Application wizard used 106-118
   server desktop publishing, Publish Application wizard used 138-148
   streaming application publishing, Publish Application wizard used 118-130
application list, pilot farm plan
   creating 29, 30
   Java 33, 34
   Microsoft Office applications 32, 33
   testing 31, 32
application streaming
   about 157
   components 161
   Group Policy setting 160
   plugin, selecting 162
   system requirements 159, 160
   using, benefits 158
ApplicationType command 364
Apply customized settings at every logon checkbox 224
Apply customized settings checkbox 223
architecture, XenApp
   Brick Unit Construction structure, diagram 24
   designing 23-25
audio configuration, for user session
   steps 280, 281

audio configuration, policy used
  about 276
  bandwidth settings 279, 280
  quality settings 277, 278
Audio redirection bandwidth limit percent setting 279, 280
Audio redirection bandwidth limit setting 279
auto-creation policy, printer implementation
  client machine printers, auto-creating 238
  network printers, auto-creating 238

B

best practices, Citrix policies 193
BrickDocProject 30
BrickExpenses 30
BrickTime 30
Brick Unit Constructions 17
BRICKXA01 server
  License Server, installing 43, 44
  web interface roles, installing 43, 44
BrowserName command 364

C

C#.NET application
  cmdlet, running 373
  creating 371
  parameters, passing to cmdlets 376
  references, adding 371, 372
  results, displaying 373-376
  runspace, creating 372, 373
  runspace, opening 372, 373
Certificate Status textbox 352
Citrix
  administrators, managing 95
  CitrixManagement Consoles 194
  design validation farm 19
  Management Consoles 78
  pilot farm 19
  Production farm 19
Citrix Access Management Console. *See* **Citrix Delivery Services Console**
Citrix administrators
  Actions pane 99
  adding 95-98
  disabling 99, 100
  Privileges page, options 95
  properties, modifying 100, 101
Citrix Computer policy settings
  ICA keep alives, configuring 308
  ICA keep alive timeout, configuring 308
Citrix Dazzle 20
Citrix Delivery Services Console
  about 78, 195, 295
  Filters tab 196
  opening 78-80
  Settings tab 196
  Summary tab 196
  using 78
Citrix farm
  Microsoft Office 2010, publishing 183-187
Citrix Group Policy Modeling Wizard 208
Citrix HDX
  session management 289
  technologies 254
  updates 291
Citrix HDX technologies
  HDX 3D Image Acceleration 254
  HDX 3D Progressive Display 254
  HDX Broadcast Browser 254
  HDX Broadcast Display 254
  HDX MediaStream for Flash 254
  HDX MediaStream Multimedia Acceleration 254
Citrix Licenses
  installing 46-48
Citrix License Server
  configuring 44, 45
Citrix Merchandising Server 2 set up
  about 335
  administrator users, configuring 341-343
  browser requirements 335
  Certificate Signing Request, creating 350, 351
  deliveries, creating 346-348
  deploying, on VMware 336, 337
  Hypervisors 335
  plugins, installing 343, 344
  recipient rules, creating 344, 345
  self-signed SSL certificate, creating 349, 350
  signing request for Microsoft certificate services, creating 352

software, installing 335
SSL certificates, configuring 348, 349
SSL certificates, importing 351
SSL certificates, installing on client machines 353
steps 340, 341
system requirements 335
virtual appliance, installing in Citrix XenServer 338-340

Citrix Online plug-in 16
about 16
Special Folder Redirection, enabling 321, 322

Citrix policies
about 191
applying, to sessions 202
computer policy settings 191
creating 198
creating, Citrix Delivery Services Console used 198-202
setting configuration, best practices 193
settings, turning on/off 192
troubleshooting 206
user policy settings 191
working with 192, 193
working with, guidelines 193

Citrix policies, applying to sessions
access control filter 203
Client IP address filter 203
Client name filter 203
multiple policies, using 205
unfiltered policies 203, 204
user filter 203
Worker group filter 203

Citrix Receiver
about 20, 325
deploying, for internal users with administrative rights 328
deploying, for internal users without administrative rights 331, 332
deploying, for Mac users 333, 334
deploying, for remote users 332, 333
features 326
installing 328
plugin compatibility 326, 327
system requirements, for Macintosh users 327

system requirements, for Windows users 327

Citrix Receiver installation, for Macintosh
system requirements 328

Citrix Receiver installation, for Windows machine
browser versions 327
operating systems 327
system requirements 327

Citrix SSL Relay Configuration tool 93

Citrix Universal Printer
about 230
auto-creating 233
benefits 230
configuring 231, 232
configuring, on sessions 235, 236
default settings, changing 236
driver priority, setting up 233
limitations 230
preview preference, setting up 236
using, ways 231
versions 231, 234

Citrix Web Interface server configuration
authentication methods, configuring 66, 68
Published Resource Type, options 69, 70
XenApp Services site, creating 70, 71
XenApp Services Sites 64
XenApp website, creating 64, 65
XenApp Web Sites 64

Citrix XenApp
about 7
client local printing 219, 220
client network printing 220
network printers, assigning, to users 221
printing on 217, 218
printing pathway 218
print job, remote spooling 221
server network printing 221

Citrix XenApp 6 Migration Tool
URL 213

Citrix XenApp on Windows Server 2008 R2 (64-bit) option 386
Client audio redirection settings 278
Client microphone redirection policy 278
Client printer names policy 239
CMD.EXE file 177
cmdlet 356

CommandLineExecutable command 364
components, application streaming
  Administration (server farm) 161
  Citrix plugins 161
  Citrix streaming profiler 161
  licensing 161
concurrent connections
  about 311
  application instances, limiting 312, 313
  connection denial events, logging 313, 314
  connections, sharing 314, 315
  sessions, sharing 314, 315
  sessions per server count, limiting 311, 312
  user connections during farm maintenance, preventing 315, 316
Configuration tab 347
Configure advanced application settings now checkbox 187
configuring
  Citrix License Server 44, 45
  Citrix Web Interface server 64
  Remote Desktop licensing 72
  Windows components 36
  XenApp 6 35, 36
  XenApp 6, on BRICKXA02 49-52
  XenApp 6, on BRICKXA03 62-64
Connect Virtual Hard Disk page 392
content redirection
  about 148
  disabling 153-155
  enabling 153, 154
  enabling, from client to server 149, 150
  enabling, from server to client 148, 149
  file types associations, updating 151-153
  published applications, associating with file types 150, 151
CONTROL.EXE file 177
ConvertTo-HTML command 362
CPU to GPU processing migration
  reducing 258
CtxCertifyPrinters
  URL 226

D

data collector, farm architecture 20
Datastore page 397

data stores, installing
  Microsoft SQL Server 2008 database server 57, 58
  Microsoft SQL Server 2008 Express database server 55-57
  options 55
  Oracle database server 59-62
Decrease Priority button 206
Deliver Now option 347
design validation farm 19
Desktop Experience feature 263
Display Mode Degrade Preference setting 259, 260
DisplayName command 364
Do not create option 228
Download Receiver button 329

E

Enabled option 227
Enable this policy checkbox 202
Enable WPFHook key 258
Enhanced Security Configuration. *See* IE ESC
Enter System Out-of-Box Experience (OOBE) option 405
Export-CSV command 362

F

farm architecture
  worker group 19
  zones 19
farm terminology
  Citrix Dazzle 20
  Citrix Receiver 20
  data collector 19
  farm Architecture 19
  infrastructure servers 20
  merchandising Server 20
  multi-user environment 18
  remote desktop services 18
  Worker group 19
  XenApp application servers 18
  XenApp infrastructure servers 18
  XenApp server 18

XenApp server farm 19
features, XenApp 6
  Active Directory Federation Services support 11
  Application gateway 11
  applications access 11
  Installation Manager 11
  Network Management Console Integration 11
  Novell eDirectory and NDS Support 11
  power and capacity management 12
  Single Sign-On 12
  SmartAuditor 12
  Web interface 12
Filters tab 212
Finish screen 339
Flash
  HDX MediaStream, using for Flash content optimization 267-274
Flash event logging setting 272
Flash latency threshold setting 272
Flash quality adjustment setting 268
Flash server-side content fetching whitelist setting 273
Flash System Verifier option 284
Flash URL Blacklist setting 273
FolderPath command 364

G

Get-Help command 359
Group Policy
  Computer Configuration 191
  User Configuration 191
  using, for Special Folder redirection 322, 323
Group Policy Management console 199
Group Policy Object (GPO) 213
guests 380

H

hardware virtualization 380
HDX 253
HDX 3D Image Acceleration
  about 254
  using, for bandwidth reduction 255, 256
HDX 3D Progressive Display
  about 254
  using, for image display improvement 256-258
HDX 3D technologies
  CPU to GPU processing migration 258
  HDX 3D Image Acceleration, using 255, 256
  HDX 3D Progressive Display, using 256-258
  using, for image display improvement 254, 255
HDX Broadcast Display setting
  using 259-262
HDX MediaStream
  enabling, at server side 268
  using, for Flash content optimization 267-274
HDX MediaStream, for Flash
  configuring 270
  enabling, at server side 268
  Flash Acceleration, disabling 271
  Flash Acceleration, enabling 270
  Flash Acceleration, setting up 271
  installing 269
  options 268
  server-side event logging, enabling 271-276
  system requirements 269
  uninstalling 269
HDX MediaStream for Flash page 283
HDX MediaStream Multimedia Acceleration
  client machine requirement 262, 263
  configuring, Citrix policies used 264-267
  CPU use 262
  echo cancellation, configuring 267
  network bandwidth 262
HDX Monitor
  Default Domain Group Policy setting, enabling 285
  for XenApp 281
  Graphics page 282, 283
  HDX MediaStream for Flash page 283
  homepage 282

Printer Redirection page 286
Printing Network Performance option 286
Smart Card page 286
USB page 285
HideWhenDisabled parameter 365
Home Server page 387
Home server screen 338
hosted application
  about 103
  publishing, Publish Application wizard used 106, 110-118
HP Proliant Support Pack Cleaner tool 383
HTTPS Redirection option 349
HTTP streaming 188
Hydra 7
Hyper-V
  for Microsoft Hyper-V Server 2008 R2 version 390
  Windows Server 2008 R2 version 390

I

ICA 289
ICA keep alive feature 307
IE ESC
  configuring 39
  disabling 39
IMA 104
Image caching setting 260
Increase Priority button 206
Independent Computing Architecture. *See* ICA
Independent Management Architecture. *See* IMA
infrastructure servers
  access infrastructure 20
  virtualization infrastructure 20
installation, Citrix Receiver
  for Macintosh 331
  for Windows 329
  methods 328
  on XenApp servers 330
  sample download page editing, instructions 334
installing
  Citrix Licenses 46, 47, 48
  License Server, in BRICKXA01 server 43
  XenApp, Wizard-based Server Role Manager used 40-42
  XenApp 6 35, 36
  XenApp 6, on BRICKXA02 49-52
  XenApp 6, on BRICKXA03 62-64
Intel Hyper-Threading (HT) 382

J

Java
  applications, testing 34
  versions 33
Join an existing server farm option 62

K

Key Management Service (KMS) 163

L

License Administration Console
  about 80
  Administration 81
  Alert Configuration tab 84
  Dashboard 81
  default view 81
  Import License icon 86
  New User icon 82
  Server Configuration tab 85
  System Information tab 82
  URL 80
  User Configuration tab 82
  Vendor Daemon Configuration tab 85
Local Special Folders redirection, in XenApp sessions
  about 319, 320
  enabling, for Citrix online plugin 321, 322
  enabling, in web interface 320, 321
  Group Policy, using 322, 323
Lossy Compression Level
  configuring 255
Lossy Compression Threshold Value setting 256

M

macdownloadLocation parameter 334
Management Consoles
  about 194

Citrix Delivery Services Console 78
Delivery Services Console, using 195, 196
Group Policy Management Console, using 194
License Administration Console 80
Local Group Policy Editor, using 196, 197
Web Interface Console 86
Maximum allowed color depth setting 261
merchandising Server 20
MFCOM
  and PowerShell 355, 356
MFCOM scripts
  converting, to PowerShell 376, 377
Microsoft Office 2010
  configuring 163
  installation, customizing 165-167
  profiler workstation, installing 163, 164
  profiling 163, 173-183
  publishing, on Citrix farm 183-187
  trusted servers, specifying 187, 188
Microsoft Office 2010, issues
  ActiveX controls and COM DLLs add-ins 33
  Microsoft Access MDE/ADE/ACCDE files 33
  Visual Basic for Applications (VBA) 33
Microsoft Office 2010 installation, customizing
  KMS port number, setting on 32-bit machines 171-173
  KMS port number, setting on 64-bit machines 170, 171
  KMS server name, setting on 32-bit machines 169
  KMS server name, setting on 64-bit machines 170
  Office popups, disabling 168, 169
  Office Welcome Screen, disabling 168
MLCFG32.CPL file 178
mobile users
  bandwidth printing, limiting 246, 247
  printer, configuring 245, 246
  printing performance, improving 246
  proximity printing 245
  SmoothRoaming 245
Modeling Results tab 211
MSVCR80.DLL file 177

multi-user environment 18
Multiple Activation Key (MAK) 163

N

Netscaler. *See* Access Gateway, access infrastructure
network printers, assigning, to users
  about 221
  default printer, setting 222, 223
  server local printers 224
  server local printers, configuring 225
  session printers setting, adding to Citrix policy 221, 222
  sessions printer setting, modifying 223
New ISO Library link 386
New User Filter dialog box 204
Notify user when display mode is degraded setting 261
Notify User When Display Mode is Degraded setting 260

O

Offline plug-in 16
Out-File command 362

P

Parameters.Add option 376
pilot farm
  about 19
  plan 25
pilot farm plan
  Active Directory integration, designing 26, 27
  application list, creating 29, 30
  application list, testing 31
  Citrix farm components, graphics 28, 29
  small test farm, building 27
  tasks 25, 26
  XenAppDesign Validation Farm, deploying 25
Pipeline.Invoke method 373
plugin, Citrix Receiver
  Acceleration plugin 5.5 326
  Citrix Receiver for Mac 2.x 326
  Communication plugin for Mac 3.0 327

Dazzle plugin 1.1.2 326
EasyCall 3.x 326
MS Application Virtualization Desktop Client 4.5 326
Offline plugin 6.x 326
Online plugin 11.2 327
Online plugin 12.x 326
Profile Management plugin 2.0 326
Receiver for Windows 2.x 326
Secure Access plugin 1.2 for Mac 327
Secure Access plugin 4.6.2 326
Service Monitoring plugin 5.3 326

PowerShell
and MFCOM 355, 356
Citrix XenApp Commands snap-in, installing 358, 359
commands, using from .NET applications 366
using, for basic administrative tasks 358
using, for farm management 360-365

PowerShell commands
Get-XAPrinterDriver 229
Start-XAPrinterDriverReplication 229
Update-XAPrinterDriver 229

printer driver
about 226
automatic installation, controlling 226, 227
compatibility list, modifying 227-229
replicating, in XenApp 229, 230

printer implementation
auto-creation policy 237
auto-creation settings, configuring 238, 239
ICA Client Printer Configuration tool, publishing 241
legacy client printer support, configuring 239
printing preference changes, storing 244
user provisioning 240
users' printer properties, storing 241, 242
users printer properties, storing 242
Windows Add Printer wizard, publishing 240, 241

printer provisioning
dynamic 237
static 236

Printer Redirection page 286

Printing\Universal Printing policy settings 231

printing concepts, Windows
network printer 216
printer driver 216
printers 215
printing device 215
print job 216
print queue 216
print server 216
print spooler 216

Printing Network Performance option 286

printing pathway, Citrix XenApp
client printing pathway 219
network printing pathway 219

print job
about 216
spooled print jobs, printing 217
spooling 216

Print Management Administrative Tool 229
production farm 19
Progressive Compression Threshold Value 257
Progressive heavyweight compression setting 258

Publish Application wizard
content, publishing 130-138
hosted application, publishing 106-122
server desktop, publishing 138
streamed application, publishing 118-130

Q

Queueing and tossing setting 262

R

Remote Desktop licensing
configuring 72
Remote Desktop licensing configuration
about 72
Group Policy, using 74
on XenApp Servers 72-74
Remote Desktop Protocol (RDP) 211
remote desktop services 18
Remote Desktop Session Host Configuration 193

Remove button 400
rendering 217
Replace with option 228
Resultant Set of Policy 206
right virtualization platform
   selecting 382, 383
Role-based Setup Wizard 10
RUNAS command 106
RunspaceConfiguration class 368
Run the modeling wizard 207

S

Save Changes and Sync button 342
Schedule tab 347
Search Files button 377
Secure Sockets Layer. See SSL
Select Applications screen 180
Send Message dialog 295
ServerManagerCmd.exe command 13
ServerName property 374
ServerNames command 364
session
   active state 290
   disconnected state 290
   open state 290
session activity, maintaining
   automatic client reconnection, configuring 305, 306
   features 304
   ICA keep-alive, configuring 307, 308
   Session Reliability, configuring 304, 305
   Session reliability connections 305
   Session reliability connections setting 304
   Session reliability timeout setting 305
Session Reliability Port Number policy setting 305
Session reliability timeout setting 305
sessions
   Citrix ICA, using 289
Session sharing checkbox 315
Settings tab 212
Shadow button 297
Shadow Session dialog 298
Shadow taskbar 94
Shift + F10 300
silos 19

Specify Name and Location page 391
SpeedScreen Latency Reduction Manager
   about 94
   Local Text Echo 94
   Mouse Click Feedback 94
spooling 216
ss3config folder 319
SSL 23
SSL certificate
   configuring 348
   creating, options 349
Stop-XASession command 364
streamed applications
   about 104
   publishing, Publish Application wizard used 118-130
Sysinternals tools 32
System Preparation Tool (SYSPREP) 405
system requirements, XenApp 6
   about 12
   Citrix Delivery Services Console, installing 14, 15
   clients 16
   data store databases 14
   license server 15
   port settings 13
   XenApp Server Role Manager 13
   XenApp Server Role Manager, software deployment 15

T

terminal services. See remote desktop services
Terminal Services Configuration on Windows Server 2003. See Remote Desktop Session Host Configuration
third-party printing solutions
   ThinPrint 247
   UniPrint 247
TLS 23
Transport Layer Security. See TLS
troubleshooting, Citrix policies
   Citrix Policy Modeling Wizard, using 207
   connection scenarios, simulating 207-211
   existing policies, importing 213
   existing policies, migrating 213

policies, searching 211-213
Resultant Set of Policy, calculating 206
settings, searching 211-213
Windows settings precedence 211
types, access infrastructure
  Access Gateway 22
  Secure Gateway 23
  web interface 22
types, virtualization servers
  Citrix licensing 21
  Citrix XML Broker 21
  Citrix XML Service 21
  data store database 21
  Power and Capacity Management 22
  provisioning services 22
  service monitoring 22
  single sign-on 21
  SmartAuditor 22

U

unattended install
  XenApp 6 406
  XenApp components 407-410
Uninstall a program option 269
Universal Printing feature 227
user-to-user shadowing XenApp sessions
  enabling 300
  shadowing policy, creating 301-303
user environments customization, in XenApp
  about 308
  audio, redirecting 310
  COM ports, redirecting 310
  device access, controlling 309, 310
  drives, mapping 310
  port access, controlling 309, 310
  user logons appearance, controlling 309
user sessions optimization, XenApp
  about 316
  local text echo 317, 318
  mouse click feedback 316, 317
  SpeedScreen Latency Reduction, configuring 318
Users who can shadow other users setting 302

V

VB.NET application
  cmdlet, running 368
  creating 366
  parameters, passing to cmdlets 371
  references, adding 366, 367
  results, displaying 369, 370
  runspace, creating 367, 368
  runspace, opening 367, 368
VBA 33
Vendor Daemon Configuration tab 85
versions, Citrix Universal Printer
  EMF (Enhanced Metafile Format) 234
  PCL4 234
  PCL5c 234
  PS (PostScript) 234
  XML Paper Specification 234
Very High or Ultra-High option 257
View New Plug-ins link 344
Virtual Machine Version page 397
Visual Basic for Applications. *See* **VBA**
VMware vSphere Hypervisor (ESXi) 395

W

Web Interface Console
  access methods 89
  Authentication Methods option 88
  Client-side Proxy task, using 91
  Manage SessionPreferences task 91
  published resources, accessing 90
  Resource Types option 90
  screenshot 87
  Server Farms option 87
  Site Maintenance task, options 92
  sites, configuring 86
  Workspace Control task 92
  XML Broker, using 87
web Interface roles
  License Server, in BRICKXA01 server 43, 44
window modes, Citrix Online plugin
  Non-seamless window Mode 314
  Seamless window Mode 314
Windows
  printing concepts 215

Windows 32-bit on Windows 64-bit. *See* WOW64
Windows components configuration
  about 36
  IE ESC, configuring 39
  Windows Firewall, configuring 37, 38
Windows Firewall
  configuring 37
  configuring, for XenApp 38
WinFrame 7
WinView 7
worker group, farm architecture 19
WorkingDirectory command 364
WOW64 31

X

XenAppSetupConsole.exe command 406
XenAppConfigConsole.exe command 406
XenApp
  access infrastructure, types 22
  architecture, designing 23
  Citrix Group policy engine 202
  client-side application virtualization 18
  client printers, auto-creating 237
  HDX Monitor 281
  infrastructure servers, access infrastructure 20
  infrastructure servers, virtualization infrastructure 20
  printer provisioning 236
  published resources access, providing 103
  server-side application virtualization 18
  setting search, order 244
  user environments, customizing 308
  user sessions, optimizing 316
  virtualization Infrastructure, types 21
  VM hosted application virtualization 19
XenApp 6
  about 8, 18
  Active Directory Group Policy integration 9
  administration tools 93
  Citrix Dazzle 9
  Citrix Delivery Services Console 8
  Citrix HDX technologies 9
  Citrix Receiver 9
  configuring 35, 36
  deploying, in virtualized environment 379
  features 11
  highlights 8
  installing 35, 36
  installing on BRICKXA02, Wizard-based Server Role Manager used 49-52
  Microsoft App-V integration 10
  Multi-lingual User Interface (MUI) 11
  pilot farm, deploying 36
  PowerShell Support 9
  Support for Windows portable USB devices 10
  system requirements 12-15
  unattended install 406
  virtualizing, benefits 380
  virtualizing, limitations 380, 381
  Windows service isolation for streamed applications 9
XenApp 6, on BRICKXA03
  configuring 62-64
  installing 62-64
XenApp 6.0 RTM
  installation, options 232
XenApp 6 deploying, in virtualized environment
  about 379
  host scalability 381, 382
  virtual machine performance 381, 382
XenApp 6 deploying, on Citrix XenServer
  about 383
  new VM, creating 385-389
  reference documentation 384
  XenApp Evaluation Virtual Appliance, installing 384, 385
XenApp 6 deploying, on Microsoft Hyper-V
  about 389, 390
  new VM, creating 392-395
  XenApp Evaluation Virtual Appliance, installing 390-392
XenApp 6 deploying, on VMware vSphere
  about 395
  ESXi, limitations 395
  new VM, creating in vSphere 396-402
  virtual machines, cloning 403-406
XenApp application servers 18

XenApp Commands installation
  Citrix XenApp 6 PowerShell SDK,
    installing 357
  on XenApp Servers 356
  options 356
  PowerShell commands, installing 357
XenApp components
  /DSNFilc parameter 409
  /exclude parameter 408
  /ExecutionMode parameter 409
  /FarmName parameter 409
  /install parameter 407
  /LicenseServerNameparameter 410
  /Log parameter 410
  /OdbcPassword parameter 410
  /OdbcUserName parameter 410
  /Platinum parameter 408
  /ZoneName parameter 410
  unattended install 407
XenApp configuration
  Wizard-based Server Configuration tool,
    using 52
XenApp configuration, Wizard-based Server Configuration tool used
  about 52
  data stores, installing 54
  first XenApp server, configuring 53, 54
XenApp farms
  managing 75
XenApp installation
  Wizard-based Server Role Manager, using
    40-42
XenApp Printing Optimization Pack
  optimization defaults 250
  Universal EMF processing mode 248, 249
  Universal printing image compression limit
    249
  Universal printing print quality limit 251
  XA600W2K8R2X64010.msp file 248
  XenAppGPMX64.msi file 248
  XenAppGPMX86.msi file 248

XenApp server farm 19
XenApp Server
  about 18
  XenApp Commands, installing on 356
XenApp Session Reliability feature 289
XenApp sessions
  disconnecting 293, 294
  installation process 296
  Local Special Folders, redirecting 319
  logging, enabling 299, 300
  logging, enabling in central file 299
  logging, enabling in Windows Event Log
    299
  logging off 293, 294
  managing 293
  messages, sending to user 295, 296
  monitoring 291, 292
  process, terminating 294, 295
  process terminating 295
  resetting 293, 294
  shadowing 296
  user-to-user shadowing, enabling 300
  viewing 296-300
XenApp sessions viewing, Shadow Taskbar used
  Available users list 298
  Shadowed users list 298
  shadowing, initiating 298
  shadowing session, ending 299
  Shadow Session dialog box 298
  starting with 298
  steps 297
XenServer 5.6 Installation Guide 384
**XenServer 5.6 Virtual Machine Installation
  Guide 384**
XenServer Administrator's Guide 384

Z

ZoneName parameter 371
zones, farm architecture 19

Thank you for buying
Getting Started with Citrix XenApp 6

About Packt Publishing

Packt, pronounced 'packed', published its first book "Mastering phpMyAdmin for Effective MySQL Management" in April 2004 and subsequently continued to specialize in publishing highly focused books on specific technologies and solutions.

Our books and publications share the experiences of your fellow IT professionals in adapting and customizing today's systems, applications, and frameworks. Our solution based books give you the knowledge and power to customize the software and technologies you're using to get the job done. Packt books are more specific and less general than the IT books you have seen in the past. Our unique business model allows us to bring you more focused information, giving you more of what you need to know, and less of what you don't.

Packt is a modern, yet unique publishing company, which focuses on producing quality, cutting-edge books for communities of developers, administrators, and newbies alike. For more information, please visit our website: www.packtpub.com.

About Packt Enterprise

In 2010, Packt launched two new brands, Packt Enterprise and Packt Open Source, in order to continue its focus on specialization. This book is part of the Packt Enterprise brand, home to books published on enterprise software – software created by major vendors, including (but not limited to) IBM, Microsoft and Oracle, often for use in other corporations. Its titles will offer information relevant to a range of users of this software, including administrators, developers, architects, and end users.

Writing for Packt

We welcome all inquiries from people who are interested in authoring. Book proposals should be sent to author@packtpub.com. If your book idea is still at an early stage and you would like to discuss it first before writing a formal book proposal, contact us; one of our commissioning editors will get in touch with you.

We're not just looking for published authors; if you have strong technical skills but no writing experience, our experienced editors can help you develop a writing career, or simply get some additional reward for your expertise.

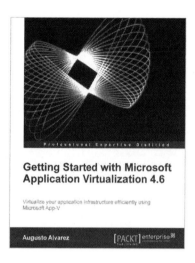

Getting Started with Microsoft Application Virtualization 4.6

ISBN: 978-1-849681-26-1   Paperback: 308 pages

Virtualize your application infrastructure efficiently using Microsoft App-V

1. Publish, deploy, and manage your virtual applications with App-V
2. Understand how Microsoft App-V can fit into your company
3. Guidelines for planning and designing an App-V environment
4. Step-by-step explanations to plan and implement the virtualization of your application infrastructure

Oracle VM Manager 2.1.2

ISBN: 13 : 978-1-847197-12-2   Paperback: 244 pages

Manage a Flexible and Elastic Data Center with Oracle VM Manager

1. Learn quickly to install Oracle VM Manager and Oracle VM Servers
2. Learn to manage your Virtual Data Center using Oracle VM Manager
3. Import VMs from the Web, template, repositories, and other VM formats such as VMware
4. Learn powerful Xen Hypervisor utilities such as xm, xentop, and virsh

Please check **www.PacktPub.com** for information on our titles

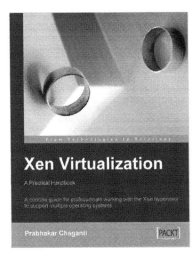

Xen Virtualization

ISBN: 978-1-847192-48-6   Paperback: 148 pages

A fast and practical guide to supporting multiple operating systems with the Xen hypervisor

1. Installing and configuring Xen
2. Managing and administering Xen servers and virtual machines
3. Setting up networking, storage, and encryption
4. Backup and migration

Microsoft Azure: Enterprise Application Development

ISBN: 978-1-849680-98-1   Paperback: 248 pages

Straight talking advice on how to design and build enterprise applications for the cloud

1. Build scalable enterprise applications using Microsoft Azure
2. The perfect fast-paced case study for developers and architects wanting to enhance core business processes
3. Packed with examples to illustrate concepts
4. Written in the context of building an online portal for the case-study application

Please check **www.PacktPub.com** for information on our titles

Made in the USA
Lexington, KY
26 January 2012